Federal Regulations

Ethical Issues
and Social Research

AAAS Selected Symposia Series

Published by Westview Press
5500 Central Avenue, Boulder, Colorado

for the

American Association for the Advancement of Science
1776 Massachusetts Ave., N.W., Washington, D.C.

Federal Regulations

Ethical Issues
and Social Research

Edited by
Murray L. Wax and Joan Cassell

AAAS Selected Symposium **36**

AAAS Selected Symposia Series

Published in 1979 in the United States of America by
     Westview Press, Inc.
     5500 Central Avenue
     Boulder, Colorado 80301
     Frederick A. Praeger, Publisher

Library of Congress Catalog Card Number: 78-21189
ISBN: 0-89158-487-0

Printed and bound in the United States of America

About the Book

As the federal government elaborates its networks of control over social research, some investigators feel that federal regulations mean only increased costs and constricted research opportunities; others see the possibility of better research through the informed interaction between investigator and subjects that can be brought about by these same regulations. This book--in which responsible social research is defended as essential for intelligent social policy--presents the effects of federal regulations on various research methodologies, with particular attention to their differential impact on qualitative and quantitative studies. It also presents material on the formation and nature of the federal regulatory system, the effects of research on the different kinds of populations studies, and the conflicts among professional associations with regard to regulation.

About the Series

The *AAAS Selected Symposia Series* was begun in 1977 to provide a means for more permanently recording and more widely disseminating some of the valuable material which is discussed at the AAAS Annual National Meetings. The volumes in this *Series* are based on symposia held at the Meetings which address topics of current and continuing significance, both within and among the sciences, and in the areas in which science and technology impact on public policy. The *Series* format is designed to provide for rapid dissemination of information, so the papers are not typeset but are reproduced directly from the camera-copy submitted by the authors, without copy editing. The papers are organized and edited by the symposium arrangers who then become the editors of the various volumes. Most papers published in this *Series* are original contributions which have not been previously published, although in some cases additional papers from other sources have been added by an editor to provide a more comprehensive view of a particular topic. Symposia may be reports of new research or reviews of established work, particularly work of an interdisciplinary nature, since the AAAS Annual Meetings typically embrace the full range of the sciences and their societal implications.

WILLIAM D. CAREY
Executive Officer
American Association for
the Advancement of Science

Contents

Acknowledgments

Joan Cassell's "Regulating Fieldwork: Of Subjects, Subjection, and Intersubjectivity" incorporates portions of her earlier essay "Risk and Benefit to Subjects of Fieldwork" as published in The American Sociologist (Volume 13, August 1978), which are reprinted here with the kind permission of the editors of that journal.

"Some Perspectives on Ethical/Political Issues in Social Science Research" by M. Brewster Smith is reprinted with the permission of the editors of Personality and Social Psychology Bulletin.

Manuscript production was coordinated by Sophia Goodman; additional typing was performed by Pat Rutherford. We are also grateful to the typists in the offices of Clark C. Abt, Robert Boruch, Bradford Gray, Virginia Olesen, and M. Brewster Smith.

About the Editors and Authors

Murray L. Wax, a professor in the Department of Sociology and Anthropology at Washington University, has extensive experience in qualitative methodology, ethics, comparative study of religion, and education. He has directed two research projects on Indian education and he serves as an editor *of* Human Organization, Sociological Quarterly, *and* Phylon. *He has held numerous offices with professional associations, including president of the Council on Anthropology and Education and of the Society for Applied Anthropology, and he is a fellow of the American Anthropological Association, the American Sociological Association, and other organizations. He is the author of some 50 publications, including* Indian Americans: Unity and Diversity *(Prentice-Hall, 1971), and the editor of* Solving "The Indian Problem": The White Man's Burdensome Business *(with R. W. Buchanan; New Viewpoints/ Franklin Watts, 1975) and* Anthropological Perspectives on Education *(with S. Diamond and F. O. Gearing; Basic Books, 1971).*

Joan Cassell, research associate at the Center for Policy Research in New York, has studied ethical problems of fieldwork, social movements, and women's issues, and is currently executive director of a project investigating the ethical problems of fieldwork. She is a member of the Human Subjects Committee and the Committee on Professional Anthropology of the Society for Applied Anthropology, a visiting member of the Hastings Institute Research Group on Death and Dying, and a fellow of the American Anthropological Association and of the Royal Anthropological Institute. *Her publications include* A Group Called Women: Sisterhood and Symbolism in the Feminist Movement *(McKay, 1977).*

Clark C. Abt, founder and president of Abt Associates Inc., a social science research and development firm located in Cambridge, Massachusetts, has over 20 years experience

*directing social science research, operations research, sys-
tems engineering, and interdisciplinary analysis. He is the
author of numerous articles and two books,* Serious Games
(Viking, 1970) and The Social Audit for Management *(American
Management, 1977), and the editor of* The Evaluation of Social
Programs *(Sage, 1977).*

    *Robert F. Boruch is a professor in the Department of
Pyschology and director of the Division of Methodology and
Evaluation Research at Northwestern University. He is past
president and director of the Council for Applied Social
Research, chairman of the Social Science Research Council
Committee on Evaluation Research, a member of the Committee
on Privacy and Confidentiality as Factors in Survey Response
of the National Academy of Sciences, and a member of the
American Psychological Association's Task Force on Privacy
and Confidentiality. He has published over 40 articles on
program evaluation methods and policy, research methods, and
privacy and confidentiality. His several books include*
Social Experimentation *(H. W. Riecken, coeditor; Academic
Press, 1974).*

    *Joseph S. Cecil is a research associate with the Depart-
ment of Psychology at Northwestern University.*

    *Janet M. Fitchen, an instructor in the Department of
Anthropology at Ithaca College, specializes in applied
anthropology, poverty, and the contemporary United States.
She has conducted fieldwork among the rural poor in the
United States, designed and consulted on poverty programs,
and developed training materials and workshops for personnel
working with low-income families. A fellow of the American
Anthropological Association and the Society for Applied
Anthropology, she has published articles and reports on her
areas of interest.*

    *Edith E. Graber, assistant professor in the Department
of Sociology at Washington University, has studied the areas
of social theory and sociology of law. She conducted research at the Max Weber Institute of the University of Munich
and the Bavarian Academy of Sciences under research grants
from the German Academic Exchange Service and Washington
University. Her publications include articles on sociolegal
change in a mountain community, Max Weber's interpretive
sociology, and police undercover agents.*

    *Bradford H. Gray, professional associate with the
Institute of Medicine of the National Academy of Sciences, is
studying the sociology of medicine. He previously served on
the staff of the National Commission for the Protection of*

Human Subjects of Biomedical and Behavioral Research, and has published articles on the conduct and regulation of research involving human subjects, informed consent, the functions of human subjects review committees, and the epidemiology of coronary heart disease. He is the author of Human Subjects in Medical Experimentation *(Wiley-Interscience, 1975).*

Lynne Kipnis is a research assistant in the Department of Pediatrics at Washington University Medical School. She received a Bachelor of Liberal Arts from Washington University in 1978, where she studied child psychology.

Virginia Olesen, professor of sociology at the University of California-San Francisco, is interested in social psychology, occupations and professions, medical sociology, and women's roles. She is a former member of the UCSF Committee for the Protection of Human Subjects, and she organized a panel on the problematics of informed consent for the Southwest Anthropological Association in 1977. She was also responsible for organizing a national conference on the Unanticipated Aspects of Informed Consent at UCSF in 1975 and editing the proceedings.

Eleanor Singer, research associate at the Center for Social Sciences at Columbia University, is working in the fields of social psychology and research methods. She has published articles on the effects of informed consent on response rates and response quality in surveys, and she is the editor of The Public Opinion Quarterly.

M. Brewster Smith, professor of psychology at Stevenson College, University of California-Santa Cruz, specializes in social and personality psychology. He is president of the American Psychological Association (1978), former president of the Society for the Psychological Study of Social Issues, and former editor of the Journal of Social Issues *and the* Journal of Abnormal and Social Psychology. *He has published four books, including* Social Psychology and Human Values *(Aldine, 1969) and* Humanizing Social Psychology *(Jossey-Bass, 1974).*

Federal Regulations

Ethical Issues
and Social Research

Overview

Murray L. Wax and Joan Cassell

As the federal government elaborates its networks of
control upon social research, investigators are both challenged and disconcerted, chastened and outraged. Some fear
that over-regulation will destroy honest and creative research;
others contend that the possibility of such research has already been undercut by the unthinking abuses of earlier
investigations. Some caution that the difficulties and costs
of research will escalate; others respond that by establishing informed interaction between researcher and subjects, the
regulations will ease present difficulties. Again, some
complain that the new bureaucratic regulations are forcing
all modalities of research into the same constricted mold;
while others note that the shaping has already been achieved
by the requirements of the review processes of federal
funding agencies.

The issues are important, not only to the small band of
social researchers, but to the republic as a whole, and possibly to even larger groups. Research is an essential contribution to the framing of intelligent social policy,not merely a
pastime of academicians and scholars. Sound policy may emerge
by accident, but in a world whose complexity and interrelationships we are only now just beginning to comprehend,
intelligent and efficient research becomes increasingly
important. For centuries political and moral philosophers
have been cautioning that right conduct is dependent upon
knowledge. Such knowledge does not derive from instinct or
from abstract principles, but from research on conduct, the
behavior of specific people, the lives of actual groups. It
is a frequent, if sophomoric, delusion that adherence to some
abstract universal principle can obviate the need for detail
and insight into empirical social reality. The disappointing
careers of many plans, advocated by persons of integrity and
determination, testify to the limitations of such simplistic

1

approaches. If science without morality is catastrophic,
morality without knowledge is foolhardy.

The foregoing applies equally well to the framing and
enforcing of the recent federal regulations. The government
has decided that it is necessary to monitor the conduct of
social researchers and to require that they protect the welfare and privacy of their subjects. Well meant as is this
attempt, it has suffered from being established with too little
knowledge of social research and too little input from social
researchers. Significant ethical principles (e.g. informed
consent, positive risk/benefit ratios) have been elaborated
and applied without regard to the specific kinds of research,
or the expressed interests or needs of those who are studied,
or the problems of those planning research. Worst of all,
there has been a failure to relate the process of research
inquiry to the civil rights of citizens; for, some of the
process of regulation comes close to infringing upon the civil
liberties of the investigator. By now, it has become a standard joke in cartoons and skits for the inquisitive stranger
at the door to be revealed as a common snoop rather than the
survey researcher from the polling organization. Yet the
serious implication of that joke is the reminder that, much
as investigators would seek to differentiate themselves professionally from the merely curious populace, nonetheless
many of their techniques are similar. In consequence, whatever infringes upon the rights of researchers to inquire and
observe may threaten the civil rights of ordinary citizens.

This makes salient a number of issues which have not
been systematically analyzed. Researchers are citizens and
should enjoy the privileges and responsibilities of citizen-
ship; many researchers are members of the academy and are
thereby accorded additional privileges or responsibilities.
Correspondingly, the academically based researcher enjoys
support from the broader community (for example, via university endowments or legislative subventions). Professional
researchers occupy a position of trust in the eyes of many
members of the public; thus, when persons are convinced that
they are confronting professional researchers, they are
usually more willing to enter into an interview and therein
to reveal intimate details of their lives. Yet, the researchers, because of their organization and competencies,
have the methodologies to forge links among data, and to
develop interpretations that could be embarrassing or detri-
mental to their respondents. Clearly, then, researchers have
special privileges, special competencies, and special
responsibilities.

Frequently, social research is funded by the federal

government, and, since those funds derive from the public by means of taxes, there is a legitimate interest that the research not be harmful either to the public generally or to those who participate in the investigation. Put most crassly, researchers funded by the government should not be at liberty to inflict harm on those who support their efforts. We perceive a dilemma of some proportions. On the one hand, we should not wish professional researchers to be denied ordinary rights of social interaction and inquiry, so that the moment persons became qualified as social researchers, they were so restricted as to be more ignorant than lay citizens. Yet, on the other hand, society does have the right to monitor their conduct and to insure that they do not abuse the trust and responsibilities which are vested in them. The resolution of this dilemma might more ethically be achieved if we had more knowledge about the processes and hazards of the various kinds of research, while confronting seriously the conflicts among the rights and privileges of various groups in the population.

In a critical review of early anthropological theories of religion, the eminent scholar, E. E. Evans-Pritchard (1965:436), characterizes them as having been developed on the logic of "If I were a horse...!" ("If I were a horse, I would do what horses do on account of one or other feeling that horses may be supposed to have.") Instead of trying empirically to discover how other peoples reason, feel, and believe, too many theorists imputed to "primitive peoples" a process of reasoning or a set of attitudes and sentiments which they imagined that they should have or feel under the same circumstances. The present governmental regulations of social research have a similar quality: instead of trying to discover how various kinds of subjects of various kinds of research apprehend the moral quality of their experience, there is a rush to judgment. This is especially troublesome in social research because there are so many different kinds of research methodologies and techniques, each with its distinctive moral climate, each with distinctive risks, benefits, hopes, and temptations. In addition, there are so many kinds of people who become involved in research, and so many research roles: subjects, informants, respondents, hosts, guides, interpreters, et al.

In a sense this set of written papers, and the discussions that have been underway at annual meetings of the AAAS and affiliated professional associations, are a belated contribution to the making of federal policy in this troublesome area. Unhappily, at the time when the regulations were being drafted to protect the human subjects of research, the professional associations of anthropologists, sociologists, etc. had too little awareness and power to affect these developments.

It would have been well had they been solicited to appear,
and had the association officers in turn been in a position
to alert their memberships to the implications of the regulatory systems. Only as the systems went into operation, and
their regulations came to affect the conduct of researchers,
was there an expression of concern and the beginnings of an
organized professional effort to influence federal policies.

In designing the AAAS session at which some of these
papers were presented, we tried to preserve a balance among
the different kinds of research methodology, particularly
between the qualitative and the quantitative, between those
which relied upon "interpretive understanding" and those which
utilized survey research methods with questionnaire schedules.
In amplifying that session for the present volume, we have
tried to preserve that same balance, because we wished to
demonstrate to readers that the various federal regulations
have differential effects upon the different methods (and the
different kinds of populations studied). Where this volume
differs from the contents of that session is in having a bit
more material on the formation and nature of the federal
regulatory system and the inner conflicts among the professional associations.

Thus, the first set of papers in this volume provides
the reader with a general guide to both federal regulations
and the ethical issues in social research, without regard to
the specifics of different methods. The several papers by
Brewster Smith, Edith Graber, and Bradford Gray furnish a
background in some of the history and development of the
regulations and terminologies, including the activities of
legislatures and the decisions of courts. (Readers who seek
further historical detail are referred to the volume compiled
by Bower and de Gasparis [1976].) The paper by Murray Wax
details the history of a project which has been used by many
as a paradigm of unethical research, from which populations
should be protected by federal and professional regulations.
Wax shows that the realities differ greatly from the myths
about Camelot, and that it is important to comprehend these
realities if we are to avoid making similar mistakes.

M. Brewster Smith was involved with the drafting of an
ethical code for the American Psychological Association in
1973 and, so, has long and thoughtful familiarity with such
concepts as "informed consent" and "risk/benefit analysis"
which have become crucial in the regulatory process. His
argument clarifies the different scope of the two concepts,
noting that each is rooted in a different tradition of ethical
analysis. We are struck also by the fact that whereas the
federal regulations talk of "risk/benefit" comparisons, Smith

is far more precise in writing of "harm/benefit."

Edith Graber focuses her essay upon <u>privacy</u>, beginning
with the analyses of the concept in both the judicial and the
social-scientific literatures. After tracing the legal standing of the concept through a series of decisions by the
Supreme Court, she then turns to a review of the kinds of
effects upon social research. Here, the regulatory mechanisms
are just beginning to come into operation, and, as in the case
of the human subjects protective system, we surmise that,
while scientists will applaud the spirit and intent of the
regulations, they may find some of their applications restrictive of investigations that might otherwise be judged of great
social value. If a review process akin to that designed to
protect human subjects should be instituted in agencies receiving research funds from the federal government, projects
such as the one described by Janet Fitchen (later in the
volume) may be ruled out of order. The principle, which
abstractly seems excellent, that records deriving from research are to be separated from those having to do with agency
activities, would in the cases she describes be so interpreted
as to prevent the assistance her project has provided to the
local community. Again, here is another instance where lack
of knowledge of specific methodologies and of specific populations might lead to an unwise regulatory system.

Bradford Gray was for many years the Staff Sociologist
for the National Commission for the Protection of Human Subjects of Biomedical and Behavioral Research. In that capacity,
he was involved with the survey conducted for the Commission
by the Survey Research Center, Ann Arbor, on the functioning
of the system of institutional review boards. He also served,
less formally, as the voice of sociology within the offices
of the Commission. He reports here on some of the pertinent
results of the survey and then uses this as the point from
which to review the changes in the protective system which
the Commission has proposed to institute during 1978-79. As
is characteristic of Gray, he is able to discuss objectively,
yet sympathetically, both the goals of the Commission and the
criticisms of the protective system by such investigators as
Abt, Cassell, Olesen, and Wax and Cassell. He is especially
aware of the problems faced by the Commission in trying to
bring under a common system of regulation the enormous variety
of researches that involve "human subjects."

Not only does social research often have ethical problems
different from those of biomedical research, but qualitative
social research is even more different. Because the survey
was designed to cover all research, it is of little help in
assessing how the system is affecting social researchers

within their institutional bases. For example, we do not
know what proportion of graduate students in social sciences
have radically altered their dissertation   plans because of
anticipated encounters with the Human Subjects Protective
System of their universities, nor do we know whether such
alterations derive from an increased sensibility or from fear
of such bureaucratic red tape, as was experienced by Lynne
Kipnis (described in the final case study in this volume).

Murray L. Wax illustrates another facet of the problems
created by abstract moralizing in detachment from factual
knowledge. During the 1960s a tremendous volume of criticism
of U. S. foreign policy and of the Defense Department was
stimulated by the intervention in Southeast Asia (and earlier
in the Dominican Republic, as later in Chile). Much of this
criticism was intensely moral, defending the rights and freedoms of local populations. Yet, intrinsically, the criticisms
were political in that they were defending indigenous revolutionary activities and the resultant governments, as opposed
to political interventions which attempted to maintain or
institute local oligarchies dependent upon the U. S. In this
politicized atmosphere, an attempt, underwritten by the
Department of Defense, publicly to research the conditions of
social change and revolution came under a variety of domestic
and foreign attacks. The critics included the U.S. State
Department, the Soviet Foreign Ministry, Chilean intellectuals,
political leaders, and radical politicians, as well as U.S.
academicians, and perhaps the C.I.A. Amidst this critical
barrage, the issues implicit in Camelot never received a comprehensive discussion, and only recently have some of them
been indicated in the volume by Deitchman. Wax uses the
occasion of that volume to review the case, the critics, and
to elicit their implications for what regulations do and
should do.

Sociologists (e.g. Becker 1963: chap.8) have coined the
phrase "moral entrepeneur" to delineate the role of those who
make careers by emphasizing a particular social problem and
becoming spokesmen of the associations or agencies devoted to
its solution. Following in this tradition, Broadhead and
Rist (1976, 1978) have argued that the new federal emphasis
upon ethical research has been associated with a distinctive
group of entrepeneurs whose activities have not only created
a set of regulations and a bureaucratic apparatus but,
more importantly, have helped to restrict the range of scientific activity. For, if research on an organization can only
be conducted with its official permission ("informed consent")
and with the proviso that its personnel be benefited more than
harmed (risk/benefit ratio), then with rare exceptions the
only projects which will be funded and allowed into operation

are those which will be uncritical of the organization or
which will present their criticism in an acceptable format
("positive criticism"). Any social researcher who has tried
to conduct projects within institutions such as schools or
hospitals has had abundant demonstration of what can be involved, even prior to the institution of the present regula-
tive network. Such organizations are extremely sensitive
about their public image and attempt to co-opt research
projects. The only research projects which are acceptable
are those designed to conclude that institutional defects,
whatever they may prove to be, are not organic but instead
derive from lack of funds and lack of community support. We
need not accept all of the implications of the analyses by
Broadhead and Rist, but their discussion does alert us to the
pressing need for knowledge of the effects of the regulatory
system upon the conduct of social research. Are the regulations encouraging researchers to behave in a more ethical
fashion? Are there effects upon the kinds of projects being
designed and conducted, and is one such effect a bias against
investigations which are radical and critical of existing
institutions?

The survey designed and directed by Gray for the National
Commission for the Protection of Human Subjects of Biomedical
and Behavioral Research is a small initial effort toward dealing with such questions. Because of the vastness of the total
research enterprise directed at human beings, and because of
the relatively small proportion which is conducted by social
scientists, that survey just begins to make evident the impact
of the regulations upon social researchers. Again, because
of the small number of social researchers, there was no
possibility of differentiating the kinds of problems that
the regulations cause for the various methods of research.

8 *Wax and Cassell*

References Cited

Becker, Howard S.
  1963 Outsiders: Studies in the Sociology of Deviance.
    New York: Free Press.

Bower, Robert T., and Priscilla R. de Gasparis
  1976 The Protection of Subjects in Social Research.
    Summary Report to National Institute of Mental Health.
    Washington, D.C.: Bureau of Social Science Research.
    Forthcoming as: Ethics in Social Research: Protecting
    the Interests of Human Subjects. New York: Praeger 1978?

Broadhead, Robert S., and Ray C. Rist
  1976 Gatekeepers and the Social Control of Social Research.
    Social Problems 23:325-336.
  1978 Ethical Research: The New Moral Crusade in Social
    Science. Social Policy. (forthcoming)

Evans-Pritchard, E. E.
  1965 Theories of Primitive Religion. Oxford: Clarendon.

Part I
Background

Some Perspectives on Ethical/Political Issues in Social Science Research

M. Brewster Smith

Contrasting Frames of Reference for Research Ethics

Current deliberation about the ethics of social science research draws upon two quite different primary reference frames that fit with each other only awkwardly and uncomfortably. One is the libertarian, voluntaristic, "humanistic" frame captured in the tag phrase "informed consent," which philosophers tell me finds a home in the Kantian "deontological" tradition. It is good if people make their significant decisions for themselves, and they ought even to have the right to make self-sacrificial choices that result in harm to themselves. It is bad for them to be coerced, conned, or manipulated, even for their own good. The other frame, that of the participant's welfare or harm, fits in the "utilitarian" tradition of Bentham and the Mills. It does not depend upon the assumption of free will. It sounds more objective, and lends itself to expression in the currently fashionable terms of cost/benefit analysis. The ten principles adopted by the American Psychological Association, which I had a hand in formulating (Ad hoc Committee 1973), assume both evaluative frames. So do the regulations pro -mulgated by HEW.

In fact, all of our recent discussion has taken the two frames so much for granted that we seldom notice that they emerge from different philosophical traditions and, although they can be made to mesh with each other, they do not fall

Published in Personality and Social Psychology Bulletin (1976) and reprinted here with the consent of the editors. Adapted from a paper prepared for the Symposium on Ethical Issues in Social Science Research, University of Minnesota, April 7-8, 1976. Written during my tenure as a Senior Research Fellow of the National Endowment for the Humanities.

into place jointly in any obviously natural way. Either
frame by itself could be made a Procrustean basis for a log-
ically consistent stance on the entire range of issues involved in research on human participants. It seems, also,
that the two frames are differentially relevant to biomedical
and to social research. The likely harms in most (but not
all) social research are trivial as compared with the life-
and-death outcomes in some medical research, whereas issues
of informed consent have proved to be particularly salient
and difficult in the social arena. Each of the evaluative
frames presents its special problems when it is applied in
judgments about the ethical acceptability of things that
psychologists and social scientists actually are doing and
want to do in the course of their research.

Problems Involved in
Informed Consent

First for the voluntaristic principle of informed con-
sent. For some positivistically-oriented researchers whose
deterministic metatheory has no place for voluntary decision,
the principle is inherently objectionable because it seems
to them meaningless. My own metapsychology is different so I
have little patience with this objection. All the same, it
does call to attention a real puzzle: how do you distinguish
between coercive incentives to participate, like food to the
starving, reduced sentences for prisoners, etc.--obviously
unacceptable--from other presumably acceptable incentives
like modest payments? Both may tip the balance toward a
decision to participate; both manipulate voluntary consent.
I see no clear dividing line, but review groups and investigators themselves have to draw one.

Among the many problems that arise from the requirement
of informed consent, there are three main types. Some kinds
of procedures that many social scientists regard as essential
simply cannot meet the requirement; and there are difficulties of interpretation as to what "informed" really means.

What are we to do about children, or the infirm aged, or
the mentally retarded or psychotic, who cannot speak respon-
sibly for themselves? The law steps in with definitive answers in some of these cases, saying who has the legal responsibility. But the range of possible administrative and
ethical interpretations as they apply to research in schools
and in other institutions extends from a scrupulosity that
would severely hamper research and work to the disadvantage
of the given class of possible participants themselves, to a
flexible policy that would delegate to institutional authorities consent for procedures that involve essentially minor

variations in the normal experience of the participant with
the institution, and might assume implicit consent if those
who are legally responsible are notified about what is proposed and do not object. Proposed HEW guidelines for research on children were of a highly restrictive, over-scrup-
ulous sort, and have been held in abeyance since the affected
research community rose up in protest. The issues are still
not resolved.

    Many procedures that seem essential to well-designed in-
quiry capable of producing dependable knowledge are incompatible with any strict interpretation of informed consent.
The most delicate and controversial issue concerns the use
of deception in social research. Social psychology since
World War II has come to depend very heavily on deception for
its major experimental strategies. In attempting to understand psychological topics like interpersonal influence,
interpersonal attraction and hostility, or strains towards
consistency in the reorganization of people's beliefs and
attitudes, it has seemed important to create social reality
under the experimenter's control in the laboratory, usually
by providing a plausible reason for the procedures to dis-
tract the participant's attention from the hypotheses really
under study. The rationale for deception here is much the
same as in the use of placebo controls in studying the
effects of new drugs, also a deviation from ideal informed
consent: if the person were to understand the true purpose
of the study, he might behave so as to conform to expecta-
tions--or to <u>nonconform</u> to them. In either case, the person's ordinary, natural reactions would have eluded the researcher's grasp.

    The way that most responsible investigators quiet their
ethical qualms about deception is <u>debriefing</u>--explaining,
after the experiment is over, what was really going on and
why. This <u>can</u> be a valuable bit of education, and, if participants who have been upset by the whole procedure are given
the opportunity to withdraw their data from use by the researcher, a retroactive gesture is made toward the principle
of consent. But the ideal of informed consent is still not
really met at all, and the rationale for debriefing lies
primarily in terms of the harm/benefit principle. Debriefing
seeks to undo possible harm from the deception. The use of
so-called "role playing," in which the participant is let in
on the true nature of the situation but asked to act "as if"
it were real, has been proposed by Kelman (1967) as an alternative to deception, but it leaves unsettled the question of
whether the "as if" behavior is the same as genuine, natural
behavior, unless the researcher also does parallel studies
that employ deceptive stage management--again throwing us

back into conflict with the principle of informed consent.
Field studies of the behavior in question in its natural setting have their own ethical problems to which we turn next,
and if they avoid manipulative deception, they also give up
the virtues of experimental control for causal analysis.

Also in violation of the canon of informed consent are
the field studies that depend on inobtrusive observation,
often advocated by ideological opponents of manipulative experimentation. If you watch people, record (tape-record?)
observations about them, and draw inferences from what you
have seen and heard, without declaring yourself or asking
permission, are you committing an ethical violation? If you
do not affect their lives, and preserve their anonymity so
that others cannot use your observations to affect them,
most of us think not. But this is not informed consent.
What if you stage deceptive episodes in the real world, so
as to evoke real, natural behaviors in response to controlled
causes? This is what Latané and Darley (1970) did in their
highly regarded study of the innocent bystander problem--why
the bystander doesn't help, and what Stanley Milgram's (1970)
students have done in exploring some of the psychological dimensions of the quality of urban life. This is not informed
consent either, but again since people's lives are not much
affected, the issue of consent doesn't seem to be crucial.

We find ourselves wanting to shift to the other major
criterion: what harm is done? And the harm done, if any,
seems more likely to lie in the poltergeist-like disruption
of normal, honest social intercourse than in harm to the un-
witting participant. Are such investigators tearing at the
normal social fabric like mischievous cats? How big, how
tolerable, a nuisance are they? seems the main question.
And, if their ruses were discovered, how badly would our
necessary mutual complicity in the usual implicit social
contract be violated? When the principle of informed consent fails us, we turn to harm/benefit analysis. There are
those (I think particularly of Diana Baumrind [1975, 1976])
who say that this is a self-serving cop-out for investigators
who give too absolute priority to the advancement of knowledge.

Anthropological research in premodern societies poses a
similar set of dilemmas, which lie half way between the
issues touched on in relation to special classes of not fully
volitional participants and those involved in inobtrusive
participant observation. How can the anthropologist explain
to the "native" what he is really up to? Surely, he or she
tries, but real success is impossible without sending the
informants and cohabitants to graduate school. And who can

explain the possible consequences of invasion of the traditional cultural privacy? It just can't be done, except in
compromise ways that meet political or pragmatic criteria,
hardly ethical ones. The protection here must be on the
harm/benefit side, not on that of informed consent. Politics, of course, is a useful corrective to obscure ethics.
Nowadays, harm/benefit considerations are looked at closely
if not always wisely by the new Third World governments, and
the consent given or withheld by governments may effectively
stand in for the less meaningful consent of the actual participants.

     The anthropologist's case leads us directly to my third
major class of problems with informed consent: what do we
mean by "informed"? We say that we mean: informed at least
about those considerations that might reasonably affect a
person's decision as to whether or not to participate. "Reasonably" is a weasel word, and in any case, how can these
subtleties be explained across cultural gulfs? What, in
general, ought the potential participant to know in order to
be able to give or withhold appropriately informed consent to
participate? This is a highly judgmental matter on which the
investigator's vested interest in the advancement of knowledge will surely produce bias. So there is good reason for
jury-like reconsideration by review groups.

     A special problem arises in regard to the scientific
uses to which an investigator might want to put the data that
have been obtained, and an even more difficult one in regard
to further scientific uses to which other investigators might
later want to put them, in so-called "secondary analyses" of
important bodies of data that, fortunately for science and
society, have not been discarded. Is consent of the original
participants ethically required before old data can be researched for their bearing on new problems? If so, the value
of the advancement of knowledge will be severely impaired.

     I see no foreordained ethical solution to this dilemma.
For myself as a person committed both to scientific and to
other competing values, I like Donald Campbell's (1976) recent proposal: so long as the individual anonymity of the
original participants is scrupulously preserved (and there
are very fancy ways of doing that [Campbell et al. 1975]),
the participant has no special right of consent with respect
to the analytic uses to which the data to which he has contributed will be put. The participant's personal welfare is
protected, and the social and scientific need to use old data
for unanticipated new purposes, or to use new data for purposes obscure or maybe unwelcome to the participant, is also
recognized. The political, and maybe ethical, issues that

lurk here involve the interests of members of ethnic groups
and other social categories in how their own category may
appear in the light of social science. Should males and fe-
males, Blacks and Whites, have to give their informed consent
to plans for analysis by sex and race before participating in
a survey interview? I return to another aspect of this issue
later on.

Problems Involved in the
Harm/Benefit Frame

Now let us turn to problems and issues that are involved
in the second primary frame for ethical evaulation of research with human participants: that of harm/benefit. A
first observation is that, as the group preparing the A.P.A.
code discovered early on, there is just no way at all to con-
ceive of a workable cost/benefit formula that could resolve
actual issues of research ethics in the social sciences, even
though an accounting of potential harms and benefits does
provide a useful framework for considering the issues. Even
a rough and ready formula is out of the question in principle
because, for the crucial issues, the benefits claimed are to
science and society at large but the costs to be considered
are to the participant individual. How can you add that up?
The common assumption that the equivalent of a formula solution is possible comes from a mistaken analogy to a major
type of clinical research in medicine, in which it is indeed
possible to weigh the risks to the patient of an "experimental" treatment against the patient's possible gains from it.
Except in the case of social experimentation on social programs, there is no parallel in social research. Of course,
not even the medical case can be reduced to a quantitative
formula. The issue is inherently judgmental, and until the
research is done, the probabilities and values of both risk
and benefit are matters of guesswork: "informed judgment."

In social and psychological research in which the harms
at risk are usually not obvious matters of life and limb, a
second set of problems arises: who is to determine what is a
harm or a benefit, and how consequential it is? Who, in
effect, is to decide what is good for people? To raise this
question is to suggest a possible interaction with our first
basic framework, the voluntaristic principle of informed consent, which says that only the participant is in a position
to make that decision. Consider a couple of examples.

In an intensive exploratory study, done a number of years
ago, Stuart Cook, the principle architect of our A.P.A. code,
brought highly prejudiced White students into the laboratory
under a pretext (without their informed consent) and put them

through a set of social experiences that were contrived to make them less prejudiced toward Negroes. He held back from carrying out the other half of the design, of testing the power of analogous procedures to increase the prejudice of racial liberals. Even so, he was worried about the ethical acceptability of the study, and went ahead with it only because he thought, after much consultative discussion, that the possible gains in understanding warranted the ethical compromise. Would the prejudiced participants regard a reduction of their prejudice as a benefit? Would they have given their voluntary consent had they known what was up?

Another example. Stanley Milgram has, on occasion, argued in justification of his important and famous study of obedience (Milgram 1974) that participants who comply to the "experimenter's" outrageous demands (and might be thought to suffer a telling blow to their self-esteem) learn in the debriefing something important about themselves that they are often grateful for. Maybe so--but it does take considerable chutzpah to regard the bestowal of unwelcome truths about themselves as a benefit to them--even if, after the fact, people say they like it.

The possible harms to be weighed in social and psychological research range from the very trivial--surely temporary boredom is the most common harm in much research that psychology undergraduates get subjected to under semivoluntary conditions--to temporary stress that can readily be alleviated afterwards, to more serious stresses and indignities. One class of potential harms is beginning to be treated as an ethical consideration in its own right, and is beginning to receive legal definition and clarification: the invasion of privacy. Because the ethical-legal status of privacy as a primary right is still unclear--and in conflict with the simultaneously emerging value of the public "right to know"--I assimilate it here to the harm/benefit frame. Penetration of privacy is a harm because of the other harms that may follow from it in the lack of safeguards: disclosure of guilty secrets, deflation of self-esteem, constriction of one's scope of free action, and, in particular cases, the risk of a variety of unwelcome social and perhaps legal consequences. Rigorous measures to protect the confidentiality of all private information gained through the research relationship, often by guaranteeing its anonymity, are commonly thought to provide an adequate resolution of problems in this area.

Again, considerations of informed consent make a difference. Prospective participants must know the degree of confidentiality they can really count on before they are invited

to disclose private things about themselves. The power of
subpoena presents legal problems here, but Boruch (1971),
Campbell (Campbell et al. 1975), and others have suggested
some ingenious practical solutions.

Our consideration of the frames of voluntary participation and harm/benefit surely adds weight to the judgment I
have implied along the way that the ethical conflicts inherent in doing research do not lend themselves to solution by
abstract analysis or formula. Complex human judgments are
involved, ad hoc judgments guided by precedent and debate, in
which movement toward consensus can be stimulated but hardly
dictated by ethical analysis.

Two Debatable Extensions of
Consent and Harm/Benefit

I turn now, very briefly, to two possible extensions of
these frames of judgment, both of which go beyond the assumption that the individual is locus of value, implied in the
foregoing discussion. The first has my sympathy as a cogent
extension; the second does not.

Harm to the Normative Order

In the A.P.A. code, the harms to be weighed, avoided, or
counteracted are always to the participant individual. In
the great preponderance of social and psychological research
that I know about, such harms are either readily recognized
and consensually condemned, or they are quite trivial. But
there is another kind of harm to be considered in doing deceptive, manipulative research, research that is not respectful of the participant's human dignity. That is harm to the
normative order of the society and culture in which the scientist participates, and harm to the integrity of the scientist him/herself as a participant in that order. I have already touched on this in my comments on possible Poltergeist
effects. I believe that such harm is what Diana Baumrind
(1964) had mostly in mind in her early critique of the Milgram experiments and in her subsequent discussions (Baumrind
1975, 1976), which are too absolutistic for my taste. It is
not a good defense to argue, as I have heard Milgram, that
ordinary business practices are no better. It seems to me
that psychology and social science should aspire to a higher
standard; that the practice of research should follow the
canons of mutually respectful human relations, not fly in
their face. The argument that participants in experiments
differentiate clearly between such experiences and everyday
life, and can be helped to do so by appropriate debriefing,
is countered by the potential "modeling" impact of deceitful-

ness by professors and practitioners of psychology, made more dubious ethically when psychologists take evident glee in clever deceits in their formal or informal teaching. I do not follow Baumrind to hold that deceit in research should be flatly forbidden for this reason. But I agree with her that the harm is real, and that although it eludes measurement it should still be considered in coming to decisions about the ethical conflicts in our research enterprise.

Rights of Social Groups or Categories

The second extension would regard social groups and categories, or organizations and institutions, as having ethical rights akin to those of individuals. The claim is made particularly in regard to research that touches on hot issues of gender, race, and ethnicity, but it has its parallel in some research on organizations. It applies on both the consent side and on the harm/benefit side.

As for the harm/benefit frame, I agree with Donald Campbell (1976), that it would be radically subversive of the pursuit of knowledge and of the role of social knowledge in the democratic process if, as has been seriously advocated, we should engrave a new Commandment, "Thou shalt not discover or publish information that is unwelcome to members of a social category." True, social scientists have a general ethical obligation to be concerned with the use and misuse of their findings—but this is a different matter, and one that does not lend itself to flat prescription or proscription.

On the consent side, the extension to social categories also gets us into absurdities. Who can speak for a social category—Blacks, the poor, patients, prisoners, or consumers of human services—in the absence of any formal institutions of representative democracy? It makes sense to have members of affected categories on project advisory committees and on institutional review groups that pass on the ethical acceptability of social research: such persons can enlarge the ethical perspective of the review group and sensitize it to considerations that it would otherwise neglect. I don't think it makes sense, however, to regard them as representatives of their category, with the implicit ethical right to give or withhold informed consent on its behalf.

Here is a point where it seems to me essential to disentangle pragmatic political considerations from ethical ones. Any social scientist who wants to do research with Blacks or other groups that for good reason are sensitive about their autonomy and dignity needs to take special steps to engage their cooperation—better, collaboration—in the endeavor.

Tact and good human judgment are essential throughout, up to
and including the reporting of results, if the research is
to be accomplished at all and be of any use, and if other researchers are to be able to follow in the same path. This is
elementary, but I see it as a matter of pragmatics or politics, not of ethics. To interpret the issue as ethical, and
especially to erect it into administrative regulations, would
seem to me dangerously stultifying.

There remain genuine ethical issues of individual consent in this connection that cannot readily be dismissed.
Cook (Ref. Note 1) suggests an actual case. "Black students
take intelligence tests presented to them as useful to their
guidance in school settings. Along comes a researcher studying the organization of intelligence who wants to factor
analyze the test items in order to determine whether the
blacks are superior to or inferior to whites on one or another of the factors of intellect uncovered. The blacks who
took the test would never have done so had they known that
this use was to be made of their responses." The dilemma is
real. While I would tend to follow Campbell in resolving it
toward favoring the full scientific use of information, the
closer this use gets to the original collection of the data
for other, personally acceptable purposes, the more uncomfortable I become. Perhaps some equivalent of a "statute of
limitations" would help psychologically if not ethically!

Normative Practice vs. the
Forbidden Extreme Case

A final word. The administrative regulation of research
ethics inevitably focuses on the extreme, unacceptable case,
the case to be forbidden. Ethically responsible members of
the social scientific community, and of the informed general
public, might properly be more concerned with the ethical
level of what is general normative practice in our fields.
For myself, I find it quite possible to justify a Milgram
study, as a carefully weighed exception, an important study
that raises serious ethical questions but can be undertaken
with heavy ethical responsibility falling on the investigator's shoulders. I wouldn't do such a study, but I really
respect Milgram's right to have done it. I find it much har-
der to defend the almost total dependence on deception that
characterized a decade of experimental social psychology.
Somehow the whole field got corrupted, an ethical fact that
also has its pragmatic consequences: our subjects don't believe us, and sometimes there arises doubt as to who is con-
ning whom. Campus review committees can play a significant
part in encouraging a gradual shift in the ethical quality of
normative practice through their important consultative role.

Reference Note

1. Stuart W. Cook, Personal communication, June 16, 1976

References Cited

Ad Hoc Committee on Ethical Standards in Psychological Research
    1973 Ethical Principles in the Conduct of Research with Human Participants. Washington, D.C.: American Psychological Association.

Boruch, R.F.
    1971 Maintaining Confidentiality in Educational Research: A systematic Approach. American Psychologist 26:413-430.

Baumrind, D.
    1964 Some Thoughts on the Ethics of Research: After Reading Milgram's "Behavioral Study of Obedience." American Psychologist 19:421-423.

Baumrind, D.
    1975 Metaethical and Normative Consideration. In Human Rights and Psychological Research. E.C. Kennedy, ed. New York: Thomas Y. Crowell.

Baumrind, D.
    1976 Nature and Definition of Informed Consent in Research Involving Deception. (Mimeo) Prepared for the National Commission for the Protection of Human Subjects of Biomedical and Behavioral Research.

Campbell, D.T., R.F. Boruch, R.D. Schwartz, and J. Steinberg
    1975 Confidentiality-preserving Modes of Access to Files and to Interfile Exchange for Useful Statistical Analysis. Appendix A in Rivlin et al.

Campbell, D.T.
    1976 Protection of the Rights and Interests of Human Subjects in Program Evaluation, Social Indicators, Social Experimentation, and Statistical Analyses Based upon Administrative Records. (Mimeo) Prepared for the National Commission for the Protection of Human Subjects of Biomedical and Behavioral Research.

Kelman, H.C.
    1967 The Human Use of Human Subjects: The Problem of Deception in Social Psychological Experiments. Psychological Bulletin 67:1-11.

Latané, B., and J.M. Darley
   1970   The Unresponsive Bystander: Why Doesn't He Help?
      New York: Appleton-Century-Crofts.

Milgram, S.
   1970   The Experience of Living in Cities.   Science 167:
      1461-1468.

Milgram, S.
   1974   Obedience to Authority: An Experimental View.   New
      York: Harper and Row.

Rivlin, A., et al.
   1975   Protecting Individual Privacy in Evaluation Research.
      Final report of the National Research Council Committee
      on Federal Agency Evaluation Research.   Washington, D.
      C.:   National Research Council, National Academy of
      Sciences.

Smith, M.B.
   1976   Some Perspectives on Ethical/Political Issues in
      Social Science Research.   Personality and Social Psy-
      chology Bulletin 2:445-453.

2

Privacy
and Social Research

Edith E. Graber

Introduction

The _privacy_ of a person refers to the flow of information
between the self and a possible audience or to freedom from
intrusion into personal spheres. By excluding others from the
opportunity to observe or interact, by releasing information
selectively, by governing one's affairs as to permit the minimum of intrusion by outsiders--in short by conduct characterized by reserve or concealment that preserves areas as con-
fidential--a person maintains a boundary against other social
aggregates.

Though legal scholars have long focused attention on the
definition and delineation of privacy, social scientists have
left privacy largely unexamined. Now with government regulation of what was once a largely semi-private preserve--the
relationships between researcher, subject or informant, and
sponsoring institution--social scientists are finding it useful to explore and argue various aspects of privacy protection
in order to examine ethical requirements of research and to
maintain their freedom and autonomy to work.

The Concept of Privacy

Most considerations of privacy have to do with the civil
rights of the individual. Thus individual privacy may be
invaded when people's mail is opened, their telephone line
tapped, when information or communication they sought to keep
to themselves is given publicity, when sensitive information
in a file or dossier is given circulation beyond the legitimate purpose for which it was collected, when people are under
surveillance that does not fulfill a legitimate social purpose,
or when a search of someone's person is made without lawful
sanction and procedural protection.

But it is also possible to speak of the privacy of the small group vis-a-vis the society. One speaks of a private party or meeting in contrast to a public gathering, of the privacy of the family, of the private home or club, of the freedom to communicate with a friend in private. Privacy of the group has connotations of exclusiveness, of intimacy, of confidentiality, and of the relaxation of public postures, or of joining together in a common purpose which may be at variance with--or more specialized--than the general thrust of the society.

Hence, privacy refers to the relationship between the small social unit (most often the individual but sometimes also the group) and the society. The crucial question for privacy is who determines access? If it is the individual (or group), then he/she is presumed to have, or to be able to regulate the degree of privacy wanted. But privacy is not an absolute right or claim. We could not have a society if individuals or groups were permitted to control all information about themselves, their actions and their resources. The relationship between the individual and the society is a reciprocal one with information, benefits and controls flowing both ways. Consequently, social norms have developed which at times permit the individual to deny access and control, even when challenged, and at times permit access by society, even when resisted.

A second major question for the issue of privacy is why access is sought? Is it for some larger social good, such as the acquisition of knowledge? Or to determine whether the individual is eligible for some benefit? To persuade and influence the individual? To exercise social control? Is the purpose socially acceptable or desirable? Is it lawful?

The definition of privacy has occupied many socio-legal scholars. The majority of discussions have focused around two general definitions which have some standing in the field of law. These are <u>privacy as the control over information about the self</u> (or group) and <u>privacy as autonomy</u>. This paper examines these as defined in court cases and recent statutes and explores the application of these two concepts to the field of social research. I shall pay particular attention to the privacy and confidentiality of information imparted to researchers by subjects or informants.

Privacy as Control over Information

Alan F. Westin, legal scholar and author of several seminal works on privacy (Westin 1966, 1967; Westin & Baker 1972), defines privacy as--

the claim of individuals, groups or institutions
to determine for themselves when, how, and to
what extent information about them is communicated
to others (Westin 1967:7).

This view of privacy as the voluntary control of information
has a long history. It is similar to the definition used by
Warren and Brandeis in their 1890 article, "The Right to Privacy," which expressed concern about the protection from unwanted intrusion using the concept of privacy. Their discussion suggests that

(T)he common law secures to each individual the
right of determining, ordinarily, to what extent
his thoughts, sentiments and emotions shall be
communicated to others (Warren & Brandeis 1890:
189; see also Fried 1968; Miller 1972;& Gross
1967).

Edward Shils uses a similar definition; he differentiates
privacy from the related concept of secrecy:

Privacy is the voluntary withholding of information
reinforced by a willing indifference. Secrecy is
the compulsory withholding of knowledge, reinforced
by the prospect of sanctions for disclosure. Both
are enemies, in principle, of publicity (Shils 1956:
26-7).

Westin's definition refers to the individual and the
collective dimension of privacy. He contends that group
privacy is more than simply the sum of the privacies of individual members. Rather, it represents protection of the functions served by groups as independent entities between the
individual and the society (Westin 1967:42).

The word "privacy" is not found in the Constitution or in
the Bill of Rights. Yet over the years, the United States
Supreme Court has carefully specified a legally defensible
right to privacy through case by case judicial inclusion and
exclusion. It has found the Constitutional basis for this
legal claim in the Bill of Rights, particularly in the First,
Fourth, Fifth, Ninth and Fourteenth Amendments.

Though Supreme Court justices and legal scholars view a
1965 case, <u>Griswold v. Connecticut</u>, as the "first" privacy
case, there are a number of earlier cases which protect privacy interests and which are directed to the issue of who has
control over certain kinds of information about the self.
Before 1965, such cases were identified as "search and seizure"

or "Fourth Amendment" cases. Only after <u>Griswold</u> are two
cases in this class defined by the court as "privacy" cases.
The issue in a number of these cases was to specify under what
conditions agents of government could have access to information about individuals. (Invasion of privacy is also a tort--
a private or civil wrong or injury. However, most of the
significant privacy cases have involved intrusion not by private parties but by agents of government.)

In an early case, pre-dating the appearance of the Warren
and Brandeis article, <u>Boyd v. United States</u>, 1886, the court
considered the consitutionality of a statute which held that
unwillingness to produce business records demanded by the
government constituted an admission of guilt. The court found
the act unconstitutional; it held that the Fourth Amendment
proscribing "unlawful searches and seizures" and the Fifth
Amendment protecting the individual against self-incrimination

> apply to all invasions on the part of the govern-
> ment and its employees of the sanctity of a man's
> home and the privacies of his life. It is not the
> breaking of his doors, and the rummaging of his
> drawers, that constitutes the essence of the offence;
> but it is the invasion of his indefeasible right
> of personal security, personal liberty and private
> property. . . It is the duty of courts to be
> watchful for the constitutional rights of the
> citizen, and against any stealthy encroachments
> thereon (<u>Boyd v. United States</u> 1886:532, 535).

Here and in some additional early cases, the word "privacy" appears in the decision. However, the right to privacy
was not the point of law on which the judgment was based.
Instead, it was that the compulsory production of papers under
the conditions cited constituted an unlawful search and
seizure.

A later series of cases focused on the "physical intrusion" concept of privacy. In <u>Olmstead v. United States</u> (1928),
the court held that wiretapping was not within the conventional meaning of "search" as used in the Fourth Amendment and
that therefore the tapping of telephone lines of a business
engaged in the illegal sale of liquor in violation of the
National Prohibition Act did not constitute an unlawful
search and seizure. The fact that the wiretapping had been
done "without trespass" was one of the deciding factors.

Louis D. Brandeis, the co-author of the "Right to Privacy"
article was now a justice on the Supreme Court. In his
eloquent dissent in <u>Olmstead,</u> he argued that the tapping of

telephone lines invaded the privacy of persons at both ends
of the lines and that the founding fathers

> conferred, as against the government, the right to
> be let alone--the most comprehensive of rights and
> the right valued by civilized men. To protect that
> right, every unjustifiable intrusion by the govern-
> ment upon the privacy of the individual, whatever
> the means employed, must be deemed a violation of
> the Fourth Amendment (Olmstead v. United States
> 1928:572).

Similarly, in Goldman v. United States (1942), where a
wiretapping device had not penetrated the wall of a room, no
intrusion and hence, no invasion of privacy had occurred. In
Silverman v. United States (1961) where a spike microphone did
penetrate the wall, there was a violation of the Fourth Amendment and an unlawful search and seizure.

Not until Katz v. United States (1967) did the court
reverse the Olmstead decision. This Fourth Amendment case
was decided after the "first" privacy case (see below).
Though it is similar to the cases discussed above in determining how information about the individual is obtained, and
whether the government has a legal right to such access, it is
defined by the court in its subsequent discussions as a "privacy" case.

Katz was charged with transmitting betting information by
telephone across inter-state lines; evidence corroborating
this was secured by F.B.I. agents who attached a listening
and recording device to the outside of a telephone booth. In
its decision, the Court found that Fourth Amendment problems
were not solved by determining whether physical intrusion had
occurred or by specifying "constitutionally protected areas":

> For the Fourth Amendment protects people, not places.
> What a person knowingly exposes to the public, even
> in his own home or office, is not a subject of
> Fourth Amendment protection. . . But what he seeks
> to preserve as private, even in an area accessible to
> the public, may be constitutionally protected (Katz
> v. United States 1967:511).

In this series of Fourth Amendment "search and seizure"
cases, the court had come increasingly to identify the claim
to protection against certain kinds of unreasonable searches
and seizures with the "right to privacy." But the Court
warned against an overclose identification of the Fourth
Amendment with the right to privacy:

> The Fourth Amendment cannot be translated into a
> general constitutional "right to privacy." That
> Amendment protects individual privacy against
> certain kinds of governmental intrusion, but its
> protections go further and often have nothing to
> do with privacy at all (<u>Katz v. United States</u>
> 1967:510).

Hence, though protection against searches and seizures overlap with the right to privacy, each offers protections the
other does not.

Westin's definition of privacy goes farther than others
in extending the concept of privacy as the <u>voluntary control
over information from</u> individuals to groups and institutions.
This definition implies that information about the structure,
purposes and membership of organizations may be protected.
In its decisions, the Supreme Court has also extended a very
limited legal right of privacy to groups. Terming this an
"associational privacy," the Court ruled in 1958 that an Alabama law which required that the National Association for the
Advancement of Colored People turn over to the state of Alabama its membership and officer lists in order to be recognized as an out-of-state corporation was unconstitutional.
The Court upheld the right to keep this information private:

> This Court has recognized the vital relationship
> between freedom to associate and privacy in one's
> associations. . . Inviolability of privacy in
> group association may in many circumstances be in-
> dispensable to freedom of association, particularly
> where a group espouses dissident beliefs (<u>NAACP v.
> Alabama</u> 1958:449).

The Court found that in the face of possible hostility
and reprisals, the disclosure of names of members and officers
might prejudice the liberty to associate in joint or group
interests. This right has been affirmed in a series of subsequent cases.

The concept of privacy as control over information about
the self and the group thus has had certain limited and carefully specified legal application.

Privacy as Autonomy

Privacy as <u>control over information</u> is a concept which
is very broad in its scope. But an alternative formulation--
<u>privacy as autonomy or freedom from intrusion</u>--is even broad-
er. Yet it is the latter concept which forms the basis of

the legally defensible right to privacy in a series of cases
beginning with Griswold v. Connecticut in 1965. Again,
through case-by-case specification and delimitation, the
Court has indicated where privacy may be reasonably expected
and legally protected.

In Griswold--which legal scholars have termed the "first
privacy case"--the Court declared unconstitutional a Connecticut statute of 1879 which made the use of contraceptives a
criminal offense. An accessory statute made anyone who as-
sisted, abetted, counseled, caused, hired or commanded this
crime subject to the same sanctions. Thus, in this instance,
the government attempted to regulate rather than learn about
personal affairs.

The Court found that the enforcement of such laws presented obvious problems. But the very intrusion of the state
into a private relationship was a more compelling issue.
Justice Douglas, writing for the majority, held that a zone
of privacy was created by several fundamental constitutional
provisions. The state's law forbidding the use of contraceptives was an intrusion into that zone of privacy and would
have a destructive impact on the marital relationship. He
continued, "We deal with a right of privacy older than the
Bill of Rights. . .older than our school system" (Griswold,
1965:486). It was Justice Goldberg, in a concurring opinion,
who termed this the "right of marital privacy" (Griswold
1965:487).

In Eisenstadt v. Baird (1972), the Court extended the
Griswold right to unmarried persons on equal protection
grounds:

> If the right of privacy means anything, it is the
> right of the individual, married or single, to be
> free from unwarranted governmental intrusion into
> matters so fundamentally affecting a person as the
> decision whether to bear or begat a child (Eisenstadt
> v. Baird, 1972:1038).

In the abortion case, Roe v. Wade (1973), the Court held
that "This right of privacy. . .is broad enough to encompass
a women's decision whether or not to terminate her pregnancy"
(Roe v. Wade 1973:727). The Court also noted that the right
to privacy could extend to activities such as "marriage. . .
procreation. . .contraception. . .family relationships. . .
and child rearing and education" (Roe v. Wade 1973:726).
Two earlier cases, one establishing the right of parents to
educate their children in a private school which met state
standards, and another sustaining the right to study the

German language in a private school, were incorporated into the new right to privacy (Pierce v. Society of Sisters 1925 and Meyer v. Nebraska 1923).

The fundamental concept protected in these cases is that of the right of persons to be free from state interference in the intimate relationships and decisions of procreation and family life. The Court has, however, let stand a lower court ruling that the State has the right to penalize sodomy between consenting adults in private (Doe v. Commonwealth's Attorney 1976).

In Stanley v. Georgia (1968), the Court considered another type of privacy invasion; it held that the state may not prevent an individual from looking at obscene materials in his or her own home; in a subsequent case, however, it supported the right of the state to forbid the showing of obscene movies in adult theaters and suggested that "the proposition that conduct involving consenting adults only is always beyond state regulation is a step we are unable to take" (Paris v. Slaton 1973:2641). In additional cases, the Court asserted that the state may forbid importation, sale or giving away of obscene materials.

Thus, in a series of recent cases, the Court has set forth specific areas where the individual may be free from state interference and regulation. In these areas, the individual or small group have specified rights to be self-governing.

The Federal Privacy Statutes

Until 1974, the major legal protection of privacy was based on Constitutional principles and case law. Privacy protection thus issued largely from the judicial branch of government. In 1974 Congress, prompted in part by the Watergate scandal, passed two major pieces of comprehensive legislation on privacy protection.

The first of these statutes, the Privacy Act of 1974 is directed to Federal agencies in the executive branch of government. Its goal is to ensure that the information about an individual maintained by a Federal agency is sufficiently accurate, timely, complete and relevant to base a fair decision about that individual. It tightens standards for keeping Government records and gives private citizens the right to examine their records and to correct inaccuracies.

The second statute, the Family Educational Rights and Privacy Act (hereinafter referred to as FERPA) provides that no funds shall be available under any federal education program to any educational institution or agency that denies access to school records to parents or students; it also provides for the correction and amendment of records and for restricted disclosure of records to third parties.

Both of these statutes are directed toward the concept of privacy as control over information about the self.

The two definitions of privacy are related in several ways. Privacy as autonomy may be viewed as a larger category incorporating the concept of privacy as control over information. One desires to keep certain kinds of information from the public domain at least partially because one wishes to maintain independence and freedom of movement. In this sense, control over information is an instrumental means toward preserving autonomy. Both aspects of the concept also include keeping some parts of the self confidential because they are not within the domain of the public, even in its governmental capacity, to know about or control.

Yet the two concepts may also be distinguished. If the restricted definition encompasses control over information, the larger concept (privacy as autonomy) also refers to control over actions and decisions. It has its roots partially in the concept that privacy sustains and enhances individuality, and more broadly in the political doctrine that ultimate power in a democratic society is vested in and flows from the people; their integrity and freedom must thus be protected.

Privacy and Research

The rise of empirical social research has largely been a phenomenon of this century. The social sciences advanced through the inte.r r.elated development of theory and accumulation of research findings. Social research, therefore, generates and rests upon information--and information is absolutely necessary in order to build theories about social phenomena.

The persons who make up the social world are inevitably the subjects of the search for social science information. A variety of groups seek information from these persons. Government is undoubtedly the largest consumer. But the media, businesses, social institutions, and social researchers also request data. And, where there is a request for information of an individual and personal nature, there is the potential for invasion of privacy.

I have suggested earlier that where privacy is threatened, two questions become significant. The first question,
"Who controls access to information?" can help determine the
conditions under which privacy is invaded. The second, "Why
is access sought?" may help assess the legitimacy of a particular claim to privacy.

Who Determines Access?

Under Westin's definition, the person (or group) with
privacy is the one who is able to determine "when, how and to
what extent information about them is communicated to others"
(Westin 1967:7). By this definition, persons who give consent, well informed and freely tendered, are not suffering an
invasion of privacy, even though they may be transmitting information of a highly personal nature, so long as the conditions are honored under which the information was transmitted.

In the prescription for securing informed consent, there
is an overlap between concern for privacy and the DHEW regulations regarding the protection of human subjects. The interests of privacy as control over information and privacy
as autonomy over the private sphere of the self are both
served when the securing of consent is made specific.

Federal regulations refer to all persons at risk in biomedical or behavioral science research as "subjects." The
definitions of privacy under consideration would support a
conceptual distinction between "subjects" and "informants."

The person about whom information is sought by direct or
indirect means is clearly the subject of the investigation.
To the extent they desire such persons should be able to maintain privacy--at least, in the face of direct inquiry. There
are few, if any, academic social research projects in which
the subject would be required or mandated to give information
about the self. To a very considerable extent, subjects have
had essential control over information before current Federal
regulations were issued; they could simply refuse to answer
or decline to cooperate. Cooperation was thus a form of implied consent.

But the respondent may have felt only partially free to
refuse, perhaps out of an unwillingness to embarrass the
researcher-subject relationship, however temporary, by non-
cooperation. In this sense, the securing of "informed consent" where subjects are involved can serve the useful function of reminding them that the control over information about
the self is theirs alone. A useful inclusion is the reminder
that the subject may withdraw from the research relationship

at any time or, in some instances, that participation may be selective (e.g., participation may continue even though not all questions are answered).

If the subject is to retain control over information about the self, it is necessary that he or she be given a fair representation about the nature of the information sought and the uses to which it will be put. A subject cannot give informed consent if the research purpose is disguised or if the researcher deceives the subject as to its real purpose. Yet, in deciding whether or not to participate in an investigation, the subject may give most attention to other features of the interaction than are contained in the usual formal description, and, in particular, may render a judgment based mostly on an assessment of the character of the person conducting the inquiry. Furthermore, as has been noted by Cassell and Wax, field investigators usually forecast neither the exact course of their research nor the likely outcome in publication, and so they are not able to provide the subject with a precise formal account of what might be entailed by participation.

Though there is some risk to privacy in the information gathering process itself, the larger threat comes with publicity, publication and dissemination. Here most threats to privacy are obviated by the aggregation of data, by anonymity for individual subjects, by disguise of particular identifiers or by the securing of consent if the identity of the individual is to be traceable in the published report.

A person who is a subject may be differentiated from one who is an informant by the nature of the information sought. While the subject is queried regarding information about the self and the attitudes, ideas and actions associated with the self, the informant is sought not for personal but for general information. The informant may be an expert in the area the researcher is examining or a participant in the social process at issue, e.g., state legislators being interviewed to determine the effect of an open meetings law on the legislative process (Graber 1974). An informant can thus give valuable information and perspective regarding the area being examined.

To the extent that informants do not give personal information about themselves (and thus are not concerned with protecting that class of information), it would appear that no privacy implications are involved under our definitions. However, the informants may not want their identity attached to the disclosures they make. Or they may not want to cause discomfiture or embarrassment to other members of the group or category about whom they furnish information and interpretation. In these instances, informants are usually promised confidentiality or anonymity; either the information will not be used directly; or, if so used, will not be identified with or traceable to them. To the extent that such a promise can be kept, the control over information obtains.

But at this juncture, the control over the information begins to pass from informant to researcher. Researchers can ensure the control over the information only to the extent that they can deliver the promised confidentiality and anonymity.

The problem is that control can pass inadvertently from the researcher to agents of government outside the two-party relationship. Under present law, only in limited instances is confidential personally identifiable information gathered by social science researchers immune from compulsory disclosure upon requests by law enforcement and court officials. Under the Comprehensive Drug Abuse Prevention and Control Act of 1970, Congress gave to the Secretary of the Department of Health, Education and Welfare the power to grant to persons engaged in mental health, alcohol and drug abuse research an absolute right to withhold the identity of subjects in all civil, criminal, administrative or legislative proceedings at federal, state or local levels (42 U.S.C. 4582). The Law Enforcement Assistance Administration not only grants immunity from compulsory legal process of individually identifiable information furnished under the statute but also specifically prohibits voluntary disclosure of such information other than for the purpose for which the information was gathered (42 U.S.C. 3371).

In other instances, the researcher may be compelled to furnish information on the identity of subjects, even though there has been an explicit or implied promise of confidentiality. Charles Knerr has cited the following examples:

> Researchers in Pueblo, Colorado, who were also counselors at a rape crisis center, were subpoenaed to produce their files on two young rape victims they had counselled. They refused and went to jail.

> A sociologist, as a participant-observer, studied police trainees. Accumulated research notes and oral testimony in a civil suit were subpoenaed. The researcher refused and was able to get the matter dropped.

> Another sociologist, studying the behavior and attitudes of sex crime victims, threatened to destroy

his files rather than breach confidences in complying with a local prosecutor's subpoena. Faced with imprisonment, he subsequently complied with four subpoenas.

Research on crime victimization revealed that in certain parts of a city only a small percentage of crimes were actually reported. The City's police chief disputed the findings and publicly demanded the names of all the interviewees. The researcher refused to cooperate since he had given assurances of confidentiality to the subjects.

Local narcotics officers took an interest in research on the behavior of drug addicts. They wanted the names of the study's subjects. Knowing that cooperation with the police would sever his contacts with the addicts, the researcher refused to deal with the officers and took special precautions to protect his data. His home was "burglarized" and a dummy codebook of the addicts' identities was taken (Privacy Journal 1977:4).

Some scholars have suggested that the researcher-subject relationship be given the same immunity from compelled disclosure of confidential communications that has long been granted in many jurisdictions to the lawyer-client, the doctor-patient and the husband-wife relationships (Boness and Cordes 1973). However, courts have in recent years been very reluctant to create new testimonial privileges. Further, in a 1972 case, Branzburg v. Hayes, (408 U.S. 665) the Supreme Court held that despite the First Amendment protection of freedom of speech and of the press, even newsmen can be compelled to testify before grand juries regarding their confidential sources and information (Nejelski and Finsterbusch 1973). Thus there is little hope for the securing of an additional confidential communication privilege for the researcher-subject relationship.

Ingenious methods by which the researcher can maintain control over personally identifiable information in his possession range from destroying data as soon as feasible, destroying identifying information which link subjects to confidential data, keeping separate files on identity of subjects and on data gathered and keeping the linking file in a safe place such as a foreign country (termed "link file brokerage"), warning subjects of the possible inability to honor commitments of confidentiality, etc. (Committee on Federal Agency Evaluation Research 1975:5-21). All of these are neither absolute nor wholly satisfactory.

The findings of the Privacy Protection Study Commission cited in its report Personal Privacy in an Information Society

point to a possible partial solution. The Commission was
established as a result of the Privacy Act of 1974. Its
many areas of inquiry included an examination of methods to
protect privacy interests of individuals who are subjects of
research collected by Federal agencies or with Federal funds.
While the Commission's recommendations for legislation are
lengthy and specific, their guiding principle is that there
be "functional separation" of data gathered for research and
statistical activities from those gathered for policy and
decision-making. To some extent, the Commission found, there
is already organizational separation of these functions. However, where one agency serves both purposes or where there
are requests from program or policy personnel to research and
statistical personnel, the need for protection remains. The
aim of such separation is to prevent individually identifiable information gathered for a research or statistical purpose with explicit, implied or expected confidentiality to be
used for influencing decisions made about the individual without his consent. Accordingly, the Commission recommended:

> that the Congress provide by statute that no
> record or information contained therein collect-
> ed or maintained for a research or statistical
> purpose under Federal authority or with Federal
> funds may be used in individually indentifiable
> form to make any decision or take any action
> directly affecting the individual to whom the
> record pertains, except within the context of the
> research plan or protocol, or with the specific
> authorization of such individual (The Privacy
> Protection Study Commission 1977:574).

If legislation complying with the principle of "functional separation" were passed by the Congress, there would
be some potential for greater control over information by
the subject or informant and by the researcher. The subject
could have greater confidence that information entrusted to
a Federal agency or to a Federally funded researcher would
be used only for the research or statistical purpose for
which it was collected or that it would be used chiefly for
a policy purpose.   In either case, more specific and reliable indication of the use of information could be given to
the person supplying it. For the Federally funded researcher, there would be statutory authority for resisting the
transmission of data gathered in a research function from
being used for decision-making functions.

The principle of "functional separation" is directed to
Federal agencies and to Federally funded research. To the
extent that this principle is also extended to privately

funded and unfunded social research (a common development in
the history of Federal regulations), some additional clarity
of expectation obtains.

But the Commission also recommended two classes of statutory exceptions to the principle. One is for disclosures
for auditing purposes. The Congress is charged with an over-
sight function over the public funds it dispenses. Where
authorized by statute, agencies such as the General Accounting Office may need access to data in order to hold agencies
and research contractors accountable.

The other exception is for disclosures in response to
compulsory process. This matter is explored more fully in
the next section. However, it is possible that even under
the Commission's recommendation a number of the requests for
identities of research subjects cited by Knerr would still
need to be honored. The threshold for law enforcement officials, both national and local, may be higher; they may have
to justify their request. But the researchers may still be
forced against their will to reveal identities of subjects
and informants, and these respondents may lose control over
communicated information. That many of the requests for such
information are legitimate and socially desirable is granted.
The ethical researcher, however, will need to assess and convey to the persons he queries a realistic estimate of the
subsequent course of the information.

It is ironic that the government requires, requests and
funds "social impact" evaluations of pending or enacted legislation but also, at present, maintains ultimate control
under conditions that may "chill" or deter research. Thus
researchers may tend to avoid projects where the inadvertent
and compelled production of information may prejudice the
interests of respondents. Or there may be increasing refusal
by subjects and informants to participate in research if they
realize that the expected confidentiality cannot be ensured.
The inability to protect confidentiality remains as a threat
to the privacy of the research subject and to the integrity
of the ongoing social science research relationship.

Why Is Access Sought?

Knowledge is power and wide-ranging knowledge or information about an individual contains the potential of wide-ranging power over him. It is not a coincidence that a totalitar-
ian or absolute government significantly enlarges surveillance of its citizens.

The concept of privacy, both as control over information and as freedom from governmental intrusion, derives from the principle of limited government. There is a private sphere which is beyond the province of society in its collective capacity to know about or to regulate. But there is also a public sphere in which the rights of the individual may need to be curtailed in the public interest.

Modern societies value the free flow of information in the belief that knowledge will facilitate rational and efficient decision-making. Technology has dramatically augmented the societal capacity to gather, store and use information. There is therefore pressure to acquire still more data to further increase the efficiency of decision-making and to further minimize the risk of unwise choices. The societal "right to know" must be weighed against the individual right to privacy.

Such balancing of individual and social interests and rights occurs where rights are in conflict. A compelling social interest can sometimes justify regulation in some spheres of intimacy, e.g., the removal of a baby from child-abusing parents. And in the public sphere a compelling interest in privacy can sometimes stem the flow of information even though such transmission serves a legitimate social purpose.

Academic researchers cannot, as does government, compel the granting of access. Nor can they often offer a reciprocal exchange of benefits for information as does government. But they can present a cogent argument that the respondents can furnish significant assistance to the understanding of social processes by their contribution to the research.

In addition to the balancing of the privacy rights of the individual against the public interest in information and regulation, another balancing process may be involved. In this instance, it is between two competing social interests-- between the public right to know and the public interest in the protection of the research process and particularly, in the protection of confidentiality. The balancing process is problematic in the field of law enforcement and particularly when the subjects are deviants or those who have relatively little power. To the extent, for instance, that the phenomenon of deviance needs to be better understood, it is in the societal interest to conduct social research. However, when the research purpose is encumbered with law enforcement purposes and when the researcher is in effect made an information-gathering arm of the law there are serious risks not only to the interests of subjects but to the research process itself (Nejelski and Lerman 1971:119-1123; Reynolds 1972, 706-718). The Privacy Protection Commission found that

> when an individual is asked to reveal information
> about himself in confidence--less for his own than
> for society's benefit--the disadvantages of making
> the information available for purposes other than
> those stated to the individual outweight the advan-
> tages accruing to other users. This is particularly
> true when the information is available through com-
> pulsory process because the disadvantages of this
> type of disclosure to researcher and subject far out-
> weigh the advantage to any law enforcement investi-
> gation. . .the Commission believes the present legal
> protections are unacceptably ambiguous and far too
> limited (The Privacy Protection Study Commission
> 1977:577).

The Commission concluded that the privacy interest of the individual together with the Fifth Amendment right to refuse to incriminate oneself require that "research and statistical records be generally immune from judicial order." However, total immunity was seen as potentially against soc-ietal interests.

> If a research activity is suspected of having unneces-
> sarily endangered research subjects, as in the infam-
> ous Central Intelligence Agency research on LSD, for
> example, or if a researcher is suspected of fraud,
> access to confidential research records may well be
> the only way to establish guilt or innocence (The
> Privacy Protection Study Commission 1977:579).

Thus, again, in the extreme case, a balancing process is involved. Under the Commission's recommendation however, the burden of proof would favor the confidentiality of individu-ally identifiable research and statistical data and greater recognition would be given to the interests of the subject, the researcher, and the research process.

Ultimately, there is a strong societal interest in the protection of the academic social research process itself. The protection of academic freedom is analogous to privacy as autonomy and freedom from governmental regulation. Indeed, in Griswold v. Connecticut, Justice Douglas drew on the Court's protection of academic freedom to support the con-cept of privacy as freedom from governmental regulation in limited spheres. He wrote that while the word "privacy" was not mentioned in the Constitution nor in the Bill of Rights, neither was the right of parents to educate their child in a

school of their choice or the right to study a foreign language or other particular subject. Yet the High Court had
secured those rights on Constitutional principles in Pierce
v. Society of Sisters and Meyer v. Nebraska. He continued:

> In other words, the State may not consistently with
> the spirit of the First Amendment, contract the
> spectrum of available knowledge. The right of free-
> dom of speech and press includes not only the right
> to utter or to print, but the right to distribute,
> the right to receive, the right to read. . .and
> freedom of inquiry, freedom of thought, and freedom
> to teach. . .indeed the freedom of the entire uni-
> versity community. . .Without those peripheral
> rights the specific rights would be less secure.
> And so we reaffirm the principle of the Pierce and
> the Meyer cases (Griswold v. Connecticut 1965:482-3).

Freedom of inquiry can be chilled both by encumbering
governmental regulation and by intrusion into the research
process. For good or ill, government is now a third party in
the research relationship. A large share of research funds
are furnished directly or indirectly by government. It is to
be expected that regulations would follow to ensure accounta-
bility for use of funds and to secure adherence to legitima-
ted social values and Constitutional principles, such as the
right to privacy.

But the researcher-respondent relationship is ultimately
a fiduciary relationship. The researcher seeks to overcome
an initial resistance and reluctance of the subject to participate in research by demonstrating competence, by giving
evidence of trustworthiness and by citing the social benefits
to be gained from the inquiry (Glazer 1971). The subject
entrusts information which is committed for selective publication. The protection of privacy--whether defined as the control over information about the self or an autonomy and freedom from governmental regulation in limited spheres--requires
that researchers have a healthy respect for the integrity and
vulnerability of their subjects. And it requires that govem-
ment, as an inevitable third party in the relationship, minimize intrusiveness to that required for a compelling social
purpose.

References Cited

Boness, F.H.,and Cordes, J.F.
   1973   The Researcher Subject Relationship: The Need For
      Protection and a Model Statute.   Georgetown Law Journal
      62:243-272.
Committee on Federal Agency Evaluation Research, National
Research Council
   1975   Protecting   Individual Privacy in Evaluation Research.
      Washington, D.C.: National Academy of Sciences.
Fried, Charles
   1968   Privacy.   The Yale Law Journal 77:475-493.
Glazer, Myron
   1972   The Research Adventure: Promise and Problems of Field
      Work.   New York: Random House.
Gross, Hyman
   1967   The Concept of Privacy.   New York University Law
      Review 42:34-54.
Graber, Edith E.
   1974   Group Privacy and the Legislative Process.   Unpublish-
      ed Ph.D. dissertation, University of Denver.
Miller, Arthur R.
   1972   The Assault on Privacy.   New York: New American Li-
      brary (A Mentor Book).
Nejelski, Paul,and Kurt Finsterbusch
   1973   The Prosecutor and the Researcher: Present and Pros-
      pective Variations on the Supreme Court's Branzburg
      Decision.   Social Problems 21:3-21.
Nejelski, Paul,and Lindsey Miller Lerman
   1971   A Researcher-subject Testimonial Privilege: What To
      Do Before The Subpoena Arrives.   Wisconsin Law Review
      1085-1148.
Privacy Journal
   1977   Protecting Crime Research. Privacy Journal 3:4.
The Privacy Protection Study Commission
   1977   Personal Privacy In An Information Society.   Washing-
      ton, D.C.:   U.S. Government Printing Office.
Reynolds, Paul Davidson
   1972   On The Protection of Human Subjects and Social Sci-
      ence.   International Social Science Journal 24:693-719.
Shils, Edward A.
   1956   The Torment of Secrecy: The Background and Conse-
      quences of American Security Policies.   New York: The
      Free Press.
Warren, Samuel D.,and Louis D. Brandeis
   1890   The Right To Privacy. Harvard Law Review 4:193-220.
Westin, Alan F.
   1966   Science, Privacy and Freedom: Issues and Proposals
      For the 1970s.   Columbia Law Review 66:1003-1050; 1205-
      1253.

Westin, Alan F.
  1967 Privacy and Freedom. New York: Atheneum.
Westin, Alan, and Michael A. Baker
  1972 Databanks in Free Society: Computers, Record-Keeping
     and Privacy. New York: Quadrangle.

U.S. Supreme Court Cases

Boyd v. United States. 6S. Ct. 524 (1886)
Branzburg v. Hayes. 408 U.S. 665 (1972)
Doe v. Commonwealth's Attorney. 96 S. Ct. 1489, 1976
Eisenstadt v. Baird. 92 S. Ct. 1029, 1972.
Goldman v. United States. 62 S. Ct. 993, 1942
Griswold v. Connecticut. 381 U.S. 479, 1965
Katz v. United States. 88 S. Ct. 507, 1967
Meyer v. Nebraska. 43 S. Ct. 625, 1923
N.A.A.C.P. v. Alabama. 78 S. Ct. 1163, 1958
Olmstead v. United States. 48 S. Ct. 564, 1928
Paris Adult Theatre I et al. v. Slaton. 93 S. Ct. 2628, 1973
Pierce v. Society of Sisters. 45 S. Ct. 571, 1925
Roe v. Wade. 93 S. Ct., 705, 1973
Silverman v. United States. 81 S. Ct. 679, 1961
Stanley v. Georgia, 394 U.S. 557, 1968

3

Human Subjects Review Committees and Social Research

Bradford H. Gray

It may surprise many social scientists to learn that DHEW requirements for institutional review of research involving human subjects have explicitly applied to social research for a dozen years, and that the original requirements acknowledged some characteristics of social research that required flexibility in the interpretation of the policy. On February 8, 1966, then Surgeon General William Stewart issued the Public Health Service policy document that initiated DHEW's institutional review requirement.[1] In response to questions that arose in subsequent months, he issued a "clarification" on December 12, 1966, in which he stated that the policy of institutional review "refers to all investigations that involve human subjects, including investigations in the behavioral and social sciences."[2] The policy itself, as revised on July 1, 1966, contained the following statement about social research:

> . . . there is a large range of social and behavioral research in which no personal risk to the subject is involved. In these circumstances, regardless of whether the investigation is classified as behavioral, social, medical, or other, the issues of concern are the fully voluntary nature of the participation of the subject, the maintenance of confidentiality of information obtained from the subject, and the protection of the subject from misuse of the findings."[3]

The July 1 statement also indicated that the social and behavioral sciences sometimes used procedures which "may in many instances not require the fully informed consent of the subject or even his knowledgeable participation."

The institutional review requirements have undergone several changes over the years. They have become more formalized, changing from Public Health Service policy, to DHEW policy, to a matter of federal statute and DHEW regulations. The requirements have also become more detailed and explicit, and the composition requirements for review committees have been broadened. Specific mention of social or behavioral research has disappeared. In addition, the review requirement, which originally applied only to research funded by the Public Health Service, was extended by the National Research Act of 1974 to all research involving human subjects that is conducted at institutions that receive funds for such research under the Public Health Service Act. The National Commission for the Protection of Human Subjects recommends that the requirement be extended still further.

In the past few years, social scientists have become increasingly vocal in expressing a variety of reservations about DHEW's regulation of research involving human subjects. Professional associations such as the American Sociological Association and the American Psychological Association have begun to hear from members about particular experiences with institutional review boards (IRBs); the American Sociological Association has reorganized its committee structure so as to be able more adequately to keep abreast of regulatory developments that might affect social research; the professional newsletters in the social sciences frequently contain articles and letters about these matters; conferences have been held; and conventions in the social science disciplines now commonly have a session or two devoted to ethical and regulatory questions.

Two other developments among social researchers in recent years are also worthy of note. First, empirical studies have begun to appear on the effects of ethical requirements on research and research data.[4] None of these studies have shown variations in consent procedures or assurances of confidentiality to have a marked effect in the context of survey research. (Many, but not all, of the complaints about current regulations have come from survey researchers.) Second, creative work has been undertaken to find methodological "solutions" to some of the ethical concerns, particularly regarding privacy and confidentiality, that have prompted federal regulation.[5]

Like all members of the public, social scientists had an opportunity to comment on the DHEW regulations when they were proposed in 1973. Whether many did so is doubtful, and there is little indication that they had any impact. Unfortunately the files containing the public's responses to the 1973 proposed regulations were mislaid after being sent to storage at DHEW. Various persons who were responsible for developing those regulations seem to have little recollection of any appreciable response from social scientists. I have examined a summary of the public's comments that was prepared at the time at N.I.H., and it contains a few hints of responses from social scientists. For instance, the summary indicates that someone suggested that there be developed separate policies for biomedical and behavioral research; the term "sociological risk", which was used in the proposed regulations, was criticized as meaningless; and note was taken of the implications for the quality of data of the requirement that the purpose of research procedures be disclosed to subjects.

(Interestingly, back in 1966 the Surgeon-General proposed that a separate policy for social research be developed by the Public Health Service. In that instance, according to documents in DHEW files, a major social science professional society--the Society for the Study of Social Problems--developed an official response to the proposal. They objected to it. Whether this had anything to do with the scrapping of the idea, I do not know. I doubt it, however, because the outcome was that the Surgeon-General issued the clarification stating that the previously announced PHS policy for the protection of human subjects was intended to apply to social research supported by PHS. This was not the outcome sought by SSSP.)

If social scientists did not make their views known when the 1973 regulations were proposed, it can be attributed to several factors. Few social scientists ordinarily read the Federal Register. Many of the professional associations-- such as the American Sociological Association--have not been organized so as to facilitate their taking an official position on an issue in a short period of time, such as the comment period allowed when regulations are proposed. Furthermore, there is a considerable lack of consensus among social scientists regarding many ethical issues in research. Finally, many of the implications of the regulations became apparent only through their application. If one distinguishes between what the regulations require, on the one hand, and how those regulations are applied and interpreted by IRBs, on the other hand, it is largely the latter that has produced the situations in which social scientists perceive that requirements are being imposed that add little to the protection of human subjects while complicating and inhibiting the conduct of social research. To state it a bit differently, the present regulations appear to contain sufficient flexibility to allow for reasonable applicability to social research, even though they do not reflect any specific attention to the nature of social research or the issues that arise therein. Thus, most of the specific instances that

have prompted complaint from social scientists have to do
with discretionary behavior by local institutional review
boards.   This may suggest the need for clarification of the
regulations, but it does not suggest that social research is
incompatable with some basic principle embodied in the regulations themselves.

National Commission for
the Protection of Human Subjects

The National Commission for the Protection of Human Subjects of Biomedical and Behavioral Research is an advisory
body that was created by Congress in the National Research
Act of 1974 and directed to advise DHEW and Congress about a
number of complex topics, including issues that arise in research involving populations such as human fetuses, children,
prisoners, and the institutionalized mentally ill and mentally retarded.   Two points about the Commission's mandate
are worthy of special note.

First, the Commission was not asked to proceed by determining whether subjects had been harmed in research and rec-
ommending ways to prevent future harms.   Instead, the Commission was directed to begin by identifying a set of ethical
principles and then to recommend ways to ensure that research
is conducted in accordance with those principles.   The focus
on affirmation of principle rather than an avoidance of harm
should not be regarded as either trivial or accidental.

Today, most serious analyses of the ethics of research
involving human subjects see the investigator's obligations
to subjects in terms of respect for their personal integrity
and autonomy, not only (or even primarily) in terms of avoidance of harm.[6]   Some of the instances that have drawn public
and governmental attention to the ethics of research involving human subjects were instances in which there was no evidence of harm to subjects.   This was true, for example, in
the scandal at the Jewish Chronic Disease Hospital in the
early 1960s when researchers injected live cancer cells be-
neath the skin of non-consenting geriatric patients.[7]   Most
critics of this research did not rest their objections on
arguments that subjects had been physically harmed; objections rested instead on the perception that a moral harm had
been committed, a transgression against the autonomy and integrity of the subjects, a violation of their rights.   Criticisms of the ethics of some social and psychological research
(e.g., research involving deception or disguised observation)
often rest on similar grounds.   From this perspective, the
argument that few people have been harmed in research--which
is true enough[8]-is largely irrelevant.   The purpose of the

DHEW regulations, the review procedures, and the Commission
goes beyond the prevention of harm to subjects, and researchers who act with disregard for the autonomy or dignity of
their subjects are as likely (or more likely) to bring societal wrath onto research as are those whose research results
in physical harm to subjects, particularly if the harm occurs
in research in which there is good quality of informed consent.

The second noteworthy point about the Commission's mandate is that, although the words "social research" appear no-
where in the legislation ("behavioral research" is left unde-
fined) and there is little evidence that particular concern
about social research had any role in the creation of the
Commission,[9] the Commission's fulfillment of its mandate has
inevitable implications for research in the social sciences.
The Commission was directed "to identify the basic ethical
principles that should underlie the conduct of research involving human subjects." It would be difficult for social
scientists to convince anyone that the rubric "research involving human subjects" does not include much empirical work
in the social sciences, although the term "subject" is not
always used in such research. It would also be difficult to
argue that social and biomedical research should be conducted
according to different sets of basic ethical principles.
(There may nevertheless be some relevant differences among
research methodologies regarding, for example, the extent to
which the procedures used in the research (a) are constitutionally protected and (b) would require informed consent
whether or not they were being used for research purposes.)
There are also clear implications for social research in the
Commission's mandate to recommend ethical guidelines and administrative actions to implement them and, specifically, to
make recommendations regarding institutional review boards
(IRBs). A significant part of the research reviewed by IRBs
is social research.

Social Researchers and the Commission

Social scientists who follow these matters were dis-
tressed when Secretary Weinberger's appointments to the Commission were announced in late 1974, and no social scientists
were included. The Act specified that no more than 5 of the
11 members of the Commission could be persons who had conducted research involving human subjects. Three physicians
and two psychologists filled those slots. The Commission has
been aware of this limitation in its composition, and has not
been insensitive to issues brought to its attention by me, as
a staff member, or by social researchers who have written to
the Commission or appeared at its hearings.

Table I   Attitudes of Different Types of Investigators and Review Committee Members Toward the Review Procedure and Committees

| | Percent Agreeing With Each Statement | | | | | |
| | Review Board Members | | | Research Investigators | | |
	Biomedical Sciences (N=370)*	Behavioral & Social Sci. (N=135)*	Other (N=220)*	Biomedical Sciences (N=940)*	Behavioral & Social Sci. (N=395)	Other (N=180)
The human subjects review procedure has protected the rights and welfare of human subjects--at least to some extent.	99%	99%	99%	99%	96%	98%
The review procedure has improved the quality of scientific research done at this institution--at least to some extent.	78	62	70	69	55	83
The review procedure runs with reasonable efficiency--at least to some extent.	99	96	99	96	94	94
The review procedure is an unwarranted intrusion on an investigator's autonomy--at least to some extent.	13	11	6	25	38	23
The review committee gets into areas which are not appropriate to its function--at least to some extent.	39	24	27	50	49	39
The review committee makes judgments that it is not qualified to make--at least to some extent.	28	21	20	43	49	25
The review procedure has impeded the progress of research done at this institution--at least to some extent.	26	30	22	43	54	36

* N's are approximate since non-response varied from item to item.

It is impossible to know how the presence of a social researcher on the Commission might have affected its recommendations. As the Commission's staff sociologist, one of my responsibilities was to be a resource to the Commission on issues in social research. One way that I fulfilled that role was to try to see that the Commission was always aware of the implications for social research of the recommendations or language that it was considering. Knowing that there are disputes among social scientists with regard to the ethics of social research, I have not been altogether comfortable with being perceived as being able to represent the concerns of social scientists. For that reason, I was pleased that social scientists were active in making their views known to the Commission, both in correspondence and in hearings.[10] Furthermore, the Commission was willing to seek the perspective of social scientists when undertaking those sections of the mandate to which those views seemed relevant.[11] It seems likely, however, that the same views expressed by a member of the Commission would have greater impact.

Survey of Human Subjects Review Committees

In preparing for its deliberation, the Commission decided to use the methods of social research to obtain information about the functioning of IRBs and the research that they review. This study was conducted for the Commission by the Survey Research Center at the University of Michigan, and involved a sample of 61 institutions (medical schools, universities, hospitals, etc.). More than 2,000 investigators were interviewed about their research and their experiences with IRBs, and more than 800 review board members were interviewed.[12] Although this is not the place to describe the major findings of the study, some data bear on the topic at hand.

Research investigators were by and large supportive of the existing review process (Table 1). Almost all said that the human subjects review procedure has protected the rights and welfare of human subjects, at least to some extent; two-thirds said that the review procedure has improved the quality of research done at the institution; and, interestingly enough, almost all said that the procedure runs with reasonable efficiency. However, substantial minorities—ranging from one quarter to nearly one-half—of the investigators indicated that they felt that the review process is an unwarranted intrusion on the investigator's autonomy, that the IRB gets into areas that are not appropriate to its function, that it makes judgments that it is not qualified to make, and that it has impeded the process of research. On balance, however, fewer than 10 percent of the investigators felt that

the difficulties of the review procedure outweigh its benefits
in protecting human subjects (data not shown).

However, on the various attitude measures about the review process, Table 1 also shows a consistent tendency for
"behavioral researchers" (mostly psychologists and sociologists) to have less favorable attitudes than biomedical researchers. For example, on the question whether the review
procedure is an unwarranted intrusion on the investigator's
autonomy--38 percent of the behavioral researchers agree, as
compared with 25 percent of the biomedical researchers. Perceptions of unfairness by IRBs were also more common among
behavioral researchers than among biomedical researchers.
Asked whether their IRB treats all departments fairly, 61 percent of biomedical researchers, but only 43 percent of behavioral researchers, said so. Eight percent of the behavioral
researchers (and two percent of the biomedical researchers)
said that some departments are favored (the others did not
know). Twelve percent of the behavioral researchers found
the difficulties of the review procedure to outweigh its benefits; seven percent of the biomedical researchers felt this
way.

What accounts for the less favorable attitudes among behavioral researchers? The data have not been analyzed enough
to answer this question adequately. However, we know that it
is not due to behavioral researchers more frequently having
their research proposals modified by IRBs. (Incidently,
very few proposals are actually turned down by IRBs. When
asked if they had ever had a proposal turned down by an IRB,
six percent of the biomedical researchers and one percent of
the behavioral researchers said yes. This difference, may
be due in part to the fact that, on average, bio-medical researchers had had more proposals reviewed by IRBs.)

The most frequent modifications made by IRBs pertained to
informed consent, a frequent topic of contention among social
scientists who have complained about existing DHEW regulations. Yet, biomedical projects (27%) were more likely than
behavioral projects (20%) to have undergone consent modifications at the hands of an IRB.

A number of explanations could be advanced to account for
behavioral researchers' less favorable attitudes toward the
review process. I will mention two possibilities.

The first follows from the finding that little research
is turned down by IRBs but that much is modified in some way.
IRB modifications of social research may be more likely to
have implications for the validity or methodological rigor of

the study than are modifications in biomedical research. As
I noted, the most frequent modifications made by IRBs pertain
to consent. In studies in which validity rests on subject
naivety or on the adequacy of a sample, such modifications
may have important implications for the soundness of the research. In biomedical research, more elaborate consent procedures may make it more difficult to recruit subjects, but
will usually have no further methodological implications.
Where nonresponse is a serious methodological concern (as opposed to a practical concern about the simple need for numbers), anything that increases the nonresponse rate is likely
to raise the researcher's concern about bias.

A second explanation posits a difference between biomedical and behavioral researchers in their orientation toward
authority structures and in their awareness of the politics
of research. For both historical and organizational reasons,
the behavioral researcher may be more likely than the biomedical researcher to perceive the review process as inconsis-
tent with the concept of freedom of inquiry. Hospitals and
medical schools have authority structures that differ from
the university; few in medical schools, for example, question
the department chairperson's right to have significant influence over the program of research carried out in his or her
department. That would be a major contention in a university.
In addition, the content of social research is more frequently manifestly political than is that of biomedical research;
no one would want someone who is ideologically hostile to
have control over one's research.

Recommendations of the Commission

Under the recommendations of the National Commission for
the Protection of Human Subjects, institutional review boards
would continue to play the central procedural role in the
protection of human subjects; the recommendations are directed at improving their performance and clarifying their responsibilities.[*] The Commission did not find it necessary or
useful to issue separate recommendations for biomedical and
behavioral or social research. However, it concluded that
IRB deliberations should take into account a wide variety of
characteristics that distinguish research projects one from
another. In this section, I will not attempt an overall sum-

---

[*] This paper, revised in May, 1978, reviews a number of actions
taken by the Commission. Although the recommendations mentioned herein have been agreed upon by the Commission, its
report on institutional review boards has not yet been re-
leased and may vary slightly from the draft on which this
summary is based.

mary of the Commission's recommendations. Rather, I will
summarize only one aspect of those recommendations--the actions that bear on concerns that social researchers have expressed about existing regulations. Thus, I will only mention in passing some aspects of the recommendations that
should improve the protection of the rights and welfare of
human subjects, even though that has remained the Commission's
primary concern.

The lack of a definition of "human subject" in the DHEW
regulations has resulted in considerable uncertainty regarding the applicability of those guidelines in certain research
situations. There have been reports of IRBs insisting on reviewing studies of anonymous records or data, studies of published materials such as newspapers, studies of unidentified
tissue or blood samples that had been obtained for other purposes, and studies in which observations were to be made of
public behavior. In some cases, IRBs have apparently tried
to impose informed consent requirements on such research.

Although "human subject" might seem like a simple term,
it is in fact difficult to define in a way that does not
raise problems. The term is not used in some fields of research, and it is seen as implying aspects of subordination
or relative powerlessness that frequently do not exist. One
can attempt to define it in terms of the studies in which informed consent is necessary or in terms of studies which
should be reviewed by an IRB. The Commission chose the latter course, with the result that it recognizes studies that
should be reviewed but for which informed consent of subjects
may not be necessary. The definition states that a human
subject is a person about whom an investigator conducting
scientific research obtains (1) data through intervention or
interaction with the person or (2) identifiable private information. Thus, for example, the four categories of research I mentioned above would not need to be reviewed.
Studies in which observation is combined with an intervention
or studies of, for example, medical records would need to be
reviewed.

The Commission's recommendations regarding the determinations that an IRB should make in reviewing proposed research
have several features that may reduce confusion when IRBs review research from a broad number of fields. First, the
methods of the research are to be judged, not in terms of
some abstract concept of "scientific soundness," but in terms
of the objectives of the research and the field of study in
which the research is being conducted. This may help with
the complaint sometimes raised, particularly at biomedically-
dominated review boards, that inappropriate standards of

scientific rigor are applied to interview or observational studies.

Second, although the Commission still sees it appropriate for risks to be considered in the framework of the benefits of the research, it recognizes that no precise weighing is possible. Thus, the Commission recommends that an IRB should judge whether the risks to subjects are reasonable in relation to anticipated benefits to subjects and the importance of the knowledge. As long as such a reasonable relationship exists, the Commission did not wish for the IRB to substitute its judgment for the judgment of prospective subjects. In the past, there have been isolated reports of IRBs judging a proposal against a high standard of scientific rigor, finding it to fall short of the highest standards, and then rejecting it on the grounds that there are no benefits to outweigh even the risk of inconveniencing subjects by asking them if, for example, they would answer a few questions. The application of this reasoning by hospital review committees has led to some suspicion that IRBs may sometime be primarily concerned with protecting the institution from systematic scrutiny by outsiders, or that IRBs may be used to reinforce the occupational caste system within the health professions.[15] The latter complaint has come from nurses who contend that nursing research is discriminated against in some medical school/hospital review boards. The Commission also stated that IRBs should consider only the risks of the research, not the risk that might result from applying the findings.

Regarding informed consent, the Commission endeavored to make informed consent more of a reality in situations where it is an appropriate requirement. Thus, the Commission would make IRBs responsible for considering the circumstances in which consent is to be obtained to assure that the possibility of coercion is minimized; it is to pay attention to the language to be used in obtaining consent to assure that it is likely to be understood by subjects; and, most importantly, it recognizes the distinction between informed consent and consent forms.[16] The Commission would give IRBs discretion to waive the written documentation of informed consent when this would unduly burden the research while adding little protection to subjects. When such research entails no more than "minimal" risk--that is, no risk greater than the risks of everyday life or routine medical or psychological examinations--and when it involves no procedures for which written consent is a usual requirement outside of the research context, written documentation is not deemed necessary, under the recommendations. The recommendations also recognize that the requirement for written consent may result in the creation of a written record identifying the subject,

thereby increasing the risk of disclosure. This is a particular problem in studies of illegal or stigmatized behavior
and is exacerbated by the fact that the researcher's records
may be vulnerable to subpoena.[17] The documentation requirement
could be waived on these grounds, under the Commission's recommendations. Fortunately, such subpoenas for research records have been rare.[18]

The recommendations also call the problem of confidentiality to the attention of IRBs by requiring that they review
the investigator's plans for maintaining confidentiality,
particularly when data are being gathered the disclosure of
which to a third party could be harmful to the subjects.

The recommendations make clear the criterion that is to
be applied in deciding what should be disclosed to subjects
when informed consent is obtained: they should be given the
information that persons in their situation could "reasonably
be expected to desire" in considering whether or not to participate. This may sound very simple and reasonable, but it
is a significant improvement from providing a list of topics
and inevitably suggesting that disclosure of the topics on
that list constitutes an adequate disclosure. The recommendations contain a list of topics, but make clear that in some
cases an item on the list might not be appropriate under the
standard of what a prospective subject would want to know:
more frequently, research may involve elements that are not
on the list but which a subject could reasonably be expected
to want to know. In other words, the Commission tried to
move things away from the rote application of a formula, to a
more thoughtful consideration of what one is trying to accomplish in the consent procedure.

The recommendations also make provision, under certain
circumstances, for the withholding of certain information
about research (particularly the purpose of research procedures) when disclosure would affect the validity of the data.
It also provides for deception, for the same purpose. There
can be no deception or withholding regarding risk, however,
and the IRB is called upon to assure that those practices are
essential to the purpose of the research.

The recommendations also state that in studies of documents, records, or pathological specimens, informed consent
may be deemed unnecessary, provided that the IRB assures the
protection of subjects' interests. The Commission did not
consider this in detail, since the Privacy Protection Study
Commission had recently made recommendations on the topic.[19]
(The Privacy Commission would have a review committee determine that the research use of the record did not violate

limitations under which the record was collected, that the use in individually identifiable form is necessary to the research purpose, that such use is warranted by the importance of the research, and that there will be no re-disclosure.)

The recommendations would also require that IRBs maintain records on the actions they take on proposals and on the basis for those actions. The IRB would have to inform investigators of the basis of decisions to disapprove or require modification of proposed research and give them an opportunity to respond in person or in writing. This might reduce some of the arbitrariness about which some have complained.

The Commission recommended that the regulations be modified to allow institutions to develop expedited review procedures for carefully defined categories of research that present no more than minimal risk. The review could be by experienced reviewers or a subcommittee. Although these categories of research would have to be defined and approved in advance of their use, this provision would allow an institution that repeatedly encounters a particular type of low risk research to develop a set of guidelines to which a study would have to conform to be approved, and then to approve particular projects that meet those guidelines, using review procedures short of full committee review. The principle of review by someone independent of the investigator would not be sacrificed, nor would the necessity that the research conform to the basic ethical principles that should underlie the conduct of research with human subjects. However, the procedure would introduce a degree of efficiency that would be very helpful at certain institutions.

A frequently made complaint concerns the cost of the review function, although the little data that exist suggest that the cost is marginal, at least at an institution that receives substantial amounts of federal funds.[20] Over time, the costs are presently recoverable under the indirect costs mechanism; however, those funds do not necessarily filter down to the institutional component that bears the cost of the review function. The Commission's report on IRBs includes a recommendation to Congress that legislation be enacted to appropriate funds to support the operation of IRBs by direct cost funding. That is, funds would be earmarked for the operation of the IRB and would at least partially compensate for costs incurred therein.

I will briefly mention five other features of the recommendations.
1. Among several recommendations to improve the composition of IRBs is one that would require IRBs to include

persons with the competence necessary to analyze accurately and thoroughly the risks and benefits of proposed projects.

2. The recommendations would require changes in the DHEW office administering the regulations to make it more responsive to issues raised by IRBs and investigators. That office would also have greater responsibility for monitoring the performance of IRBs, including making site visits, and for conducting educational activities for members of IRBs.

3. The Commission would have approval by one IRB suffice to satisfy regulatory requirements, even if research is conducted at more than one institution or the investigator is affiliated with more than one institution. This may help with the complaints about multiple reviews, although nothing can prevent an institution from requiring review by an IRB before allowing the research to be conducted there.

4. The Commission's recommendations would require IRB review only before the conduct of the research, not before it is submitted for funding consideration. This may reduce some of the burden on IRBs, since much of the research now reviewed is never funded or conducted. Furthermore, the time pressure that sometimes exists--for example, when a proposal is being submitted against a deadline in a Request for Proposal--will be eliminated. On the other hand, it may be that proposals that have not been reviewed by an IRB will have more difficulty in the funding review process, and IRBs may find themselves subjected to pressure when asked to review a project for which funds have already been approved.

5. Finally, the Commission recommended that there be uniformity in regulatory requirements across federal agencies; as more and more federal agencies adopt requirements, the slight differences from agency to agency has become an increasing problem at major research institutions.

Conclusion

There is undoubtedly much in the draft recommendations to provoke serious comment, so, in conclusion, I will indicate how the process is to run from here.

Presumably, by the time this paper is published the Commission will have forwarded its recommendations regarding review procedures to DHEW and to Congress. (Incidently, a separate report will be issued regarding the basic ethical principles that should underlie the conduct of research involving human subjects.) Under the law, the Secretary of HEW must publish the Commission's recommendations in the Federal Register within 60 days of receiving them and provide opportunity for interested persons to submit their views regarding the recommendations. Within 180 days of publication of the recommendations in the Federal Register, the Secretary is to

decide whether to accept the recommendations and, if the recommendations are not accepted, to publish the reasons.   The
next year is thus a crucial time for persons interested in
this topic to express their views, either by commenting on
the Commission's recommendations or on the regulations that
may be proposed by DHEW to implement those recommendations.

References

1. U.S. Public Health Service, PPO #129, February 8, 1966.
2. Memorandum from the Surgeon General to Heads of Institutions Receiving Public Health Service Grants, December 12, 1966.
3. U.S. Public Health Service, PPO #129, Revised, July 1, 1966.
4. Eleanor Singer, "Informed Consent: Consequences for Response Rate and Response Quality in Social Surveys," paper presented at meetings of the American Sociological Association, September 7, 1977; Lloyd Lueptow, Samuel A. Mueller, Richard R. Hamnes, and Lawrence S. Master, "The Impact of Informed Consent Regulations on Response Rate and Response Bias," Sociological Methods and Research, 6 (November 1977), pp. 183-204; Edwin D. Goldfield, Anthony G. Turner, Charles D. Cowan, John C. Scott, "Privacy and Confidentiality as Factors in Survey Response," paper presented at the meetings of the American Statistical Association, August, 1977.
5. The work of Donald Campbell, Robert Boruch, and associates at Northwestern University's Program on Methodology and Evaluation Research has been most notable.
6. See, for example, H. Tristram Engelhardt, Jr., "Basic Ethical Principles in the Conduct of Biomedical and Behavioral Research Involving Human Subjects," paper prepared for the National Commission for the Protection of Human Subjects, 1975; Paul Ramsey, The Patient as Person, New Haven: Yale University Press, 1970; Robert M. Veatch, "Three Theories of Informed Consent: Philosophical Foundations and Policy Implications," paper prepared for the National Commission for the Protection of Human Subjects, 1976.
7. This case is described in detail in Jay Katz, Experimentation with Human Beings, NY: Russell Sage, 1972, pp. 9-65.
8. See the report of the HEW Secretary's Task Force on the Compensation of Injured Research Subjects, Washington: DHEW, 1977. Their survey of research supported by the National Institutes of Health showed the risks to subjects of "nontherapeutic" research to be comparable to the risks of everyday life.
9. U.S. Senate, Hearings on the Quality of Health Care - Human Experimentation, Washington: Government Printing Office, 1973.
10. At its three hearings on institutional review procedures, for example, the Commission heard from sociologists John Clausen, Wallace Gingerich, Howard Higman, Ada Jacox, Hans Mauksch, Virginia Olesen, and Edward Rose, and heard testimony in a similar vein from researchers in psychology, education, nursing, epidemiology, and anthropology.

11. Among the papers written for the Commission were papers by Bernard Barber (on the assessment of risks and benefits in the review of proposed research), Donald Campbell (on issues in program evaluation and social experimentation), and Albert Reiss (on informed consent and confidentiality in social research).

12. Robert A. Cooke, Arnold S. Tannenbaum, and Bradford H. Gray, A Survey of Institutional Review Boards and Research Involving Human Subjects. This report is available from the National Technical Information Service, Springfield, Virginia. A summary was presented at the 1977 meetings of the American Sociological Association-- Bradford H. Gray, Robert A. Cooke, Arnold S. Tannenbaum, and Donna Hansen McCulloch, "Research Involving Human Subjects: An Empirical Report on Human Subjects Review Committees."

13. Survey Research Center, University of Michigan, Research Involving Human Subjects: A report to the National Commission for the Protection of Human Subjects of Biomedical and Behavioral Research, October 2, 1976, p. 102.

14. An explanation not examined here is that social scientists, like other scientists, are simply protective of their autonomy. On this point see Bernard Barber, "Liberalism Stops at the Laboratory Door," paper presented at the 1975 meetings of the American Sociological Association.

15. For a brief analysis of some of the latent functions of IRBs and some dangers of politicalization, see Bradford H. Gray, "The Functions of Human Subjects Review Committees," American Journal of Psychiatry, 134 (August 1977), pp. 907-910.

16. Consent problems of the sort that prompted these recommendations are described in Bradford H. Gray, Human Subjects in Medical Experimentation, NY: Wiley-Interscience, 1975, Chapter Eight.

17. These problems are examined in detail in Paul M. Nejelski (ed.), Social Research in Conflict with Law and Ethics, Cambridge, Mass.: Ballinger, 1976.

18. James D. Carroll and Charles Knerr, "The Confidentiality of Research Sources and Data," testimony presented to the Privacy Protection Study Commission, Washington, D.C. January 6, 1977.

19. Privacy Protection Study Commission, Personal Privacy in an Information Society, Washington: Government Printing Office, 1977, pp. 305-310.

20. The best study of the costs of these procedures at one institution is Eugene J. Millstein, The DHEW Requirements for the Protection of Human Subjects: Analysis and Impact at the University of California, Berkeley. Berkeley: Research Management Improvement Project, 1974.

Hegel remarks somewhere that all great world-historical facts and personages occur, as it were, twice. He has forgotten to add: the first time as tragedy, the second as farce....

Men make their own history, but they do not make it just as they please; they do not make it under circumstances chosen by themselves, but under circumstances directly found, given and transmitted from the past. The tradition of all the dead generations weighs like a nightmare on the brain of the living. And just when they seem engaged in revolutionising themselves and things, in creating something entirely new, precisely in such epochs of revolutionary crisis, they anxiously conjure up the spirits of the past to their service and borrow from their names, battle slogans and costumes in order to present the new scene of world history in this time-honoured disguise and this borrowed language.

> --Karl Marx, The Eighteenth
> Brumaire of Louis
> Napoleon, I. (1852)

Those who cannot remember the past are condemned to repeat it.

> --George Santayana, Life of
> Reason, I, Reason in
> Common Sense

The Reluctant Merlins of Camelot

4

Ethics and Politics of Overseas Research

Murray L. Wax

Among many social scientists, Project Camelot is considered the paradigm of unethical research. In its collapse, the project was the focus of intense polemic--both domestically and overseas--but the atmosphere of the times was such that key issues in the ethics and politics of social research were not confronted. The role of sponsorship and regulation by the U.S. Government was mentioned, but inadequately. I propose now to review something of the history of the Project in order that these issues should emerge more clearly.

The Fall from Grace

In the history of U.S. social-science, Project Camelot has come to occupy an exemplary status akin to "The Fall of Man" in Christian theology. Tempted by monies and the pro-spect of political influence, scientists forgot their obligation to serve humanity, or permitted themselves to be deceived about the intentions of the military establishment, and so entered into a fateful compact with the forces of imperialism. Fortunately, the scheme came to the attention of foreign colleagues who exposed and vehemently denounced the Project; whereupon a segment of U.S. scientists then joined in the critique. The foreign denunciation was initiated by Chileans who interpreted Camelot as "a plan" or conspiracy to subvert their democratic-socialistic government; this interpretation seemed to find confirmation when the Allende government was subsequently overthrown by the Chilean military with the connivance of U.S. federal agencies and business firms. In consequence, whenever today the issue of ethical responsibility in social-scientific investigation is raised, Project Camelot is presented as the exemplum of the temptation against which ethical researchers must be on guard (cf. Barnes 1977:50-56).

If Project Camelot is to play so central a role in the ethical formulations of the social sciences and in the in-

structions given to students, it would be well that the details of the case be accurately known. In principle, this
should be easy, since the Project was never secret, and its
crucial documents have always been in the public domain; moreover, many of the scientists who participated in its planning
are still alive and available for interview. Yet, several
recent texts (e.g. Boughey 1978:53-55) seem to prefer myth to
fact. Authors cite such key sources as "Horowitz 1967," but
do not seem to have troubled to digest its pages. The resultant discussion is inaccurate and even sloppy. Instead of
clear ethical analysis, the reader is presented with fantasy
and political polemic. While it is true that ethical, political, and professional issues can rarely be separated absolutely, there are important benefits from the attempt. Scientists
should be able to reach agreement on ethical codes governing
research investigation, even though they may be in significant
disagreement on political policies. But, because of the inac-
curacy, fantasy, and rhetoric surrounding the case of Camelot,
they have failed to confront dilemmas intrinsic to their roles
in the modern world. (Because it will be easier to perceive
the inaccuracies of some of the current accounts of Camelot,
I have postponed a review of them until later in this text.)

Origins and Hopes

Following the use of social-science by various branches
of the Defense Department during World War II and subsequent
engagements, a faction began to develop both within and without the Department that urged considerable more attention to the
field. In the early 1960s "a world renowned physicist" ven-
tured to prophesy to the Secretary of Defense that--

> ...While World War I might have been considered the
> chemists' war, and World War II was considered the
> physicists' war, World War III, which we might already
> be in, might well have to be considered the social-
> scientists' war (Deitchman 1976:28).

And a study by political scientists instructed the Defense
Department that "the political art of detecting internal war
potential must have priority over the military art of fighting
it" (Deitchman 1976:32):

> In a world of alliances, foreign bases, and far-
> flung power blocs, detecting in advance the instabi-
> lity of regimes and knowing how to shore them up with
> fair chances of success are among the most urgent
> imperatives of the military as well as the political
> arts.

Thus, by 1966, an innovative and reform-minded Secretary
of Defense could state:

> There is still among us an almost ineradicable tendency
> to think of our security problem as being exclusively
> a military problem.... We understand that our military
> mission to be most effective requires understanding
> of the political, social and economic setting in which
> we fulfill our responsibilities (speech of Robert S.
> McNamara,May 18,1966, cited in Yarmolinsky 1971:147).

In gaining a perspective upon such utterances, we may
permit ourselves to be reminded that during the first World
War the National Academy of Sciences offered its assistance to
the Army and that this was politely declined by an officer who
pointed out that "the Army already has a chemist"(Yarmolinsky 1971:297). For, notwithstanding the advice of such
committees, the interest in social research was confined to
specific branches of the Defense Department and to specific
individuals; among the exponents during the 1960s were Seymour
Deitchman, an engineer who was in the Office of Defense Research and Engineering, and Theodore Vallance, a psychologist,
who was head of the Army Special Operations Research Office
(SORO). These officials had their own vision of the kinds of
research that Defense ought to purchase. They were oriented
toward positivistic (or "scientistic") methodologies: in the
(masculine sexual) jargon of our times, the "soft" sciences
were to be "hardened." Systems analysis, operations research,
quantitative measures were key phrases, and the goal was to
assemble sufficient hard data so as to describe a social
system quantitatively and simulate its behavior on a computer
(Deitchman 1976:115-116). If, from the viewpoint of their
critics, the social-scientists involved in Camelot were being
tempted by Satan, one could equally well respond that, from
their own viewpoint they were sharing in the eschatological
vision of the Coming of the Kingdom of Behavioral Science.

While, from Defense standards, the sums of money were
not large, from the perspectives of the research planners,
they would enable the gathering of such large quantities of
reliable data as to enable the subjecting of received hypotheses to rigorous testing. Quantities of data would be
assembled about many different countries and focused on
numerous crucial incidents, so that there could be developed
a model of a society in conflict. Thus, it was planned

> ...to examine such historical or current events as:
> the Argentine revolution of 1943; the Peruvian coup
> of 1963; Colombia since World War II; the Egyptian

coup of 1952; the Iranian coup of 1953; the Korean
revolution of 1960; and Greece in the context of
the cold war (1976:145).

With this rich variety of hard data, the numerous theories of
social change could then be subjected to test:

> For example, some economic theories stated that
> (a) internal wars are generated by growing poverty;
> others stated that (b) internal wars result from
> rapid economic progress. Social theories postulated
> that (a) internal war is a reflection of disorder
> resulting from great social mobility, and also that
> (b) internal war is a reflection of frustration
> arising from little social mobility. Etc. (Deitch-
> man 1976:142-143).

These ambitious goals of research and theory had to be translated into project design and organization, which would be
difficult to accomplish because social scientists lacked the
experience of administering such large projects. They also
lacked the experience and training for handling an enterprise
within a monster bureaucracy such as the Department of Defense. In consequence, it was to prove difficult to reach
agreement on the basic design and goals of the emerging
project.

Army Brass

The developing Project required an administrative loca-
tion within Defense, and it seemed appropriate that this be
the Special Operations Research Office (SORO) of the Army; but
this soon exposed the rival and incompatible goals of several
different interest groups. The social scientists were being
recruited to perform basic research on conflict and social
change in modern societies. But, the key Army administrators
proposed to justify the monetary expenditures on the grounds
that these would provide immediate assistance in dealing with
problems of "insurgency." While a significant clique of officials high in the Department had hopes for the overall strategic utility of the social-sciences, there were numerous and
powerful factions within the armed services who were skeptical;
and to deflect their indictment of useless expenditures, the
Army Research Office adopted a vocabulary emphasizing "counter-
insurgency." The consequence was that--

> The various documents reveal a military vocabu-
> lary provided with an array of military justifica-
> tions, often followed (within the same document)
> by a social science vocabulary offering social

science justifications and rationalizations
(Horowitz ed. 1967:10).

It is likely that the scientists figured that the decla-
rations of the Army Research Office could be discounted as
being for political consumption, and that, once the Project
was underway, they could focus on fundamental problems as
they had hoped. In time, there might indeed have emerged a
working compromise, but meanwhile there was the need for
rapid and specific planning, made all the more urgent because
a major effort of the Project was to be overseas. True, some
modest period of time was available for refined planning since
there was agreement that the initial phases of the Project
were to be library research, first to be conducted within the
U.S. and then to be expanded to 21 countries overseas. But,
given the size of the Project and its commitment to conduct
empirical research overseas, the lack of fundamental agreement about design was disconcerting to experienced administrators, such as Deitchman (1976:149). Worse yet, as later critics were to note, inadequate attention was being given to
the question of how the Project would be received when it
sought to conduct its inquiries in foreign countries. Social
scientists were overlooking the need to take the role of the
other.

Bitter Fruit

Despite the lack of agreement as to goals, SORO felt it
had to move quickly toward staffing; this meant alerting the
wider networks of social-scientists to prepare for possible
participation. And now, the narrative enters the phases
which are particularly well-known. To head the project, SORO
hired (the late) Rex Hopper (Chairman of the Department of
Sociology, Brooklyn College), a specialist on social movements, particularly in Latin America. In April 1965, Hopper
corresponded about the project with Johan Galtung, a Norwegian
working with the U.N. in Chile, and invited him to participate in a planning conference to be held in Washington that
August. Galtung, a severe critic of American foreign policy,
discussed the implications of the letter with faculty of
Santiago University. Meanwhile, Hugo Nutini (a Chilean who
had become a naturalized citizen of the U.S.) was planning a
visit to Chile in August and secured from the project a small
sum of money on the grounds that he would "informally assess
the interest of academic and governmental officials with respect to the possibility of doing some related research in
Chile (apparently in terms of Chile as an example of orderly
social change)" (Deitchman 1976:158-159). Nutini's presence
in Chile and the nature of his responses to the inquiries and
challenges put to him were such as to allow the Chilean Left

to launch a sensationalistic media campaign. Beals (1969:164) surmises that party rivalry between the Christian Democratic Party (whose members were among the scholars first approached by Camelot) and the extreme left "no doubt played some part" in motivating the attack. In any case, the Communist news- paper El Siglo broke the story under the headline, "Yankees Study Invasion of Chile" and initiated the media custom of referring to Camelot, not as a research project (proyetco) but as a plan, a term conveying conspiratorial and authori- tarian overtones.

The Chilean government was outraged; and so too was the U.S. Ambassador. Even Chileans sympathetic to the U.S. were embarrassed and found it difficult to cope with the attack in the media. Meanwhile, within the U.S., the critics of Defense now had a conspicuous target, and an informal alliance among the State Department, leading Senators (such as J. Wm. Full- bright), and newspaper columnists (e.g. Walter Pincus of the Washington Star) went into action. The manifest complaint was the lack of notification to the Chilean Government and the American Ambassador. (In fact, the State Department was fully apprised [Deitchman 1976:171f] of the plans for Camelot, and indeed had a representative, Pio Uliassi, on the Camelot Core Planning Group [Horowitz ed. 1967:14-15]. Uliassi knew of such details as the trip by Nutini, but there had been no formal notification to the Ambassador, because there had been no plans for research within Chile.) The latent complaints were that the State Department approved neither of Camelot specifically, nor of the sponsorship of Camelot by Defense, nor of such varieties of social research, generally, no matter by whom sponsored. Pincus' columns talked of--

> State's "open-mouthed amazement" at the DOD's grow-
> ing interest in foreign policy and social science
> research; and expanded at length on State's view of
> the foolishness of trying to do research on social
> systems, and on how DOD could get research money,
> while State couldn't (Deitchman 1976:170).

State's scholarship was academically more traditional and more limited, and its budget was far smaller than that of Defense. Worse, its local and international influence were being undermined by the aggrandizement of the Defense Depart- ment.

The federal critics of Camelot were now weightily rein- forced by the many critics of the U.S. involvement in South- east Asia. The joint pressures were such that its sponsors realized that Camelot, or kindred research projects, had become impossible. The plans for Camelot were cancelled, but, the long run consequences in budget and organization were of greater import. Within Defense the design and control of funded research were placed under operational rather than scholarly authorities, and in particular, "social science research" was eliminated as a separate entity. Social researchers were now incorporated as members of larger teams working on general projects, e.g. village defence or troop training, and approval for such projects had to be cleared throughout the Department. Where social researchers still existed, they were directed to "harden" their procedures and to serve as technicians who would provide data to be utilized by those with the responsibility for making decisions.

Meanwhile, at the congressional level, there was the "Mansfield Amendment" to the Defense authorization bill for FY 1970:

> None of the funds authorized to be appropriated by this Act may be used to carry out any research project or study unless such a project or study has a direct or apparent relationship to a specific military function or operation.... We interpret 'military function or operation' in its narrowest sense (421).

The legal consequence was that Defense was now permanently enjoined from any attempt at supporting social research on issues of social change and internal conflict. The ensuing system of clearances and multiple bureaucratic approvals meant that a project could not be conducted within another country unless its officials not only approved, but specifically requested its presence. The overall resultant of the Congressional, Presidential, and Defense-Departmental regulations was to render inconceivable the vision that had inspired its participants of performing holistic, autonomous, and theoretically relevant projects (or long-range basic research) under the sponsorship of Defense. Such researchers as could now be engaged by the Department were to be in the role of technicians, working on projects of immediate utility as defined by departmental officials.

A Few Myths about Camelot

Both Boughey and Barnes write as if Chile was to have been a major and immediate locus of Camelot research. Boughey (1978:54) declares:

> Theoretical questions about order and disorder had been carefully framed, and the comparative, empirical research required to answer them had been carefully

blocked out. Questionnaires and interview schedules
were ready. Segments of the population in each
society needing to be sampled had been identified.
Methods were honed to a knife edge....

Given the actual disorganization (Deitchman 1976:146)
that characterized Camelot, this is sheer fantasy, just as
is--

Camelot misfired upon making the first tentative
contacts with social researchers in the first of the
countries scheduled to be researched, Chile (Boughey
1978:54).

Again, one of the significant characteristics of the Project
was that it was to be an--

unclassified, open project the results of which will
be made available through normal scholarly channels.
In addition it is anticipated that all the data will
be made available to other scholars, in the United
States and abroad, for their analysis ("Document
Number 4," [1965] as cited in Horowitz ed. 1967:
62-63).

Yet, Barnes (1977:51) writes of Nutini's visit to Chile:

It is not clear whether the attempt to conceal the
sponsorship, or the very existence, of the project
formed an essential part of the research design or
whether it arose by accident and bad management.

Barnes does note that the Project was not secret in the U.S.,
but implies that it may have been deliberately intended by
the administrators of the Project to keep it secret within
Chile. In making this accusation, he conveniently overlooks
the fact that from its inception, Camelot had invited foreign
scholars, such as Galtung, to participate in the planning.

Boughey and Barnes, and indeed most other critics, ignore
the tension that developed in the planning of Camelot between
those (mainly social-scientists, but some Army officials) who
sought basic research about social structure and social stability and those (mainly conservative Army officers) who
wanted a project of immediate utility in planning "counter-
insurgency." Hence, the critics write as if the participating
social-scientists had sold their autonomy to the Army, when
in fact there was underway an intense bureaucratic struggle
to determine just who would control the Project and toward
what aims.

The foregoing is especially worth mentioning because
many critics of Camelot assume a unity to the U.S. imperialistic efforts and fail to perceive the bitter rivalries among
the Defense Department, the State Department, and the C.I.A.
The role of the State Department in defeating Camelot is
clear; not so, the role of the C.I.A., and yet there is some
reason to believe that it too was among Camelot's prime enemies (Boguslaw 1967:120).

State, Defense and Social Science

Within the Department of State there seems to have been
no counterpart to the clique about Deitchman and Vallance who
were interested in how social-science might be used to assist
government programs overseas. According to Deitchman (1976:
86-87), State--

> appeared to consider problems of internal conflict a
> diversion from their normal areas of concern, outside
> the main interest of foreign policy and diplomacy, and
> something that would, if played down long enough,
> eventually be resolved in the normal course of inter-
> national relations.

And such research as was fostered by State was limited and
traditional:

> the Foreign Service...leans almost exclusively on the
> traditional historical and institutional analyses
> favored by the political realists, when it does not
> proceed simply on the basis of intuition.... The
> conservative attitude...its recruitment policies, its
> emphasis on short-term goals, its limited research
> system--all tend to discourage acquaintance with
> recent trends in social science (Lyons 1969:188 as
> cited by Deitchman 1976:87).

Thus, when Deitchman encouraged State to undertake research in
order to understand the political groups which the U.S. was
attempting to support, or oppose, by our policies in the
developing countries, and even offered to make funds available
to underwrite the projects, the response of State Department
was lack of interest (Deitchman 1976:88-89).

Perhaps here the real irony is that in this respect
Deitchman and revolutionary socialists like Kathleen Gough
are closely akin in their research interests. In 1968 (406-
407), she outlined a series of research topics that appear
remarkably like those which its social-scientific partisans
(including Deitchman) wanted to achieve by Camelot. She was

intelligent enough to perceive that kinship of research
interests and so went on to explain that--

> I may be accused of asking for Project Camelot,
> but I am not. I am asking that we should do these
> studies in <u>our</u> way, as we would study a cargo cult
> or kula ring, without the built-in biases of tainted
> financing, without the assumption that counter-
> revolution, and not revolution, is the best answer,
> and with the ultimate economic and spiritual welfare
> of our informants and of the international community,
> rather than the short run military or industrial
> profits of the Western nations, before us.

Despite these disclaimers, I should judge that there was a certain community of scientific interest between Gough and the
scientists who were recruited to Camelot.

Reflections on the Marxist Critique

Among the critiques of Camelot, those developed by
Marxists played a leading role, not merely in the initial attack within Chile and Latin America, but later within the
American professional associations. The Marxists conceptualized the United States as an imperialist power, whose struggles for economic and political hegemony have led it to
support authoritarian regimes and exploitative economies in
the nations of the non-Western world. Against this unholy
alliance of U.S. and local capitalistic elites, the only hope
for social betterment lay in a revolution which would bring
to power the oppressed classes of native peoples.

Marxism can thus be regarded as a form of revolutionary
applied anthropology, aiming generally to overthrow bourgeois
society and its capitalistic economic system. In pursuit of
its revolutionary goals, Marxist groups have generated a rich
body of social theory and analysis; nevertheless, this literature has been directed toward <u>praxis</u>: "The previous philosophers have merely described the world in many ways; the point
however is to change it!" Yet, while Marxist groups have
oriented themselves toward politics and struggle, individual
scholars have been engaged in a variety of researches--theo-
retical, historical, and even empirical in the modern social-
scientific sense. At times, some Marxist scholars have encountered difficulties in some Western countries, but for the
most part they have enjoyed great freedom in conducting and
publishing their critical inquiries. Some of these scholars
have even gained high status and wealth.

Under these circumstances, it becomes somewhat paradoxical for Leftist critics of Camelot to have denounced its "asymmetry": that is to note that whereas Camelot was oriented toward studying the social dynamics of countries other than the U.S., the Army was not concomitantly sponsoring studies of the U.S. by foreign scholars who held alien purposes. Given the number and quality of critical and revolutionary studies of the U.S.--many conducted by foreign scholars--one can only find the "asymmetry criticism" to be meretricious. The criticism becomes hypocritical when it is advanced by those who advocate the Leninist, Stalinist, Maoist, or Titoist versions of "Marxism." For these regimes have been intrinsically hostile to civil liberties, including especially the academic and scientific freedoms to investigate, teach, and publish. From the viewpoints of such repressive regimes, all social research is dangerous, unless carefully channeled by the authorities, and no clear line can be drawn between social research and military intelligence or ideological warfare. To the officials of such regimes, it would have been inconceivable that a project like Camelot should have been open and unclassified; it had to be a conspiracy. These critics approach Camelot not for what it was--in its bureaucratic complexities and rivalries--but for what it would have been, had it been sponsored by the kind of "Marxist" regime that they advocate.

The foregoing does not justify a Project Camelot, nor does it compensate for its numerous deficiencies. However, it does call into question the good faith of those Leftists who have denounced the Project as a species of unwarranted intrusion into the affairs of another State. If foreign Marxists (and their domestic allies) judge it proper within a country to study how to overthrow its bourgeoisie (or its conservative government), then ethically the agencies of the U.S. should have the same privileges and be judged by the same standards. Either both enterprises are to be deplored or both are to be judged permissible.

Occasionally, in Leftist criticisms of Camelot, reference is made to its sponsorship by the Department of Defense, rather than the Department of State. Coming from Leninists, this argument verges on heresy, since for Lenin the state was "the executive committee of the ruling class"; and so, by definition, any state-sponsored activity would conduce to the realization of its imperialistic aims. André Gunder Frank, a Marxist scholar of note, recognized this point explicitly, when he declared (1968:412):

Project Camelot was not an isolated event, and the widespread hue and cry against Defense Department

of social scientists rather misses the point that
virtually the whole of the "free" world's social
science is in effect one huge imperialist Camelot
project, whoever pays for it.

Finally, it is noteworthy and should be emphasized that
no statutes or regulations within the U.S. currently prohibit
alien scholars from conducting investigations either in the
field or using documents, in order to inquire about the potential for internal war or insurgency. Given the regulations
having to do with the issuance of visas, some persons explicitly identified as revolutionaries may find it difficult to
enter the U.S.; but it would be unusual for a scholar of
eminence to be restricted, and little would prevent his (or
her) engaging in social research on a wide variety of topics,
including that of insurgency.

Of Ethics and Politics

When Camelot burst upon the international scene, it was
subjected to criticism on ethical and political grounds, as
well as for faults in its research methodology and design.
Of these numerous criticisms, the ethical seems the least
appropriate, and much that has been proffered as ethical criticism is really political in nature. Ethical research is
that which does not bring harm to those who are studied,
whether by the interactions of the researcher with the host
peoples during the investigation or by the subsequent release
of the findings. During fieldwork, the researcher must not
exploit nor abuse the hosts but must respect their lives, the
integrity of their persons and society, and their general
wellbeing. After the fieldwork, the researcher must be careful that the distribution of the findings does not allow
others to invade their privacy or to infringe upon their well-
being. Some may argue that Projects such as Camelot would
have brought harm to the hosts because it would have supported
existing authoritarian regimes or hindered the emergence of
revolutionary movements. These are legitimate criticisms,
but must be classed as political (rather than ethical) in
nature; they rest on an analysis in which it is conceived that
revolution would improve the lot of the hosts in the long run
and that, conversely, maintenance of the existing situation
would be deleterious. Moreover, it prejudges the political
orientations of the scientists involved in Camelot, for at
least some number of them thought of themselves as advocates
of oppressed peoples and of their revolutionary aspirations
and hoped that the Project would be an instrument for effectively communicating to the Defense Department and the federal
government generally that the welfare of the U.S. was linked
positively to liberating social movements, rather than to

authoritarian regimes. Yet, whether or not Camelot would
have conduced toward or against popular revolutions is beside
the point of ethical judgment; for, after the numerous examples of exploitative tyrannies introduced by revolution and
sustained with leftist rhetoric, there is ample ground for
cautioning against the blanket linkage of popular uprisings
to the professional ethics of applied anthropologists. Our
ethics must govern our own conduct--and affect those events
for which we can be responsible--and so must not be framed as
to be dependent upon the course either of social movements or
of governmental programs, over whose development we have no
control.

The ethical principle that does seem applicable is one
in which the researcher is encouraged to involve local personnel as peers, in the investigation, and in the analysis of
the findings. Here, a paradigm for international research
would be the Project, jointly headed by William Foote Whyte
(1969) and José Matos Mar, and involving Cornell University in
the U.S. and Instituto de Estudios Peruanos in Lima, Perú.
Students, faculty, and data were exchanged between the two
institutions, and every attempt was made to institute cooperative research and training. This project was launched with
funding from a variety of U.S. agencies, together with some
funding for activities in Perú from the Instituto de Estudios
Peruanos. Despite the cooperative structure of the project,
it incurred severe criticism when in 1965 it accepted funds
from the Advanced Research Projects Agency (ARPA) of the
Department of Defense:

> The grant simply supported an expansion of the
> program which we had under way and carried with it
> no restrictions whatsoever on our freedom to plan
> the study and to publish our findings. Furthermore,
> we arranged that the ARPA funds would not be used on
> the salaries of professors and students in Peru.
> While we did not call a press conference in Lima to
> announce this grant, neither did we make any efforts
> to keep this source secret. A barrage of attacks in
> one Lima newspaper, aimed particularly at the in-
> direct link of our Peruvian associates with the Pen-
> tagon, led us to return the unexpended balance (more
> than $100,000), even though we felt we needed the
> money more than the Pentagon did (Whyte 1969:27-28,
> note 1).

In a world characterized by rival nationalisms, imperialisms, ethnic and political parties, any project of social
research can become a pawn or symbol. Political or interest
groups may assert the right to control whether or not the

research shall be performed within a group for whom they
claim to be spokesmen. Such claims pose a dilemma for the
researcher because, until the situation is known intimately,
the legitimacy of the claim is not known. (Within the U.S.,
I have noted that while some Indian leaders were denouncing
anthropologists and deploring their presence among Indian
groups, local populations often welcomed investigators whom
they knew as friends and allies.) In general, the ethical
anthropologist will respect the rights of individuals and
groups to privacy, and must especially respect their needs to
conceal particular aspects of their ritual, political, economic or personal lives. Yet, at the same time, anthropologists
must also advocate the rights to observe, inquire, and publish
not only as rights for anthropologists, but for all persons.
We have especial reason to be suspicious of those in authority
who would restrict the conduct of inquiry among their subordinates; we have equal reason to suspect those whom we suspect
of organizing a "revolution" that would bring into power another tyranny equally constrictive of civil and academic
liberties. And we have special cause to cherish that revolutionary document, the Bill of Rights to the U.S. Constitution.

The Dilemma for Applied Research

The Camelot Affair brings into high relief the conflicting responsibilities and loyalties of applied social researchers in the United States. Recognizing the imperialistic
qualities of our own nation--and the rival nationalisms and
imperialisms of its peers--what roles may a scientist ethically adopt in relationship to a militarily inferior nation or
subordinated people? It has been argued that these latter
could secure more respect and better treatment if U.S. officials had a proper knowledge of their culture and social
organization. (Such was the stance of those anthropologists
who worked in association with the Bureau of Indian Affairs,
or during World War II with the War Relocation Authority, or
the Office of Strategic Services). Contrariwise, it is also
arguable that social-scientific knowledge should be regarded
as a species of "military intelligence," and that the less
knowledge available to U.S. officials, the more the freedom
enjoyed by the subordinated and the greater their chances for
liberating political movements.

The foregoing dialectic applies to both the U.S. involve-
ments in Southeast Asia and to the Camelot Project. Assuming
that the U.S. will continue to play a predominant role in
world politics and that its military will be associated with
that role, there are two simplistic possibilities. On the
one hand, the military can remain ignorant of anthropology,
and other social-sciences, and thus approach its task as one

calling for the employment of sheer force and violence, as
epitomized by the campaign slogan of the 1964 elections:
"Bomb them (North Vietnamese) back to the Stone Age!" On the
other hand, the military could, conceivably, become sophisticated in the social-sciences and thus come to utilize a maximum of political maneuver and compromise and a minimum of
random violence. During the Vietnam War, many anthropologists
advocated a disciplinary policy of refusing to conduct research for the military, on the grounds that any such work
would in effect aid the imperialistic ambitions of the U.S.
and thereby inhibit the efforts of the Vietnamese peoples to
liberate themselves (Orlans 1973:42-49, 63-69). On the opposite pole, anthropologists, such as Gerald Hickey (1967, 1970)
and Felix Moos, and political scientists such as Ithiel de
Sola Pool (1971) argued that if the military were provided
with guidance, it might arrive at a more just policy. Specifically, these scholars contended on the basis of their
researches that the most desirable outcome of the struggle
would be a federated government, in which the numerous factions (including the various ethnic, religious, and political
groupings) would be represented. Viewed with the advantage
of hindsight, and judging by the tales of atrocities that
have followed after the evacuation of U.S. forces from Southeast Asia, their counsel of compromise does not seem unwise.
And yet the sad truth--contrary to the notions of the radical
critics of Camelot and of anthropological participation in
Vietnam--is that the military establishment was disinclined
to give any attention to the advice of social-scientists,
even when it recruited and paid them.

Merlin Neglected by Arthur

A valuable supplement to Deitchman's narrative is tne
record of the interview of Ritchie P. Lowry (1978), conducted
by Horowitz. Reflecting on his experience, and on such temptations as the desire to influence American policy, Lowry
emphasizes that--

> We thought we could humanize the military....
> We thought we could teach DOD to bring about changes
> in a humane, more democratic, less authoritarian
> fashion (Lowry 1978:71).

It was not merely that these scientists were confronting tra-
dition-bound Army brass. They had also to deal with those
persons who were identified as social-scientists and who by
longevity had achieved positions of authority in the armed
services. Many of these persons were applied-psychologists,
oriented toward measurements of training and education. Not
only did they favor statistical and quantitative techniques,

but they could not comprehend general social theories.   One
such official returned a proposal with the comment:

> This study is of no use; it merely formulates
> hypotheses and then proposes to test them; this
> isn't research which can be of any use to the
> military (Lowry 1978:70).

Most Defense officials thought that they wanted research
which could supply answers to immediate, specific, and practical problems; and, Lowry confesses, on the basis of his experience with these problems, social-science is not very good
at this sort of thing.   He does believe that social-science
can have significant impact in the development of "strategic"
policies, i.e. those which are long-range and general; but
research of this sort, he thinks, is better sponsored via a
detached organization like Rand than by one like SORO.

An even more pessimistic judgment about the disutility
of social-science to those concerned with foreign policy is
found in the description of Louis J. Halle (quoted by Nisbet
1967:324-325):

> Professors of diplomatic history, professors of Latin
> American history, professors of economics and socio-
> logy were brought to Washington for meetings at which
> the men in the State Department tried to explain their
> troubles.   But the gulf could not be bridged.   The
> professors tended to confine themselves to the general
> nature of the problems that the officials hopefully
> set before them, often speaking about the need to
> maintain the traditional idealism of our international
> conduct.   When confronted by the direct question,
> 'What shall we do?',   they fell silent.   They could
> answer every question up to that last, but that last
> was the one question for which the men in the State
> Department had to have an answer.   The experiment,
> abandoned at last, left the State Department men in a
> mood of disenchantment tinged with bitterness, such
> as often follows a frustrated courtship or a broken
> engagement.

Of course, at this point, one might recur to the advice of an
eminent natural scientist, whose researches were to prove of
enormous utility to the Defense Department:

> Be guided not by what it would be practically
> helpful to learn, but by what it is possible to
> learn (Oppenheimer 1964, as cited by von Mering
> 1968:421).

Renewed Aspirations

During the same time as Camelot, a joint committee of the
National Academy of Sciences and National Research Council had
been in session and in 1968 it issued a report on "The Behavioral Sciences and the Federal Government": In this report
the nationally eminent scientists recommended strategies in
science for each department of the government. The joint committee attempted to facilitate research in the area of foreign
affairs by resolving the bureaucratic rivalries in favor of
the State Department; long-range "behavioral science research
objectives" were to be drawn up by an interagency planning
group headed by State, and the research programs of all other
departments and agencies operating overseas, including Defense,
were to "be continually related to these long-term objectives
through the Foreign Area Research Coordination Group" (Deitchman 1976:419).

Two years later, the same Committee published another
report, "Behavioral and Social Science Research in the Department of Defense: A Framework for Management" (1971), in which
it again recommended Defense involvement in social research
on foreign areas.

The persistence of such recommendations over the course
of a generation, and during an era which was distinguished by
the unfavorable publicity ensuing upon Defense attempts to
engage in social research, is noteworthy. Despite the denun-
ciations of the State Department, congressional leaders, the
American Anthropological Association and its social-scientific allies, and despite the widespread suspicion by overseas
intellectuals of even conventional research by academic
scholars, there was hope among eminent scientists that pertinent research might be conducted. Or, to put the matter in
another perspective, there was the strong conviction that the
Departments of Defense (and State) would benefit enormously
from gaining a better and empirically-grounded understanding
of the peoples of the areas in which they are operating.

Conclusion

Within the social sciences, the interpretation of Project
Camelot that has become conventional is that it was spawned
by the military-imperialistic establishment (including not
only the Army and the Defense Department but the C.I.A. and
multinational corporations); that the essential goal of the
Project was set by its sponsors as being "counter-insurgency,"
i.e. learning how to thwart the uprisings of peoples who were
oppressed by domestic capitalism and foreign (U.S.) imperialism; and that the prospect of large sums of money as grants

and of opportunities for ambitious research enterprise seduced social-scientists into ignoring ethical norms about the treatment of fellow human beings who were involved in their researches. As is evident from our narrative, this description contains a bit of truth and much distortion. Even greater distortions are associated with a mythical Camelot, envisioned as a covert project intended to intervene actively in the domestic affairs of Chile and other vulnerable nations, and in whose activities social-scientists were either dupes (figureheads to the conspiracy) or machiavellian advisors to the process of counter-revolutionary oppression.

As has been shown above, the actuality was far more complex. In many respects Camelot was a political pawn in the interagency struggles within the U.S. (among the Defense Department, the State Department, and the C.I.A.), just as it was in the struggles among rival political parties and factions in Chile, elsewhere in Latin America, and generally through the literate world. Politics and polemics aside, Camelot did and does present problems and dilemmas of some ethical consequence for social-scientists: First, how should social-scientists encourage within the federal government a more accurate appreciation of the other societies of the world? In particular, how can the sciences help relevant agencies to perceive social change in relationship to indigenous social movements, grounded in grievances arising from oppression (and relative deprivation)rather than viewing such movements as inevitably being the product of conspiratorial groups, such as terrorists or foreign-trained revolutionaries? Second, given the involvement of the military in U.S. imperial activities, and with due allowances for the differences in ideological perspectives, under what circumstances is it permissible, perhaps even advisable, for the social-scientists to assist the military, either technically (as in operating a program in a foreign language and culture), or more wholistically (as exemplified by the research of Hickey, Pool, or others, and their discussions of political policy). Third, given the close relationships between social-scientific fieldworkers (particularly ethnographers) and their hosts, what are the proper ethical and political boundaries that would apply fairly, equally, and reciprocally? Fourth, how can social scientists resolve their moral commitments to humanity, to science, to research sponsors, to the host people, and to their own people?

Within the compass of the present article, I cannot do more than frame these questions in counterposition to the history of a single and notorious project. The questions deserve careful and dispassionate analysis, but it must be confessed that, instead, the professional associations have

been subject to the winds of political fashion: during World
War II, the political and moral norm was collaboration with
the armed services, even (by some) in the conduct of covert
intelligence; during the U.S. involvement in Southeast Asia,
the norm swung drastically in the opposite direction against
any assistance to the armed services; while, far earlier,
during World War I, the norm for support of the U.S. military
effort was such that Franz Boas became the recipient of severe
censure because of his protests against the corruption of the
neutrality of anthropological fieldworkers.

Beyond these profound questions, and historical exempli-
fications, there is the irony that, after itself (via Camelot)
being the agency that provoked the wrath of overseas critics,
it is the U.S. Government which then instituted a review system
monitoring all research projects (including social research)
which are intended to be conducted outside the U.S. (Orlans
1973:174-178).

References Cited

Barnes, J. A.
   1977 The Ethics of Inquiry in Social Science. Delhi:
      Oxford University Press.
Beals, Ralph L.
   1969 Politics of Social Research: An Inquiry into the
      Ethics and Responsibilities of Social Scientists.
      Chicago: Aldine.
Boguslaw, Robert
   1967 Ethics and the Social Scientsit. In Horowitz ed.
      Pp. 107-127.
Boughey, Howard
   1978 The Insights of Sociology: An Introduction. Boston:
      Allyn & Bacon.
Deitchman, Seymour J.
   1976 The Best-Laid Schemes: A Tale of Social Research and
      Bureaucracy. Cambridge: M.I.T. Press.
Frank, Andre Gunder
   1968 Comment on Social Responsibilities Symposium.
      Current Anthropology 9(5):412-414.
Gough, Kathleen
   1968 New Proposals for Anthropologists. Current Anthro-
      pology 9(5):403-407, 428-431.
Hickey, Gerald C.
   1967 Accommodation in South Vietnam: The Key to Socio-
      political Solidarity. P-3707. Santa Monica: Rand.
   1970 Accommodation and Coalition in South Vietnam. P-4213.
      Santa Monica: Rand.

Horowitz, Irving L., ed.
 1967 The Rise and Fall of Project Camelot: Studies in the
       Relationship between Social Science and Practical
       Politics. Cambridge: M.I.T. Press.
Lowry, Ritchie P.
 1978 From Camelot Policymaker to College Professor (inter-
       viewed by Irving Louis Horowitz). Society, January/
       February, pp. 69-75.
Lyons, Gene M.
 1969 The Uneasy Partnership. New York: Russell Sage.
Mering, Otto von
 1968 Comment on Social Responsibilities Symposium.
       Current Anthropology 9(5):421.
Nisbet, Robert A.
 1967 Project Camelot and the Science of Man. Reprinted in
       Horowitz ed. 1967:313-338.
Oppenheimer, Jules Robert
 1964 The Flying Trapeze: Three Crises for Physicists.
       New York: Oxford University Press.
Orlans, Harold
 1973 Contracting for Knowledge. San Francisco: Jossey-
       Bass.
Pool, Ithiel de Sola
 1967 The Necessity for Social Scientists Doing Research
       for Government. In Horowitz ed. 1967:267-280.
 1971 Reprints of Publications on Viet Nam: 1966-1970.
       Cambridge: M.I.T. Press.
Uhlaner, J. E.
 1974 The Research Psychologist in the Army--1917 to 1973.
       Arlington, Va.: U.S. Army Research Institute for the
       Behavioral and Social Sciences.
Whyte, William Foote
 1969 The Role of the U.S. Professor in Developing Countries.
       The American Sociologist, vol. 4, no. 1, 19-28.
Yarmolinsky, Adam
 1971 The Military Establishment: Its Impacts on American
       Society. "A Twentieth Century Fund Study." New York:
       Harper & Row.

Part II
Qualitative Methodology

Introduction to Part II

Murry L. Wax and Joan Cassell

Many anthropologists, some sociologists, and a few persons of kindred disciplines utilize a research method variously labelled as fieldwork, participant observation, ethnographic or qualitative method. Olesen prefers to speak of "interpretive sociology" (a direct translation of verstehende Soziologie, coined by Max Weber in filiation to the historiography of Wilhelm Dilthey). Labels aside, the crucial point is that between the person who studies and those who are studied the fieldwork relationship differs markedly from those of experimenter-subject (psychological and biomedical researches) of interviewer-respondent (social survey research). Thus, ethnographers assert that they have no "subjects" but only informants or hosts.

Wax and Cassell review some of the varieties of interaction between ethnographic researcher and researched, revealing a complex range of ethical problems. Because of internal political conflict, the professional associations have not been able to achieve consensus about these problems and so cannot confront the federal regulatory system with a unified critique. Finally, the authors suggest that a comparison between fieldwork and journalism would indicate that the two have similarities which are provocative, given the constitutional protection accorded the press and the lack of legal standing of ethnography.

Olesen is concerned that research should be conducted ethically, but is troubled at the application to interpretive sociology of the guidelines developed from experimental research. Qualitative research is an ongoing process, throughout which researchers are continually redefining their problems, while hosts are reappraising their relationships to researchers. Consent is therefore under constant renegotiation, becoming ever more "informed"--for both parties. Institutional review boards may "protect" hosts so that they are denied the possibility of utilizing their own judgment about the degree of their participation in this long-term and interactive process.

Cassell begins with a review of the various meanings of "subject" and then compares the risks to experimental subjects with those resulting from fieldwork. The issue is not whether fieldworkers are more or less moral than their biomedical counterparts, but the nature of the risks and hopes, harms and benefits, of the investigations. She emphasizes that in most fieldwork the major risk is violation of privacy when the findings are published, subsequent to the research. While review boards attempt to regulate fieldwork a priori, the damage (if any) is most likely to occur a posteriori. Yet, until the fieldwork is completed, we do not know what kinds of publication may inflict harm, and, until the analysis is completed, we do not know what is worthy of being published.

Fitchen worked both as a fieldworker and as an advocate of the host group in relationship to exterior agencies. Where the host people are poorly literate and subordinated, it is natural for the fieldworker to act as their spokeswoman, for in good fieldwork there is an interchange of gifts and services between researcher and hosts. Fitchen performed this role with insight and ethical sensibility. Yet, from the perspective of federal regulations, her labors were a confusion of two roles. Bureaucracies are required to separate rigidly those agencies which conduct research and those which perform services, for one would not wish that the data freely given by a person to a researcher should then find their way to those who make administrative determinations about the eligibility of that very person for services or benefits. In a small but salient way, Fitchen's essay poses dilemmas for those who wish to frame universalistic regulations for monitoring the ethics of social research.

5

Fieldwork, Ethics and Politics

The Wider Context

Murray L. Wax and Joan Cassell

In this paper we shall focus upon the ethical problems associated with that variety of social research which (depending upon the context) is called "fieldwork," "participant observation," or "ethnography." In focusing upon ethical problems we shall also be examining political conflicts and dilemmas, because, as it will become apparent, the two realms are intertwined: my ethics are your politics (cf. Rynkiewich & Spradley 1976).

Responding to the ethical problems of research involving human beings--and perhaps also to political needs and opportunities--the federal government has set forth a series of regulations which have had a marked effect upon research. Behavioral scientists and their professional associations have responded with uncertainty and perplexity. It was not until September 1976 that the American Sociological Association brought together a panel of senior researchers, charging them to develop recommendations on how the association should respond to the federal regulations. The American Anthropological Association was consulted by the ASA and chose then to leave the initiative to its larger associate. It did, however, delegate William C. Sturtevant of the Smithsonian Institution to present its needs and problems to the National Commission for the Protection of Human Subjects of Biomedical and Behavioral Research. Reading his excellent testimony, we believe he was handicapped by the absence of three classes of information: (1) he (and we) do not really know the kinds of ethical problems and infringements that have been occurring in the course of anthropological research; (2) he (and we) do not really know the effects upon different researchers and researches of the various federal regulations; and (3) finally, he (and we) have not explored the larger social, political, legal, and ethical context of ethnographic research. It is to the last question that this present paper addresses itself.

Relationships between Fieldworker and Hosts

First, let us characterize the activities and interrelationships which make up "fieldwork." This is necessary because within sociology and anthropology there is lack of clarity about the varieties of approaches that have been labelled as "fieldwork" or "participant observation." In the present context what is important is, on the one hand, the posture adopted by the researcher and, on the other hand, the status and role into which the ethnographer is placed by the host people.[1] The position of the fieldworker can best be understood as a negotiated role, a social construction, composed in part by the ways in which the host people will tolerate a stranger and in part by the temperament and interests of the investigator (cf. R. Wax 1971: ch. 4). Illustration will convey this negotiated role of the fieldworker better than abstract discussion.

Verandah Model

At one extreme, and by now historically obsolete in most parts of the world, is the verandah model of ethnographic research. Think of the fieldworker, seated comfortably on the verandah of the government station, sending out for "a native." The latter will be fetched to join him on the verandah to be subjected to several hours of systematic interrogation about his--usually "his" and not "her"--language and customs. We understand this model was utilized by A. R. Radcliffe-Brown, who questioned Andaman Island prisoners sent to him from the British gaol. This type of research is still frequently adopted in modern institutional settings, where the subordinates, (be they prisoners, students, enlisted men, or mental patients) are brought to the office of the researcher for questioning about the peculiar customs and jargon of their fellows.

Noblesse Oblige

The research model which we call noblesse oblige is exemplified by the fieldworker who moves into a substantial dwelling with a retinue of servants and assistants, coming to play in local society the role of wealthy and influential patron. This role was perhaps easiest to adopt during the imperialist era of the European presence, but it still can be played--and is, in fact, sometimes expected--by the host peoples in many areas of the world. As is evident from his diaries, this style of fieldwork was adopted by Bronislaw Malinowski (M. Wax 1972). Given the relative wealth and

technological sophistication of Western anthropologists, as
compared to the host peoples, this was a congenial style of
mutual co-adaptation, and it sometimes permitted a great deal
of informal and comfortable intercourse between the individuals of the two cultures. It worked most easily when the
fieldworder could establish a peer relationship with local
elite, as did Raymond Firth (1957) among the Tikopia. Indeed,
in many such situations, it is difficult for the Western
anthropologists not to be cast in such a role.

Going Native

The research model which we call going native is that in
which the fieldworker tries, in every conceivable fashion, to
adopt the way of life of the common people being studied: to
live in their residences, eat their food, talk their language,
participate in their ceremonials and share their lives.
Given the alien quality of the cultures of most other peoples,
and the fact that the ethnographer is a full adult from our
own society, such conduct is often difficult, if not arduous;
it is the more so because the researcher is attempting to
play the role of a local and responsible adult--itself a time
consuming task--while at the same time conducting research
and maintaining fieldnotes and a field-diary. An individual
who seems to have performed this feat with considerable grace
is Colin Turnbull (1962) in his work among the Pygmies of the
Ituri rain forest; on the other hand, David Maybury-Lewis
(1965) had a frightful time when he attempted to play native
among tribal Indians of South America. The role is most
easily handled when the fieldworker is or can be cast by the
hosts as "a native." Thus, when Joan Cassell (1977) conducted fieldwork within the contemporary American feminist
movement, she was in many ways just another recruit, one more
woman whose consciousness was being raised as she learned how
to behave (and think) like a feminist.

Undercover Agent

In the model which we call undercover agent the investigator seeks to expose the real activities of some group of
persons who are for one reason or another concealing important parts of their lives. In the vocabulary of Erving Goff-
man, this infiltration is spoken of as "penetrating fronts"
and "exposing the back-stage." It is an approach that would
be natural to radicals, for example, who wish to demonstrate
the true (i.e. self-serving) nature of "The Establishment."
The most eloquent exposition of this orientation, however,
has been written by a non-radical, Jack Douglas, who has devoted himself to exposing the actualities of conduct in sites
such as selected massage parlors and nude beaches. Indeed,

there are cases where it is precisely the contrast between
the front and backstage that gives the project its focus, as
in Laud Humphreys' Tearoom Trade (1970), where the significant contrast is between the respectable heterosexual fami-
lial life of his subjects and their discreet participation in
impersonal homosexual sex in public restrooms. In the majority of field investigations, however, penetrating fronts is
neither the focus of the ethnographer nor the essential task
of the project; and when a front is penetrated, the event is
more a rite de passage for the researcher than an exposure of
chicanery among the hosts (cf. Barth 1976).

Advocate

The model which we call advocate appears less often in
the conventional literature. But, many ethnographers study
peoples who are economically or politically depressed, and
there is a natural human tendency to intervene to help them
transform or improve their destinies. The advocacy posture
can range from the liberal (or relatively conservative) approach known as "applied anthropology" to varieties of insurgency. Equally, if not more important, the advocate can
range from being someone scarcely familiar with the hosts and
not committed in any way to their longterm condition, to
being a person both familiar and deeply committed.[2]

Kinds of Ethical Problems

From even this brief review of the varieties of fieldwork, it should be clear that there are many different kinds
of ethical problems intrinsic to each model of research. It
should also become apparent that the attempt to control this
variety of problems through a single type of bureaucratic
regulation, such as the Human Subjects Protective System, may
on occasion augment rather than resolve difficulties.

Fieldworkers enter the field as people mentally rooted
within the professional world of a scholarly discipline and
morally anchored as well in the cultural worlds where they
were nurtured. In the course of fieldwork, if it be of the
more participatory and egalitarian variety, they are gradual-
ly incorporated within the moral systems of those who are
studied and so become increasingly sensible of, and governed
by, the same moral codes as the hosts. A major difficulty
with the federal regulations and with the professional codes
of ethics, is that neither treat ethnographers as real human
beings, engaged in human interaction and subject to human
passions and frailties, as well as indigenous moral logics.
A surprising variety of parties--the federal government, the
radical reformers, the professional associations--seem intent

on transforming fieldworkers into saintly types, with super-
human responsibilities. These expectations, we would contend,
not only make for bad research, but also encourage irrespon-
sible conduct.

Critics have contended that the fieldworker, as a stranger from another and frequently technologically more advanced
society, may upset the local political and ecological balances. To some observers, such disruption may appear all to
the good, as when the researcher in a Hindu village inter-
vened to assist villagers who were being exploited by outside
landlords. Nevertheless, there may be harmful consequences
in the long run: when, after the departure of the powerful
and literate stranger, the exploiters may take revenge on
those who challenged their authority. Such situations are
sufficiently complex, exotic, and unpredictable to make it
difficult for anyone to form an adequate ethical appraisal.
The counsel which seems safe--that the fieldworker should do
nothing to disturb existing equilibria--is even more dubious,
because it assumes that a morally responsible human being
should do nothing to assist those who have been friendly and
helpful.

In many kinds of fieldwork, the ethically most problematic phase of the investigation comes when composing and pub-
lishing research reports. For, through publication, information about the lives of those who were studied will be made
available to a larger public. In the past, when host peoples
were not literate, nor in easy or rapid communication with
the "civilized" world, the consequences of publication tended
to be slow and mediated. But, today, the networks of communication are swifter, more efficient, and more extensive: and
even when the writer makes strong efforts to disguise the
identity of those studied, this screen can often be penetrated. The anthropologist, Carl Withers, went to considerable
pains to disguise the identity of the town he called,
"Plainville, USA," and even published his major report pseu-
donymously; nevertheless, the disguise was penetrated by professional anthropologists and students; and, even more important, the work circulated among the townspeople, discomfi-
ting some individuals (Gallaher 1964).

Political Conflicts among Fieldworkers

Among many of our colleagues, there is an intense distrust of the conduct of some group of their peers. In most
cases, this distrust is grounded in political differences.
For example, if we turn the clock back to the period of armed
involvement by the United States in Asia, we may recall the
moral crusades led by academic radicals. Radical anthropolo-

gists were horrified that any of their colleagues should be associated with the American military presence in Asia. As part of their crusade, the radicals initiated professional codes of ethics, which were supposed to end any association between an anthropologist and a federal agency participating in activities within Southeast Asia.

Of course, this distrust was returned. Conservative ethnographers were concerned about the ethics of their radical colleagues, fearing that their "research" was really a species of revolutionary activity--"agitprop" in the traditional Communist classification.

The conservatives believed that the fieldwork done by the radicals was a species of moral exploitation, since those who were studied were being pressured into undertaking innovative and revolutionary activities not necessarily in their own longrun interests; and, worse yet, this counsel and manipulation was proffered by persons presenting themselves as professional ethnographers, not as revolutionary agitators. Naturally, the radicals thought that the fieldwork performed by their more conventional (and presumably more conservative) colleagues was a species of exploitation of those who were studied, who were viewed as unwittingly surrendering valuable information which would then be utilized for aggrandizement by imperialist, military, or commercial enterprises.

Given such a disparity of interpretations it is not surprising that ethnographers were unable to present a common platform when confronting federal agencies and their regulatory systems. At its most simplistic, each political group would like to use the regulatory systems to monitor the activities of other groups and factions. Each political group, faction, and clique tends to regard the federal regulations as unnecessary or illegitimate in its own case, but as being useful in controlling the dubious activities of political antagonists. Unfortunately, it is the ethical relationships between fieldworkers and hosts that suffer in consequence.

The Politics of Regulation

It would be appropriate here to have a section reviewing the history and politics of the federal regulatory systems: what were the crucial incidents that became occasions for regulation; who were the moral entrepeneurs who formulated the initial provisions (Broadhead and Rist 1976, 1978); which disciplines, individuals, and factions were represented in the process; and so on (cf. Bower and de Gasparis 1976). We can only note the consequences: The federal agencies which formulate, develop, and interpret the policies have been

staffed largely by physicians, lawyers, and moral philosophers (ethicists). Despite the fact that ethnographers have,
over the generations of their disciplines, studied moral systems and their functioning in human groups, no anthropologist
or sociologist has been appointed to any of these regulatory
commissions.

We do not wish to deny the ethical problems generated by
social research generally, or fieldwork particularly. The
problems are genuine and require serious consideration. They
do, however, need to be regarded in perspective. A simple
way of exemplifying this is to examine the situation of the
Pueblo Indians. These peoples are few in number, divided
into a score of different tribes and different villages, so
that we are talking of relatively small populations. The
media tend to give considerable attention to the presence of
anthropologists among their neighbors, the Navajo, who number
perhaps 150,000 persons, as opposed to Pueblo peoples, where
a large tribe would be the Hopi, with less than 10,000 members, while some tribal-villages have only a few hundred in-
habitants. Robert Breunig, who has worked among these people
for the past ten years, notes that anthropologists have been
relatively few in number, respectful of Pueblo ways, and of
but little impact on Pueblo life. Historically, a major impact has been that of missionaries. Among some Puebloes, the
effect of the Mormon missionaries is so great, and Indian
conversion so numerous, that traditional ceremonials are
likely to vanish within a generation, because children will
no longer be trained to perform them. There have been other
intrusions into Pueblo life: the Bureau of Indian Affairs;
generations of tourists; and, most recently, members of the
counter-culture, who have read a book or two about the
Puebloes, decided that they were spiritual brothers-and-
sisters, and have descended upon them trying to share their
lives and ceremonial practices. In smaller numbers have been
journalists, novelists, social welfare workers, social reformers, and others. In moral terms, if you think of, not
only a person as having a right to privacy, but of a group as
having such a right,--then the Puebloes surely have a just
claim.

The present forms of federal regulation, such as the
Human Subjects Protective System or the Privacy Act, neither
accord with Pueblo customs nor protect them from intruders.
A Pueblo community may welcome ethnographers known to them
personally and may encourage their continued presence, but
refuse to endorse any piece of paper whatsoever, because,
like many folk peoples, they distrust legal forms and fear
that their signatures may be used against them on a later
occasion.[3] If we are to help protect the Pueblo in protect-

ing themselves from unwanted visitation, we must begin with
how <u>they feel</u> and what <u>they want</u> and how <u>they choose to act</u>,
rather than with a universalistic formulation applied by
agencies with no knowledge of Pueblo customs and needs.

Civil Rights in Conflict

As do all persons who are reasonably alert, sociable,
and intelligent, fieldworkers observe and talk to others:
they inquire about feelings and attitudes, strategies for
handling the vicissitudes of life; hopes and fears. Where
fieldworkers differ from others is that they conduct their
inquiries more systematically and record their information
with the hopes of organizing it into a written report.

We mention these similarities to emphasize their natu-
ralness and normality. Some fieldworkers we know have greet-
ed the introduction of the Human Subjects Protective regulations and of institutional review boards with an attitude of
moral outrage: They (the authorities) have no right to stop
me from observing people and talking to them. If people
don't want to talk to me, they can refuse to respond or tell
me to go to Hell. Besides, most of the people I talk to in
the course of fieldwork are my friends--people I have known
for a long time. It's impossible for me to differentiate our
casual conversations from our scientific ones, where I am in-
quiring about some particular piece of information. If they
ask me to testify for them in a court hearing, and if, while
I work with them in preparation for this, I also make inferences about their styles of interaction and organization;
why should I need to get prior approval from a university review committee which is composed of people who understand
nothing of the situation?

However critical one may be of social research, or of
the theories and practices of particular investigators, we
think that there is in this situation a dilemma of some consequence for law-makers and framers of policy. It is a far
more serious action than is realized when government presumes
to exercise prior review and restraint over its citizens in
such daily activities as associating, observing, and convers-
ing. Moreover these regulations are especially disturbing
because they are framed exclusively in terms of the rights of
the so-called subject to protection of self and of privacy.
However laudable may be these rights--and indeed they are
laudable--the regulatory system is skewed because it does not
recognize the equally essential and elementary rights to associate, observe, and converse. There is no recognition of
these alternative rights and so of course there is no attempt
to delineate how these contrary rights might be balanced

against each other in particular cases. In one sense, what
has happened is that the rights which the ethnographer shares
as a citizen or member of a relatively free and open society
are denied the moment the fieldworker thinks seriously enough
about a social problem to wish to approach it professionally.
One fieldworker we know was sufficiently disturbed by the regulatory system so that she threatened to study the institutional review board on her campus; when she mentioned this to
the chair of that committee, she learned that she would have
to submit her research design and any questionnaire schedules
to them for their approval and written consent, prior to
being able to conduct the study!

Fieldwork and Journalism

The ethical and legal issues confronting fieldworkers
can be placed in a broader perspective by means of a comparison with another profession: journalism. Although journalism
is akin to fieldwork in a number of significant respects, it
is in a privileged position because of the protections accorded by the First Amendment to the Constitution.

In the natural sciences, there may seem to be a gap of
abyssal dimensions between the activities of the scientist
and those of the journalist, but within the United States,
there has for a long time been a close linkage between much
of social research and journalism. It was the influence of
an ex-journalist that helped transform American sociology
from a reformative discipline, resting on vague historical
and evolutionary generalizations, into a discipline based on
empirical examination of contemporary life. Robert Ezra Park
(1864-1944) had had a long and successful career as a newspaper journalist before he went to Germany to study what were
considered the social-sciences (Hughes 1963). Returning to
the U.S., he became secretary to Booker T. Washington and
lived and worked in the South. Eventually (1912), he encountered a sociologist named William I. Thomas, who was so taken
with his talents that he persuaded his departmental chairman
at the University of Chicago to bring him there in 1914 on a
temporary appointment. Park's experiences as a journalist
had made him thoroughly knowledgable about urban life, and he
had no patience with the students' ignorance nor with their
sentimental programs of social betterment. Like a good newspaper editor, he sent his students out into the neighborhoods
of Chicago and later of other cities, so that they could
learn firsthand--by observing, talking and associating with
people, and sharing their lives.

W. I. Thomas had already used some of these techniques
and procedures which today would be called "urban anthropo-

logy" to study Poles in their rural villages in Europe and in
their neighborhood enclaves in Chicago. Park intensified,
systematized, and accelerated this inquiry, becoming the
guiding light of the Chicago department and of much of the
sociology of that time. At times, Park formulated sociology's
task as that of discovering "the news behind the news," i.e.
of identifying and describing the fundamental social processes that manifested themselves as newsworthy items. (In-
cidentally, it should be clear that when we speak here of a
department or profession of sociology, we are including much
of what at that time and even today would be considered anthropology. Not only in his fieldwork methods, but in his interest in worldwide comparisons, and his concern with ecological comparisons with the animal and plant kingdoms, Park
worked in the spirit of anthropology.)

Park was not the only professional whose career was an
interweaving of journalism and social-science: a significant
number of social-scientists have written regularly for non-
professional journals.[4]

Starting from the opposite pole, there have been journalists, who produced work with some of the solidity of sociology or anthropology. For example, William H. Whyte, Jr. did
fieldwork among the upper middleclass after World War II and
wrote ethnographies of the man in the gray flannel suit and
of the suburban life of young corporate executives. Nicholas
von Hoffman did ethnographic studies of the drug culture and
of the civil rights movement. And, much earlier, Lincoln
Steffens and the others denounced as "muckrakers" demonstrated the corruption of the business world and its interrela-
tionship with political parties and machines.

Journalism and Fieldwork: Legal and Ethical Considerations

We have linked journalism and fieldwork, not because we
judge the two professions to be identical, but because we
wish to broaden our ethical and legal analysis.

In judging the freedoms accorded to journalists, our
American political process looks neither to "risk/benefit
rations" nor to "prior informed consent" of those actors
deemed newsworthy. Instead the scope given to the press is
absolute and extraordinarily wide due to the compact statement in the First Amendment:

"Congress shall make no law...abridging the freedom of
speech, or of the press...." Those who drafted this Amendment were familiar with the press and knew that it could be
intrusive, adversary, and painfully critical. Nevertheless,

they were willing to give it an absolute privilege because they judged that its information and criticism were vital to the health of the republic. They might also have judged that it was worth paying the price of journalistic assaults upon privacy for the benefits of a free press to the political community as a whole.

We are not here contending that fieldwork should be accorded the same privileges as journalism, although there is some basis for making that argument and from some points of view the two activities appear extraordinarily alike. Fieldwork often generates the news behind the news, and often presents critical information about the nature of the political and social world. For example, important social and political functions similar to those of a free press were performed by Hortense Powdermaker (1939, 1966) and John Dollard when each did fieldwork in a small town of the Deep South during the 1930s and reported upon the patterns of Negro-White interrelationships.[5] We think it is fair to say that the literate public has a legitimate interest in the conduct of fieldwork, and that on occasion the grounds for differentiating fieldwork from journalism are so narrow as to cast some doubt upon the validity of the present system of federally mandated regulation.[6]

Summary and Conclusion

Let us review the argument of this paper. We have focused upon one particular methodology of social research, variously labeled as "fieldwork," "ethnography" or "participant observation." We have tried to show how varied and complex is this methodology and, at the same time, how intensely human. We have tried also to indicate some of the ethical dilemmas that arise during the course of fieldwork, precisely because it typically involves intercultural, interclass, and even international relationships. We have shown how various types of relationships between ethnographer and host peoples, described in terms of fieldwork models, generate different types of ethical problems. We have contrasted this variety and richness with the conceptual poverty of the universalistic formulations of "risk/benefit" and "informed consent" and we have contended that this bureaucratic vocabulary tends to reduce our capacities to treat fieldwork relationships with the sensibilities and care that they deserve, so that instead of protecting the peoples studied, it reduces them to a faceless and natural set of objects, "the subjects" of research. We have then noted that the responses of the professional associations of sociologists and anthropologists have been disorganized and ineffectual, partially because of their numerical and financial weakness, but even more because of the divisions of political opinion among their memberships.[7] We have further argued that in many situations, fieldworkers are not notably intrusive upon the people studied and that they are generally far more respectful of their hosts, and of lesser impact, than many other visitors whose activities are unregulated. Moreover, because many of the procedures of fieldwork are so informal and are rooted in the natural pro- cesses of human interaction and communication, it is diffi- cult to regulate the fieldwork process without seeming to deny to fieldworkers their elementary rights as citizens and human beings. As a final effort toward breaking out of the narrow conceptual scheme of federal regulations, and enlarg- ing the framework of discussion and analysis, we have com- pared fieldwork to journalism and emphasized the constitu- tional protections which have been afforded to journalism be- cause of the functions that a free press performs in sustain- ing a republican form of government.

Human activities and relationships involve conflicting interests. It is a chronic utopian illusion that such con- flicting interests can be abolished by a magical reorganiza- tion, or by the legerdemain of a moral formula that can be enforced in all situations. There is no substitute for the painstaking examination of individual cases and the careful weighing of contrary interests. Since fieldwork is such a complex human enterprise and since it brings together at least two, and sometimes several, parties of different cultu- ral backgrounds and different social perspectives, it is small wonder that ethical problems abound. Unfortunately, such problems cannot be dissolved or resolved by the fiat of "risk/benefit" rations or "informed consent."

This examination of the wider social and political con- text within which fieldwork is carried out has (we hope) en- abled us to perceive something of the magnitude and variety of the several interests which should properly be balanced against each other. By now, it should be evident that it is not sufficient to merely consider a fieldworker's desire to conduct an investigation. It is equally the case, however, that morality does not lie in simply obtaining an initial declaration of consent from a research population, especially when that group is stratified or complexly organized and does speak, or might speak, through many voices.

What distinguishes enlightened from unenlightened ethi- cal discourse is a regard for context, and for the interests and values of as many parties to interaction as can be encom- passed. Moral decisions are unsatisfactory when based solely upon the needs of the actor, or solely upon the needs of what is conceptualized as an uninformed and unsophisticated (and

on occasion, unintelligent) study population. This is one
reason why utilitarianism as a moral philosophy is so unsatisfactory: it tends to focus solely upon the actor, or upon the
community viewed simply as congeries of distinct actors.

To place fieldwork within a broader framework of ethics
and law may seem a bit of American ethnocentrism. Few other
nations regard a free press as essential to their political
system. Here we may advance the argument of Michael Polanyi
in his Science, Faith, and Society, where he contends that
freedom and democracy are not simply peculiarities of Western
bourgeois society; they are also essential ingredients of
scientific investigation.

Notes

[1] Among the several previous attempts to categorize the
interrelationships between fieldworker and host people, the
most evocative is that of Colby Hatfield (1973) who describes
three sets of statuses into which the fieldworker is placed
by the hosts: Incompetent (incompetent dope, incompetent
child, incompetent pawn); Sahib (technician, social expert);
and Fort Knox. There is also the earlier effort by Gold
(1958) who distinguished among the "complete participant,"
the "participant-as-observer," the "observer-as-participant,"
and the "complete observer." Neither of these systems of
classification cope with the issues raised in the present
essay.

[2] An important if numerically small variety of the advocate is the person whose fieldwork is really a species of
revolutionary agitation and organization. Some anthropologists have contended that this is the only ethical posture in
a world characterized by poverty, oppression, and gross dif-
ferentials in wealth, power, and status (cf. Diamond 1969).
Presumably following this lead are persons without organic or
enduring ties to depressed communities who nonetheless venture to incite them toward revolutionary action, without
carefully assessing the resources available or the terrible
forces arrayed against them.

[3] Thus Ann Fischer noted (1970: especially p. 273) that
the Houma Indians of southern Louisiana were intensely suspicious that fieldworkers (or other outsiders) would attempt to
secure signatures on documents in order to dupe the people of
their little remaining title to lands.

[4] The individuals would include at least the following:
Margaret Mead, who wrote a column regularly for Redbook;

Daniel Bell, a former editor of <u>Fortune</u>; Helen MacGill Hughes, a student of Park's who was a stringer for <u>Time</u>; Marvin Harris, a column for <u>Natural History</u>; Nathan Glazer, former editor of <u>Commentary</u>; Lewis Coser, former editor of <u>Politics</u> and then of <u>Dissent</u>. And there must be numerous others.

[5]We can likewise note the social and political values (again of a variety akin to journalism in depth) of the field work of Rosalie Hankey Wax (1971), Edward Spicer and others in the Relocation Centers where the Japanese-American were confined during World War II; or of the fieldwork by William Foote Whyte (1955) and Herbert Gans (1962) in urban Italian-American lowerclass enclaves. We can further note the fieldwork in rural Quebec by Everett (1943) and Helen Hughes and by Horace Miner who described the tension and dynamics of French-English relationships long before the separatist move-ment emerged with such power and publicity.

[6]The text was written prior to <u>Zurcher v. Stanford Daily</u>, 1978, in which the Supreme Court ruled that newspapers do not have any special right to warning of a court-approved search by law enforcement officers or an opportunity to contest such a search in the courts prior to its occurrence (Weaver 1978). From this decision, it could be inferred that, in so far as they were concerned to protect the sources of their informa-tion, social researchers would have nothing to gain from being considered as legally equivalent to journalists. And, of course, the special irony remains that it is precisely the government which insists on the privilege of invading docu-mentary files and thereby forcing a breach of the confidenti-ality pledged by journalist (and fieldworker) in order to protect the privacy of the respondents.

A small ray of hope may be found in the text of the syn-dicated columnist, Anthony Lewis, who defended the Court de-cision on the grounds that--

> It is a fundamental mistake for the press to argue
> that it is entitled to different and better treatment
> under the Constitution. The First Amendment also pro-
> tects the right of professors and pamphleteers and
> ordinary citizens to write and speak freely.

The issue thus raised by Lewis and ourselves is whether the First Amendment protects the institutional "press" (i.e. the organized media of communication) or the activity of pub-lishing (whether by journalists, scholars, or pamphleteers). The issue dealt with by the Court in <u>Zurcher v. Stanford Daily</u> is whether materials gathered by investigators (repor-ters or, conceivably, scholars) and intended as the basis of publication should be available to law enforcement officials possessing search warrants or should enjoy special protection and thus become available only via a subpoena, which could be challenged in court. By inference, Lewis is arguing that it would be easier to grant the latter protection, if "the press" were interpreted as referring to an activity rather than an institution.

Edith Graber informs us that in Great Britain, the freedom of the press is interpreted as applying to the activities of scholars and authors as much as to the institutionalized media.

[7]The intermixture (or confusion, depending on one's point of view) between the professional ethics of anthropologists and their political commitments is clearly evident in the essays by Berreman and Gough in the "Social Responsibilities Symposium" of Current Anthropology (1968) and especially in the comment by Frank (1968:413) who cites approvingly the following statement by Barbara and Alan Haber (1967:95-96):

> Radicals cannot accept without reservation the code of ethics and responsibility of their professions. Ethics are not abstract ideals. They are sanctifications of certain types of social relations, purposes and loyalties (which is no news to anthropologists so long as the reference is to other peoples' ethics rather than their own). Conventional ethics entrap us into support of things which we do not support politically and into loyalties which conflict with our own values and politics....

References Cited

American Sociological Association
   1977 Conditions of Research: Proceedings of a Conference
      on Implications for Social Research of Selected Federal
      Regulations. Washington DC.
Appell, G. N.
   1973 Basic Issues in the Dilemmas and Ethical Conflict in
      Anthropological Inquiry. MSS Modular Publications,
      Module 19.
Barth, Frederik
   1976 Ritual and Knowledge. New Haven: Yale University
      Press.
Berreman, Gerald D.
   1962 Behind Many Masks. Monograph #4, Society for Applied
      Anthropology.
   1968 Is Anthropology Alive? Social Responsibility in
      Social Anthropology. Current Anthropology 9(5):391-396.
Bower, Robert T., and Priscilla R. de Gasparis, eds.
   1976 The Protection of Subjects in Social Research.
      Summary Report submitted to National Institute of Mental
      Health. Washington DC: Bureau of Social Science Re-
      search (in press, under title, Ethics in Social Research;
      New York: Praeger Publishers, 1978?).
Broadhead, Robert S., and Ray C. Rist
   1976 Gatekeepers and the Social Control of Social Research.
      Social Problems, Vol. 23, No. 3.
   1978 Ethical Research: The New Moral Crusade in Social
      Science. Social Policy, forthcoming (May/June?).
Cassell, Joan
   1977 A Group Called Women. New York: David McKay.
Diamond, Stanley
   1969 Anthropology in Question. In Reinventing Anthropo-
      logy, ed. Dell Hymes. New York: Vintage Books.
Douglas, Jack
   1977 Investigative Social Research. Beverly Hills: Sage.
Firth, Raymond
   1957 We, The Tikopia. 2nd edition. London: George Allen
      & Unwin.
Fischer, Ann
   1970 Field Work in Five Cultures. Pp. 265-289 in Peggy
      Golde, ed. Women in the Field. Chicago: Aldine.
Frank, Andre Gunder
   1968 Comment in Social Responsibilities Symposium.
      Current Anthropology 9(5):412-414.
Gallaher, Art, Jr.
   1964 Plainville: The Twice-Studied Town. In Reflections
      on Community Studies, ed. A.J. Vidich, et al. New York:
      John Wiley.

Gans, Herbert J.
  1962   The Urban Villagers. New York: Free Press of Glencoe.
Gold, Raymond L.
  1958   Roles in Sociological Field Observations. Social
      Forces 36:217-223. Reprinted, pp. 30-38, in Issues in
      Participant Observation, edited by George J. McCall and
      J.L. Simmons (Reading, Mass.: Addison-Wesley, 1969).
Gough, Kathleen
  1968   New Proposals for Anthropologists. Current Anthropo-
      logy 9(5):403-407.
Haber, Barbara and Alan
  1967   Getting By with a Little Help from Our Friends.
      Our Generation 5(2):83-101.
Hatfield, Colby R., Jr.
  1973   Fieldwork: Toward a Model of Mutual Exploitation.
      Anthropological Quarterly 46:15-29.
Hughes, Everett C.
  1943   French Canada in Transition. Chicago: University of
      Chicago Press.
  1963   Robert E. Park. In The Founding Fathers of Social
      Science, ed. Timothy Raison. Baltimore: Penguin Books,
      1969.
Humphreys, Laud
  1970   Tearoom Trade: Impersonal Sex in Public Places.
      Chicago: Aldine.
Lewis, Anthony
  1978   The Court and the Press. St. Louis Post-Dispatch,
      June 13, p. 3C.
Maybury-Lewis, David
  1965   The Savage and the Innocent: Life with the Primitive
      Tribes of Brazil. Cleveland: World.
Polanyi, Michael
  1946   Science, Faith and Society. Chicago: University of
      Chicago Press.
Powdermaker, Hortense
  1939   After Freedom, A Cultural Study in the Deep South.
      New York: Viking.
  1966   Stranger and Friend: The Way of an Anthropologist.
      New York: Norton.
Rynkiewich, Michael A., and James P. Spradley
  1976   Ethics and Anthropology: Dilemmas in Fieldwork.
      New York: John Wiley.
Sturtevant, William C.
  1977   Testimony before the National Commission for the
      Protection of Human Subjects of Biomedical and Behavio-
      ral Research. Newsletter of the American Anthropologi-
      cal Association, 18(6):1, 10.
Turnbull, Colin
  1962   The Forest People: A Study of the Pygmies of the
      Congo. New York: Natural History Library, Anchor.

Wax, Murray L.
 1972 Tenting with Malinowski. American Sociological
       Review. Vol. 37, No. 1, pp. 1-13.
 1977 On Fieldworkers and Those Exposed to Fieldwork:
       Federal Regulations and Moral Issues. Human Organiza-
       tion. Vol. 36, No. 3 (Fall), pp. 321-328.
Wax, Rosalie H.
 1971 Doing Fieldwork: Warnings and Advice. Chicago:
       University of Chicago Press.
Weaver, Warren, Jr.
 1978 High Court Bars Newspaper Plea against Search.
       New York Times, Vol. 127 (Thursday, June 1), pp. 1, 42.
Whyte, William Foote
 1955 Street Corner Society. 2nd edition. Chicago:
       University of Chicago Press.
 1969 The Role of the U.S. Professor in Developing Countries
       The American Sociologist, Vol. 4, No. 1, pp. 19-28.
Withers, Carl
 1945 Plainville, USA by James West (pseud.). New York:
       Columbia University Press.

Federal Regulations, Institutional Review Boards and Qualitative Social Science Research

6

Comments on a Problematic Era

Virginia Olesen

When future accounts of the social sciences in the United States are written, one of the bulkiest and most controversial chapters may well be an analysis of the ethical, methodological, and political issues which have been generated by the federal regulations for conduct of human subjects research. Bulky and controversial though that chapter could be, it nevertheless may be easier to write at that future time than it would at present when the issues are still emergent and passions about the impact of the regulations run high.

This paper will explore the interaction between implementation of the regulations and conduct of research in the qualitative or interpretive social sciences, those anthropological and sociological inquiries where field methods such as participant observation and protracted interviews constitute the major data gathering modalities. These interpretive disciplines share with the experimental behavioral and biomedical sciences a great many criticisms of the regulations, e.g., perceived threats to free inquiry, as well as, it must be noted, concerns about researchers' ethical conduct. Additionally, their concerns embrace the implications of the regulations for the very place of social science inquiry in a free society (Wax 1977).

The Context

The history of the policies, regulations and guidelines which are discussed here is a history primarily read through events in medicine and experimental biomedical science and only secondarily understood through the chronology of the social sciences. This has blurred distinctions between biomedical and experimental behavioral science research and that of the qualitative sciences, coloring the regulations with the imagery of experimental research. As is well known, the

context in which the regulations initially rose was one in
which the influence of the Nuremberg and Helsinki declara-
tions prompted the U.S. Public Health Service in 1966 to generate a policy on the protection of human subjects in federally funded clinical investigations (Chalkley 1977). As
various memoranda eventually became the policy in 1971 of the
Department of Health, Education and Welfare, the behavioral
and social sciences were included in policies originally intended only to cover federally funded clinical or biomedical
research. Gray's paper elsewhere in this volume (Gray 1978)
makes clear that it is uncertain as to what, if any, impact,
the social sciences had on these developments, or, indeed, on
the passage of the National Research Act of 1974 which created
the National Commission for the Protection of Human Subjects
of Biomedical and Behavioral Research.

Further, the 1973 federal regulations do not seem to
indicate influences from the social sciences, although ethical codes had been developed in anthropology in 1967 and in
sociology in 1969. To the contrary, the regulations discuss
social or psychological consequences from social research
projects as parallel to those of risks engendered in biomedical work.[1] The experimental imagery which suffuses the rest
of the regulations permeates the discussion of social research
as well. If prominent qualitative social scientists were in
fact not consulted during the passage of the regulations, as
indeed no such scientist was later invited to sit on the
National Commission, then it would appear that serious mis-
understandings existed about the nature of these disciplines
and their divergence from biomedical experimentation. An
opportunity to influence the regulations was either never
offered or never seized, thus rendering these disciplines
themselves problematic in the field of human inquiry (Dalglish
1976, vii). We shall return to this theme after review of
new and problematic research situations which emerge for
qualitative researchers. As background, let us contrast
criteria for evaluating research in biomedical experimental
research and qualitative work.

Contrasts in Evaluation for Paradigms

Since at least the 1950's qualitative researchers have
been accustomed to presenting their work for formal review
to funding bodies in universities, foundations, state and
federal agencies, quite aside from the usual peer reviews in
the processes of publication and personnel procedures. However, the necessity to submit qualitative work for review by
an Institutional Review Board adds new dimensions to the
review process. In particular, many interpretive social
scientists would acknowledge that there may be mild risks to

participants, and occasionally, high risks to their reputations, hence would agree that appropriate evaluation to protect their rights might be acceptable. Very rarely are such risks intrinsic to the research act as is the case in biomedical work, rather, they are apt to be somewhat amorphous and usually extrinsic to the research situation (Wolfensberger 1967). Therefore, review along criteria for experimental work which are inappropriate for qualitative research, is entirely unacceptable. Being fit on that procrustean bed has cut out certain subtleties of interpretive social science which are relevant for evaluating such work while other features have been stretched in order to analyze the risk-benefit ratio and to assure informed consent.

Some instances of this may be dramatically overstated in order to establish the case, noting first that the very materials of the interpretive social sciences are fundamentally different from those of experimental research (Olesen 1974). Whereas the qualitative social sciences aim to inter-pret the mutually meaningful actions of persons, in experimental work individuals become subjects from whom objective measures are obtained in order to predict and control. The federal regulations therefore provide evaluation of risks and benefits for an experimental subject whose personhood is segmentalized and exemplified by, for instance, a venipuncture analysis, blood pressure reading,or drug dose response rate, but fall short of criteria with which to understand the consequences to and benefits for participants in qualitative work whose personhood is completely implicated, as is that of the researcher.Experimental work can provide explicit end points articulated in statistical conventions which may be invoked in understanding risks and benefits. However, the open-ended, emergent properties of field work are poorly understood, hence a fruitless search occurs for obscure and frequently unreachable terminal points.

These properties of experimental work lead to the assumption that it is possible to achieve written, informed consent in a single, perfectly rational encounter prior to the experiment, that consent being thought to endure through the experiment and beyond. The weakness of this assumption has been beautifully demonstrated by Gray's research on human subjects' experimentation (Gray 1975, esp. 202-234). By contrast, in qualitative work, particularly field work or participant observation, written consent may be difficult or impossible to achieve at the outset, but ongoing communication and renewal of the information on which consent is predicated are possible throughout the course of the field work. Informed consent in the field can be constantly revitalized and in so doing the research is re-clarified for participants, allowing

them the continual choice of the terms on which they will
participate, indeed, if they wish to participate at all.
This model of seeking informed consent accords with the
epistemological bases of interpretive research, namely the
assumption of the ongoing relatedness or intersubjectivity of
participating persons (Shipley 1977). Following those who
have conceptualized the experimental situation to acknowledge
that it, too, is an ongoing social occasion (Rosenthal, 1966;
Friedman, 1967), it may be seen that the interpretive social
scientist's potential to achieve, assure,and renew consent
might well contain the model for assurance of durable informed
consent insofar as this is ever possible, in experimental
work, too.

That the application of criteria for evaluation of experimental work to qualitative work has in fact created problems
is indicated in the responses of behavioral and social science
investigators interviewed in the National Commission's study
of institutional review board functioning. On a series of
items concerning attitudes toward the institutional review
procedure both institutional board members and research
investigators were asked to indicate their agreement about
items relating to unwarranted intrusions in the review procedure, appropriateness of evaluation, qualifications of
board members to make judgments and whether research progress
had been impeded at the board members' and investigators' own
institution. Indicating that investigators in all disciplines,
biomedical as well as social and behavioral, respond uneasily
to the review process, more investigators than review board
members agreed with perceptions of unwarranted intrusions,
and so forth.[2] However, among the investigators, there were
higher percentages of agreement among the social and behavioral scientists about intrusion and impeding of progress than
there were among the biomedical scientists. Specifically, 54
percent of social and behavioral science investigators agreed
that review impeded research progress, as compared with 43
percent of biomedical researchers, 24 percent of biomedical
board members and 30 percent of social and behavioral board
members. Since nearly 100 percent had also agreed that the
review process at their institution was being run reasonably
efficiently, and in light of the fact that most of the social
and behavioral science projects reviewed by boards in the
study were assigned "low risk" or "no subjects at risk" categories, we may infer that the attitudes of social and behavioral science investigators relate to the problems already
noted, namely, inappropriate criteria for evaluation. A "low
risk" category may be eventually assigned, but earning that
designation may involve numerous leaps over the hurdles of
inappropriate criteria.

It is possible that this has actually occurred in some cases, judging from the extensive and informed testimony from eight interpretive social scientists at the National Commission's hearings in the Spring of 1977 on review board functioning. These scholars noted, among other criticisms, collisions with human subjects review boards over the content of their work, inappropriate review and the blocking of social science work in certain sensitive areas. Another possibility in understanding the frequent assignment of "low" or "no" risk categories to interpretive research is that such assignments are made because review board members, unfamiliar with the types of risks to reputation, privacy, psychological well-being in certain types of interpretive work, failed to accurately assess risk (National Commission 1976).

The composition of such review boards may well provide further explanation for these perceived and experienced problems. There were only 23 sociologists and four anthopologists, together constituting a tiny three percent among the 760 review board members in the National Commission's study.[3] Since most of the boards in that sample were in medical schools, one would not expect the percentage of interpretive social scientists to be large, since medicine has not incorporated those disciplines to any significant extent. The three percent is still very low, considering that there were 24 university review boards, both with and without medical school assurances in the study. This general finding is mirrored in an in-depth study of the University of California (Berkeley) review board where sociology and anthropology were under-represented between 1972 and 1975, even though the board had two consecutive chairpersons from anthropology (Dalglish 1976: 176-177). Needless to say, concerns about freedom of inquiry would remain, even if review boards included more interpretive social scientists, and particularly if members representing the lay community exercise essentially political criteria in their evaluations (Gray 1977).

Consequences for Interpretive Research

Though the contours and nature of problems with the implementation of regulations to interpretive work awaits much-needed serious and wide-scale inquiry, it is possible to note several areas where the regulations have made problematic research on certain topics, among them issues in the newer sub-disciplines of urban and medical sociology and anthropology.

The first type of problem refers to research with persons or groups whose lives are "unusual" or "deviant," e.g., homosexual parents' childrearing strategies, motorbike groups'

life styles, the daily existence of petty criminals, the work
of procurers and call girls. To do research with such persons
necessitates to a high degree that the qualitative researcher
respects the privacy which shields them from the rest of
society. Undue insistence, therefore, on written informed
consent, the very act of which can place members of such
groups at risk, can deter such investigations.

Institutional review boards can waive requirements for
written consent if there is only minimal risk, or use of
written consent would invalidate objectives of considerable,
immediate importance, or reasonable alternative means of obtaining the research objectives would be less advantageous to
the subjects. Obtaining such a waiver, however, is not easily
done with boards who do not comprehend or are unsympathetic to
interpretive social science work, or when qualitative researchers do not present their protocols clearly for review.

A second set of problems relates to the study of socially
disapproved behaviors or practices within a "non-deviant" set
of persons, for instance, child abuse or wife beating in the
middle classes; extramarital sex among the clergy; substance
abuse, e.g., excessive drinking at cocktail parties; in short,
a range of behaviors customarily understood as problems about
which a great more needs to be known in order to understand
the situations in which they occur. Because of perceived
risks to privacy, confidentiality, and, unlike the first set
of persons noted above, reputation, it is difficult to persuade some review boards to sanction the research, in spite
of researcher assurances to the contrary.

Finally, a third set of problems, less dramatic, but
equally poignant, have to do with the lot of the isolated,
newly divorced, broken families, the unemployed, or those who
do unusual, but not socially stigmatized work. In proposals
to do research with these groups interpretive paradigms are
apt to be misunderstood and review board members, applying
the risk-benefit formulation to the complexities of interpretive social research are apt to rule out such research as
too far into the risk zone, particularly psychological risks
or threats to confidentiality (Robins 1977). They thus overlook participants' capacities to exercise their own controls
over the researcher, a feature of interpretive research which
few field workers or experienced interviewers would overlook
or deny.

Yet another problem emerges in this last congeries of
concerns. Would-be participants in some types of inquiries
seen as psychologically risky by review boards may be denied
the choice to participate in research crucial to their

particular situation. Such problems are apt to arise in interpretive research done in a medical setting where the researcher is also asked to secure the physician's permission for the individual patient to participate. Though no thoughtful interpretive researcher in medical anthropology or sociology would wish to observe or interview critically ill patients, for instance, where the observation or interview would prove burdensome or an intrusion, these exquisite difficulties are by no means present in every research proposal where physician permission to interview patients in addition to the patient's permission may be required. The issue of participants' civil liberties in such inquiries has yet to be explored or understood, but it adds an additional concern for interpretive research.

In sum the consequences of the inappropriate implementation of the regulations to qualitative work makes problematic these disciplines' potential to contribute to the social store of knowledge necessary to understand and deal with sensitive, painful problems (Reynolds 1972: 709). If planners and policy makers make the assumption, as is generally done, that knowledge generated from inquiries in these disciplines is useful, then the impairment of that capacity in these disciplines has more consequences than the serious ones of limiting freedom of inquiry. In the absence of interpretive social science findings, however, faculty, planners,and policy makers can only resort to conventional wisdom or information from vested interests which may or may not be the best base for understanding and decision making.

Problematics in the Conduct of Inquiry

What has also become problematic is the very conduct of interpretive research, but the consequences of this have been to generate a useful collective reflexivity, indicated by numerous panels at professional meetings and extensive self-scrutiny and colleague discourse such as the AAAS session which generated this volume.

Clearly, as it has been outlined here, the necessity to submit interpretive research to institutional review enlarges the universe of persons with whom the qualitative researcher must interact on the way to the field or interview. Review boards, secretaries of review boards,and others now are part of the interactive process that includes the field work or interview. This enlargement expands the researchers' responsibilities to explain and interpret the research explicitly and carefully so that risks and benefits are carefully understood and the means of obtaining informed consent communicated. This sometimes involves lengthier explanations of the research

and its purposes than would otherwise be the case. If interpretive disciplines are part of an open free inquiry, explanations of the purposes and research styles should not deter
such researchers. On the contrary, they should provide the
opportunity to inform other scholars about work in the interpretive sciences and the uses of these disciplines. They
should also provide the opportunity for researchers to review
for themselves what the risks and benefits of interpretive
qualitative social science are, grounding that review in the
specifics of the particular project to be pursued. A thoughtful interpretive worker would in any case probably have reviewed these in any case in preparing for the field, particularly
in this litigious era.

Once in the field, these types of explanations surely
ought to be part of a thoroughly grounded set of interactions
in which informed consent is sought and reaffirmed for the
particular project. Perhaps some participants will shy away
from the research once they understand what observations of
or interviews about their lives entail. In other instances,
participants, made curious by the explanations mandated by
the necessity to obtain informed consent, may ask pesky questions, intrude themselves into the fine points of the research,
may, as often happens in field work, become "researcher's
assistants" in a more active way than the researcher would
like.

Are these consequences negative? They happen in a good
many field projects in any event. Moreover, what sensitive
field worker would want participants to continue if in fact
they, knowing the purposes, risks, etc., of the research would
not wish to continue? Surely their information would be colored by this fact. As for pesky and intrusive participants,
their peskiness and intrusiveness may provide impetus for the
researcher to better understand his or her own work in order
that the participant, too, will understand. In point of
fact, the pesky or intrusive informant or any of the parties
involved in the explanations of research provide opportunities
to clarify the work and, invariably, as field work goes along,
to clarify some of the findings. In short, the very process
of seeking and obtaining consent, itself humanizing because
it provides participants with choices on whether they will
participate, how much they will, etc., is part of the data
gathering process (Sjoberg 1976). As the research is explored,
the field worker may find that the basic problem has not been
conceptualized in a meaningful way and that reconceptualization
to accord with the participants' view provides a more productive research experience. Further, such explanations teach
respondents what the field workers' interests are, hence
enhance the mutual data generating activities in the field,

and provide some sense of research role for the participant as well as the researcher. In many field work situations, particularly those in contemporary medical sociology and anthropology it is difficult for the researcher and the participant to engage one another in roles other than the research role. For instance, if one is a sociologist or anthropologist observing in a hospital ward, a mutually constructed set of research roles for self and participants, be they patients, physicians, nurses or what, eases interaction which would otherwise be quite difficult, since as a layperson one has no business in that setting. Moreover, the search to get informed consent while creating and sustaining research roles tends to mitigate what has been called "the friendship dilemma," the situation in which the demands and rewards of friendship take prior consideration over those of the research role (Olesen and Whittaker 1968: 39).

If we wish to agree that the impact of review boards in most university settings essentially protects the researcher and shifts the burden of complaint onto the participant, perhaps even blunting the researchers' necessity to work very carefully (Dalglish 1976: vii), then the reciprocities of interpretive work are crucial. Though we can acknowledge that the reciprocities of field work are such that the ways in which the participant in the field can assault, control, snub, hurt and deny the researcher are legion, nevertheless the burden of action, e.g., legal complaint if that becomes the case, is placed on the participant, since the university indemnifies the researcher whose protocol has been approved by the review board.

This necessitates that interpretive social science give careful thought and new analysis to dimensions of reciprocities in the observational, interview,and field work relationships with participants, much as Wax has suggested (Wax 1971). Within careful understanding of these reciprocities between field worker and participant lies the possibility of altering the increasingly crystallized and formalized adversary relationship between researcher and subject (Reis 1977). Not every field work project carries the same reciprocities between researcher and participant, hence not every set of relationships carries the same possibility of participant control of the researcher, as with formal contracts negotiated by Northwest Coast Indians with anthropologists, or for the researcher's potential to threaten privacy. In this connection we have attended far too intently to dramatic instances where ethical principles seem to have been trampled, as in the taking of auto license numbers in the Tearoom Trade study and not enough to problems in more mundane field work situations (Humphreys 1970).

Moreover, although many ethnographies contain fascinating glimpses of field workers' responses to their situation, we have little systematic or in depth knowledge of the impact that field work, dramatic or banal, has on the researcher, the work of Glass and Frankel (1968) and Alison Lurie's intriguing novel, Imaginary Friends (1965) being exceptions. Curiously, even in the experimental sciences this has not always been so: in the 17th century criticisms about crude experimentation with animals not only inveighed against the pain caused the experimental animal, but raised questions about the experimenter's virtue (Musto 1977).

This is not to suggest that a code of field work conduct should ever be articulated to meaningfully comprehend every potentially hurtful or damaging exchange between researcher and participant, but it does indicate that such a review can at least suggest the properties of mutual risk, as Robert Sommer has (Sommer 1971). This would remind the researcher that while participants can indeed control, monitor or injure the researcher, that fundamentally the researcher's role has greater power. This is not the type of power one sees vividly displayed in the poignant comments of pregnant women who were afraid to refuse to participate in certain types of abortion research (Gray 1976: 140-154), but instead the power lies in the access to the multiple possibilities of disseminating the participants' lives and persons through publishing, speaking, writing and teaching.

In sum, in the field itself we need to review carefully the mutually constructed possibilities for risks to both researcher and participant. We must at this time recall that the very processual nature of interpretive work implicates the researcher and participant in ways which mandate that the researcher shall continually affirm and explain the purposes and nature of the work. We must also reindicate good faith for the future beyond the field itself, where research reports, because of the complex dissemination networks and audiences, as always, have varied and unforeseeable impacts. In this sense, then, the guidelines have rendered problematic the very conduct of interpretive research to those who pursue it, thus providing a welcome, if unexpected opportunity for self-scrutiny.

Implications and Recommendations

What then is to be done? If interpretive social scientists are going to have to live with the federal guidelines and regulations, as it certainly seems they will, efforts to make the National Commission and other relevant bodies aware of distinct and inquiry-threatening discrepancies between

experimental criteria and appropriate interpretive criteria
for evaluation of qualitative work appear necessary. At
local levels those efforts might well also be paralleled by
placement of more interpretive social scientists on review
boards, ad hoc committees or consulting groups. Integrating
review boards could also prove mutually beneficial: the
implications of qualitative work as outlined here would inform experimentalists, the rigor of experimental work could
enrich interpretive researchers. This would surely assist in
understanding research projects where definitions of privacy
in the research setting are culturally divergent from commonly understood definitions accepted by review board members
(Roberts and Gregory 1971; Bidney 1959).

However, mechanisms for adjudication and control of
research in order to protect participants in interpretive
studies are for the most part already available and workable:
peer review within one's own university, evaluative processes
in publication and dissemination networks, criticisms of unethical research behavior (Barth 1973). Perhaps most significantly, the potential to instill a creative consciousness
of ethical issues lies in the socialization process of graduate students in these disciplines. It has been the case
until recently that textbooks and lectures did not include
such materials, a situation which has changed substantially.
Guidance of graduate student projects not only should not
place the student in situations where keen motivation to do
well leads to unethical conduct in interpretive research, but
may profitably stress the "common sense and good manners
(which) are assuredly vital to field research" (Schatzman and
Strauss 1973:145).

The Debate in Historical Perspective

This essay opened with a note regarding the future
history of the controversies around implementation of the
regulations discussed here. In closing, it is useful to return the discussion to the history of two major themes which
have shaped much of the debate around social science inquiry
since its inception and which are fundamental to understanding the current and future trajectories of the encounters
reviewed here.

The first of those major themes is the ancient dialogue
between Chance and Fate; the question is whether man, as in
the ancient Greek dramas, is cast into conflict with his lot
and his gods in inevitable ways which can only work themselves out inexorably, or whether the significant aspect of
life is its randomness, its total hazard, or its fundamental
indeterminacy (Fowles 1975; Moore 1976; Rankin 1966). We

may place the institution of the guidelines and the debate over them vis-a-vis another chapter in the dialogue over Chance and Fate; this chapter attempts to reduce some of the fundamental indeterminacy which underlies social life, but, ironically, produces further indeterminacy by providing, at least through informed consent in interpretive work, that sustained consent which maximizes choices for both participant and researcher.[4]

The second of these great themes may be found in the old question, Quis custodiet custodes? Who shall judge the intellectuals, the scholars, the interpretive social scientists? This is the critical question, since no thoughtful anthropologist or sociologist would care to suggest herself or himself above judgment. This paper has suggested that in part such judgment is now in a new set of hands outside the interpretive disciplines, formally mandated and generating a problematic situation. That judgment, however, within the interpretive disciplines--within the conduct of research-- remains, as it has previously, with participants in the field who are also judging and evaluating researchers as persons and as researchers.[5] That judgment, integral to the very act of data gathering, is perhaps the most crucial.

Certainly, this mundane evaluation coming as it does in the everyday intimacies between researcher and participants, differentiates again the fundamental nature of interpretive work in the social sciences from experimental and biomedical work. Solutions to the question of who shall judge researchers which place the answer fully outside the interpretive research situation and fully in the hands of review boards or indeed in credentialling mechanisms (Freidson 1976), lead to a type of distancing and alienation not now characteristic of interpretive work. The interpretive social sciences, rightly seeing themselves threatened by the impact of the regulations, have in fact failed to strongly argue this, a most powerful attribute at the core of their epistemology, which, with proper understanding on part of review boards, if we must have such, could well be the core of new comprehension of disciplines and their fundamentally humanizing research.

Notes

This paper reflects a number of provocative conversations over the past several years with scholars concerned about the regulations and their implementation: Anne Davis, Albert Jonsen and Christie Kiefer of the University of California, San Francisco; Murray Wax of Washington University, St. Louis; Diana Baumrind of the University of California, Berkeley; Michael Garland of the University of Oregon; Bradford Gray of the Institute of Medicine, as well as my former colleagues on the Committee for the Protection of Human Subjects, UCSF, and my students in my Spring, 1977 Seminar on the Sociology of Informed Consent. Special thanks are due Erica Heath, administrative assistant of the UCSF review board, for incisive comments on an earlier draft.

[1]The wording of the federal guidelines suggests that infusion of experimental imagery into these disciplines: "There is a wide range of medical, social, and behavioral projects and activities in which no immediate physical risk to the subject is involved, e.g., those utilizing personality inventories, interviews, questionnaires, or the use of observation, photographs, taped records, or stored data. However, some of these procedures may involve varying degrees of discomfort, harassment, invasion of privacy, or constitute a threat to the subject's dignity through the imposition of demeaning or dehumanizing conditions." Section D.2, The Institutional Guide to DHEW Policy on the Protection of Human Subjects, June 16, 1971.

[2]Table IX, 2, p. 184 of the National Commission study shows that whereas 11 percent of social and behavioral board members thought the review procedure intrusive on investigator autonomy, 38 percent of the investigators agreed with this. On the review board moving into inappropriate areas, 24 percent of the board members, as against 49 percent of the researchers from the social sciences thought this the case. Finally, on whether review committees make unqualified judgments, 21 percent of the social science board members agreed, but almost 49 percent of the social science investigators thought this (National Commission 1976).

[3]This particular problem may be changing. One review board with which this author is familiar was delayed in obtaining the requisite general assurance because the board had only one behavioral scientist among its members, when two were required, since the board reviews social science research. A second member was designated and the assurance received.

[4]As Einstein is reported to have said to Max Born in 1944,
"You believe in God playing dice and I in perfect laws in the
world of things existing as real objects which I try to grasp
in a wildly speculative way" (Rankin 1966; 504).

[5]Erica Heath has perceptively observed that when judgment
of social science research is done outside the social sciences
by biomedical reviewers, a larger amount of trust must be
accorded to the social science researcher than is granted investigators in the biomedical fields which, though often
riskier, are within the formal codes derived at Nuremberg and
Helsinki. This necessity for a larger amount of trust may
explain some resistance of biomedical reviewers to social
science work. Also at issue, as the present essay indicates,
is the lack of clear understanding on how to accord trust to
the social science researcher.

References Cited

Barth, Fredrik
    1974 On Responsibility and Humanity: Calling a Colleague
        to Account. Current Anthropology 15:99-102.
Bidney, David
    1959 The Philosophical Presuppositions of Cultural Rela-
        tivism and Cultural Absolutism. In Ethics and the Social
        Sciences. Leo R. Ward, ed. Notre Dame, Indiana: Univer-
        sity of Notre Dame Press.
Chalkley, Donald T.
    1977 Federal Constraints: Earned or Unearned? American
        Journal of Psychiatry 134:911-13.
Comments (On Jorgensen)
    1971 Current Anthropology 12:340-56.
Dalglish, Thomas Killin
    1976 Protecting Human Subjects in Social and Behavioral
        Research: Ethics, Law and the DHEW Rules: A Critique.
        Working Papers in Management Science. Center for Re-
        search in Management Science, University of California,
        Berkeley.
Fowles, John
    1975 The Aristos. New York: New American Library.
Freidson, Eliot
    1976 The Legal Protection of Social Research: Criteria for
        Definition. In Social Research in Conflict with Law and
        Ethics. Paul Nejelski, ed. Cambridge: Ballinger.

Friedman, N.
   1967   The Social Nature of Psychological Research, The
          Psychological Experiment as Social Interaction.   New
          York: Basic Books.
Glass, J.F., and H.H. Frankel
   1968   The Influence of Subjects on the Research: A Problem
          in Observing Social Interaction.   Pacific Sociological
          Review 11:57-80.
Gray, Bradford G.
   1976   Human Subjects in Medical Experimentation.   New York:
          Wiley.
   1977   The Functions of Human Subjects Review Committees.
          American Journal of Psychiatry 134:907-9.
   1978   Human Subjects Review Committees and Social Research.
          Originally prepared for the Annual Meeting of AAAS.
Lurie, Alison
   1965   Imaginary Friends.   New York: Avon.
Moore, Sally Falk
   1976   Symbol and Politics in Communal Ideology.   Ithaca:
          Cornell University Press.
Musto, David F.
   1977   Freedom of Inquiry and Subjects' Rights: Historical
          Perspective.   American Journal of Psychiatry 134:893-96.
National Commission for the Protection of Human Subjects of
      Biomedical and Behavioral Research.
   1976   Research Involving Human Subjects.   An unpublished
          report.
Olesen, Virginia, and Elvi Whittaker
   1968   The Silent Dialogue.   San Francisco: Jossey-Bass.
Olesen, Virginia
   1977   Testimony to the National Commission for the Protec-
          tion of Human Subjects in Biomedical and Behavioral
          Research.   Hearings on the Functions of Institutional
          Review Boards, April, San Francisco, California.
Rankin, Bayard
   1966   The History of Probability and the Changing Concept
          of the Individual.   Journal of the History of Ideas
          XXVII:483-504.
Read, Kenneth
   1965   The High Valley.   New York: Scribners.
Reis, David
   1977   Freedom of Inquiry and Subjects' Rights: An Intro-
          duction.   American Journal of Psychiatry 134:891-92.
Reynolds, Paul Davidson
   1972   On the Protection of Human Subjects and Social Science.
          International Social Science Journal XXIV:693-719.
Robins, Lee N.
   1977   Problems in Follow-Up Studies.   American Journal of
          Psychiatry 134:904-7.

Roberts, John M., and Thomas Gregory
  1971 Privacy, A Cultural View. In Privacy, Nomos, XII.
    J. Roland Penn and John W. Chaplan, eds. New York:
    Atherton Press.
Rosenthal, R.
  1966 Experimenter Effects in Behavioral Research. New
    York: Appleton-Century-Crofts.
Schatzman, Leonard, and Anselm S. Strauss
  1973 Field Research, Strategies for a Natural Sociology.
    New York: Prentice-Hall.
Shipley, Thorne
  1977 Misinformed Consent: An Enigma in Modern Social
    Science Research. Ethics in Science and Medicine 4:93-
    106.
Sjoberg, Gideon
  1976 The 'Hidden Side' of Bureaucracy and Social Research.
    In Social Research in Conflict with the Law and Ethics.
    Paul Nejelski, ed. Cambridge, Massachusetts: Ballinger,
    Co.
Sommer, Robert
  1971 Some Costs and Pitfalls of Field Research. Social
    Problems 19:162-66.
Turnbull, Colin
  1973 Reply. Current Anthropology 15:103.
Wax, Murray
  1977 On Fieldworkers and Those Exposed to Fieldwork:
    Federal Regulations and Moral Issues. Human Organiza-
    tion 36:321-28.
Wax, Rosalie
  1971 Doing Fieldwork: Warnings and Advice. Chicago: The
    University of Chicago Press.
Wolfensberger, Wolf
  1967 Ethical Issues in Research With Human Subjects.
    Science 155:47-51.

7

Protecting Privacy
in Action-Oriented Fieldwork

Janet M. Fitchen

Introduction

Genuine protection of informant privacy requires us to take a <u>field-centered approach</u>. Rather than using an imposed notion of privacy, as defined by U.S. bureaucratic culture, we should regard the very concept of privacy as relative or culture-specific, to be defined in each case on the basis of empirical research in the field. We must then ask what privacy means to the people with whom we are working. The pre-field commitment made by the anthropologist regarding protection of informants' privacy would then be general, to be translated into specific safeguards only after field research had determined the actual nature of privacy and the risks inherent in the particular field situation.

The field-centered approach may be especially useful in action-oriented fieldwork. In fieldwork that has an action component, as opposed to pure research, we must protect the privacy of informants during fieldwork itself, not just at the later time of publication. The standard ethnography-writing devices of pseudonyms and altered personal details, while they may satisfy the requirements of a university committee overseeing research on human subjects, are apt to be irrelevant and too late for effective protection of informants during the process of action-oriented fieldwork.

There are also heuristic benefits to be gained from treating privacy as a concept to be investigated empirically, rather than a pre-defined given. Treating privacy as a question for study will provide ethnographic insights that may help in the development of effective action projects.

The Fieldwork Context

These advantages of a field-derived concept of privacy

apply not only in cross-cultural research, but also in the
case of fieldwork conducted within our own society. To
illustrate the usefulness of this approach, I will describe
aspects of a six-year involvement (Fitchen 1973) with the
people of small rural depressed neighborhoods enclaved on
the margins of urbanized areas in upstate New York--people
who are pejoratively termed "poor white trash."

These rural enclaves have long been characterized by
chronic poverty, resulting from protracted agricultural decline, differential rural exodus, and unsatisfactory transition into the urban economy. In one such neighborhood
studied intensively from 1969 to 1975, 20 out of the 30 base-
line households have had an income hovering around the official poverty level. (At any given time, 15 households might
be eligible for food stamps, and six may be on welfare, but
all of the 20 have been eligible for or participating in
these programs at one time or another in the six years.)
Though most households have had at least one member in the
urban work force most of the time (on assembly lines, highway
crews, janitorial services), household income is low and in-
secure, periodically affected by layoffs, loss of job, injur-
ies, chronic disabilities, and temporary absence of the wage
earner from home. But intergenerational economic poverty is
only one fact of the complex problem.

A related problem in these neighborhoods is that of social marginality, which resulted from collapse of the rural
social community and incomplete incorporation of rural poor
people into the encompassing urban-suburban community.
While forced to participate in the wider society, rural poor
people are seldom able to gain satisfaction in it.

The problem of social marginality was seen as particularly important because it causes psycho-social stress,
which, in turn, exacerbates and perpetuates the economic
poverty. Therefore, a major aim of the fieldwork was to
discover the barriers to satisfactory inclusion in the
encompassing community, and to devise ways to overcome them.
The action projects followed the model of Leighton, et al.,
(Hughes, et al. 1960; Leighton 1965; Stone, Leighton and
Leighton 1966) towards reducing social marginality in depressed rural areas of Nova Scotia, where ethnographic
similarities are striking.

For the purpose of this presentation, illustrations will
be taken only from the realm of the relationship between
adults (parents) and the public schools. The children of
the rural depressed neighborhoods attend socially hetero-
geneous schools in the larger urban-suburban community--but

they stand out as failures from the day they enter to the time they drop out. The parents blame this failure on the school; the school blames the failure on the parents. Past efforts at supportive, cooperative interaction have been unable to create trust or sustain interaction. Bridging this gap was the goal of a number of school-related action projects carried out during the course of fieldwork, some of which will be described here as they relate to the issue of informant privacy.

Aspects of Protecting Privacy
In This Fieldwork

In this attempt to bring changes in the interface between an institution of the dominant community and the people of the sub-community, the anthropologist had to be sensitive to the privacy problem throughout the course of fieldwork. Each privacy-risk situation that arose had to be evaluated to determine in what way privacy might be jeopardized, and how the risk could be minimized. It was assumed that the needs of the informant took precedence over the ethnographic and action goals of the anthropologist. At times, however, the privacy needs of the informant might be superceded by other needs of the informant. And sometimes, the privacy question was spurious because there really wasn't much privacy to be protected.

Use of pseudonyms and other anonymity devices found in published field reports clearly would have been too late to offer protection during the course of action, and relatively ineffective anyway because the families were already well known to the dominant community. For example, if Mrs. Jones is upset about the treatment her son, Tim, receives at school, and I persuade her to discuss this problem with a school authority, Mary Jones obviously cannot hide behind a pseudonym as "Mrs. X." Anonymity is neither possible nor germane in such a case: of greater concern is the way the interaction is handled and what benefits Mrs. Jones derives. In other interactions, calculated risks to privacy were taken in the interest of achieving important goals. For example, if Tim's behavior in school is getting him into more than usual disciplinary trouble, I may talk with his teacher, urging her to show extra patience with Tim because he's currently undergoing a particularly rough time at home. The resulting consideration the teacher shows for Tim has been bought at the cost of revealing something about Tim's family to the teacher, and therefore, such an attempt was used only sparingly, with caution.

Another standard device for protecting privacy is to
lump individual cases into an impersonal aggregate. This
traditional safeguard has an added advantage as a means of
redefining the problem you're working on in terms of failures in structural relationships, rather than in terms of
the particular individuals who incur the difficulty. For
example, the generalizing approach could be used to help the
school redirect its efforts away from attempting to change
Tim Jones or his mother, and towards changing the patterns
of the school in which Tim and his sisters and his cousins
(whom he reckons up by dozens) and his aunts are forced
participants. However, while this approach may help in protecting individual privacy, it must be used with some caution also, for it may contribute to the dominant community's
tendency to categorize and label a separate group of people,
thus perpetuating stereotypes.

A different facet of the problem of protecting informants' privacy lies in the working relationship that develops
between the anthropologist and individual informants. The
anthropologist clearly has an obligation to his informants
to protect them from undue or uncomfortable examination. An
informant may actively protect his own privacy by refraining
from participation in the anthropologist's inquiries or
actions. An informant may be selective about when and how
much to cooperate--and the anthropologist must allow him this
control by refraining from coercion and probing. An informant may also protect his privacy by presenting an unrealis-
tically ideal image of himself and his actions. Often,
during the course of fieldwork, I was aware that an informant was trying to pull the wool over my eyes, putting on an
act of "everything's going fine" when known facts would not
substantiate such an optimistic presentation of self. At
such times, it was obviously of therapeutic benefit to the
informant to have someone believe in the image he or she was
trying to project, since image-management is a strategy for
protecting the ego from stress, a means of gaining temporary
relief from the failure-discouragement syndrome. By refraining from calling the informant's bluff, by playing the role
of a convinced audience, the anthropologist is protecting
the psychological privacy of the individual. But this notion
of protecting psychological privacy cannot usually be suf-
ficently understood or guaranteed prior to fieldwork, nor
could it be required by the agencies and committees that
oversee human subjects research.

In these various ways, the anthropologist guards against
exposing people's private lives. But there is also another
aspect of the privacy issue to which we must be sensitive:
privacy may be an indigenous concern in normal life, even

before the anthropologist steps into the picture. In the sub-community described here, privacy is a limited good, regarded by the people themselves as strategically important in the management of their relationships with each other and with the dominant community. Therefore, informant-perceived privacy needs had a definite effect on people's response to the action projects aimed at decreasing social marginality.

The Indigenous Concept of Privacy
and Its Effects on Projects Intended to
Strengthen Interaction with the Schools

What does privacy mean to the people of these rural depressed enclaves? Ethnographic study showed that privacy is not defined simply as keeping all others at a distance, or preventing all situations of personal exposure. In fact, inviolate personal space and individual seclusion is neither possible nor of great concern to people who live in these overcrowded houses and tight clusters of shacks and trailers: their personal life is rarely out of view of family, relatives and neighbors. In local thought, privacy seems to have a more limited meaning, a more instrumentally-defined meaning, in terms of exposure that entails <u>negative consequences</u>. Privacy maintenance is defined as avoidance of situations in which personal exposure would be a) status damaging, and/or b) personally threatening. Privacy means the right to shield oneself from divulging information that could be used against oneself.

Ensuring privacy is thus instrumentally important to people coping with a socially and psychologically marginal position. If this is recognized, it becomes easier to understand the failure of past efforts at increasing social integration, and to plan for more effective efforts. I'll give some specific examples, comparing approaches used by the schools to approaches devised by the anthropologist, in order to show that the anthropologist's appreciation of the indigenous concept of privacy helps him or her to plan more acceptable change strategies.

In the past, the schools' efforts to bring parents into increased contact have been through the medium of the PTA or parent-teacher conferences. Despite such extra inducements as extending special invitations, offering transportation and providing babysitting, parents from the rural depressed neighborhoods rarely show up. The school personnel, in frustration, conclude from this that the parents <u>don't care</u> about their children's education. In fact, the reason the poor parents resist these attempts is because participation in them is painful and harmful, confirming in their own eyes

and in the community's their failure and their low status.
Informant comments include: "The PTA only wants us to come
to the meeting so they can talk about us afterwards," and,
"Why should I go to a conference to have a teacher tell me
that my child is a failure as a student, that I'm a failure
as a parent?"

Obviously, different types of approaches would be needed
to enable parents to interact with the school setting and its
personnel in situations that would not be status-differentiating and failure-confirming. In one successful project, we
involved parents in enrolling their kindergarteners. We
arranged a special day for parents to come to school with
their youngsters, to have a guided tour and a cup of coffee,
and to learn about what to expect in the coming kindergarten
year, while the children were given a chance to play and explore in the kindergarten room. The event was planned so as
to minimize the stigma of neighborhood and family reputations, invidious status comparisons, and concern about proper social behavior, all of which are so noticeable and uncomfortable in standard PTA functions. Parents from the depressed neighborhoods participated on an equal footing with
the dominant-community mothers, who were equally anxious and
tentative about releasing their babies to the big wide
world. The failure labels, so much a part of parent-teacher
conferences, were also absent. No parent had to reveal anything about past school difficulties of their older children:
this was a new beginning for a new pupil, and the parents
went home feeling better about the school, about themselves,
and about the relationship between them.

For reaching outward to families, the schools had relied
on home visits by teachers, social workers and the school
nurse. These visits, however, were rarely successful in
building better relationships, for like the PTA meeting, they
were status-differentiating. The parent easily perceived the
uncomfortableness of the official visitor, who turned down
the offer of a cup of coffee, sat on the front edge of the
dingy chair, and seemed eager to depart. Additionally, these
visits were interpreted by parents as the school forcing its
way into the home to tell parents about the shortcomings of
their kids, and to inspect the family and report back to
school on unsanitary conditions, parental neglect, or other
disapproved situations. Like the forced visits of the welfare caseworker or the probation officer, visits from the
school person were perceived as an intrusion on family pri-
vacy--primarily because of the implied threat of outside
power that could be exerted on the family to correct its
ways. The only recourse for the family was to try, or to
pretend, to be away from home when the school visitor arrived.

It seemed to the anthropologist, however, that the out-
reach concept might still be salvageable as a means of building communication and interaction if families did not have to
fear that by opening the door to the visitor they would also
be opening themselves up for inspection and possible punitive
action. Therefore, the possibility was discussed among parents of having a home-school aide who would be a connector
and advocate, an intermediary to talk over school problems
with parents at home and then work towards solutions in the
school. As a parent-shaped idea that did become reality,
the aide's home visits were accepted. Her presence was not
regarded as an invasion of privacy since parents did not fear
that what this visitor saw and heard would be reported to
authorities and used against the family.

Another possible approach to strengthening the parent
position vis-à-vis the school would be to develop neighborhood cohesion around some school-related issue of common
interest. The process of involving parents in the development of the home-school aide plan was intended to have this
cohesive effect, quite apart from the benefits accruing from
the actual implementation of the plan. But deliberate attempts to form a group of neighborhood parents interested in
creating changes in the schools did not succeed. Only once
in the six years was an actual planned neighborhood parent
meeting held. It was organized for parents to voice their
concerns to the new superintendent of schools, who had been
invited by the anthropologist and an OEO community aide.
Although the small group of parents who attended gained a
new awareness that they all faced common school-related
problems, and a new hopefulness that someone in power would
actually listen to their problems, still, there was no interest in attempting subsequent group meetings or sustained
joint endeavor. Why?

In part, the resistance to group formation results from
the constant suspicion and squabbling among neighborhood
families that undermine the ties of kinship, mutual assistance and shared identity that otherwise bind them. One person will refuse to attend a meeting or event if a certain
other person is likely to be present. (The excuses people
give are usually vague, sometimes untrue, but are mostly
variations on a common theme: sex, and marital infidelity
within the neighborhood.) However, a more important and more
significant deterrent to grouping involves the indigenous
concept of privacy. Although within the confines of the
neighborhood a family may interact frequently and positively
with its neighbors, publicly participating in a neighborhood
group would represent a damaging statement about one's social
identity. Any family striving to gain acceptance for itself

in the outside community will attempt to dissociate itself
in the public eye from the low reputation of the neighborhood
and its component families. For this reason, a parent would
prefer to settle children's school problems on an individual
basis, rather than to have them merged with and tainted by
the problems of children from other families. Parents want
to be heard by the school as individual parents of individual children, not as a category labelled "low-income parents,"
and certainly not as the parent group from a particular den-
igrated neighborhood. (This realistic perception of the
need to seek a separate entry into the dominant community has
forced the anthropologist to question the value of using increased neighborhood cohesion as a means of reducing social
marginality.)

Conclusion

This empirical analysis of ways in which felt privacy
needs affect people's response to action projects points up
the advantages of using a field-centered approach to protecting the privacy of people among whom we work. In this
particular case, even though taken from our own society, it
would not have been possible to predict, in advance of ethnographic study, what constitutes privacy, how it is already
threatened or restricted in everyday life, how it is indi-
genously protected, and how it might be jeopardized by the
anthropologist.

Privacy, as any other aspect of culture, is culture-
specific. Protection of informant privacy during fieldwork, therefore, depends on the nature of the local culture
and on the nature of the fieldwork. The design of appropriate protection mechanisms can best be accomplished by the
anthropologist in situ rather than a priori.

Note

Presented as a part of a symposium entitled "Fieldwork:
Ethical Problems and Federal Regulations," chaired by Murray
L. Wax and Joan Cassell, at the annual meeting of the Society
for Applied Anthropology, April 1977, San Diego, California.
Part of the fieldwork reported on here was supported by the
National Institute of Health Training Program at Cornell
University, grant #NIGMS 1256.

References Cited

Fitchen, Janet M.
  1973 Rural Poverty in Upstate New York: The Collapse of
        Community. Doctoral dissertation (unpublished),
        Cornell University.
Hughes, Charles C., et al.
  1960 People of Cove and Woodlot: Communities from the
        Viewpoint of Social Psychiatry. Vol. II of The Stirling
        County Study of Psychiatric Disorder and Sociocultural
        Environment. New York: Basic Books.
Leighton, Alexander H.
  1965 Poverty and Social Change. Scientific American 212:
        21-27.
Stone, I. Thomas, D. C. Leighton, and A. H. Leighton
  1966 Poverty and the Individual. In Poverty Amid Afflu-
        ence. New Haven: Yale University Press.

8

Regulating Fieldwork
Of Subjects, Subjection, and Intersubjectivity

Joan Cassell

Federal regulations to protect human subjects contain an implicit model of the research process. The definition of a subject, of the relationship between subject and experimenter, of what risk is and when it occurs, and what potential benefits might be, are clear, even when they are not clearly spelled out. The paradigm for such research is biomedical experimentation, although much social science research also fits this model.

What happens when such regulations are applied across-the-board by institutional review boards to an entirely different type of research? Does that variety of social research which is called fieldwork, participant observation, or ethnography differ significantly from the biomedical model and if so how do these differences affect the application of regulations designed to protect the subjects of traditional experimentation?

Of Subjects

I am going to explore some differences between a "subject" of traditional experimentation and a fieldwork "subject," then investigate what types of risk people are exposed to in fieldwork and when that exposure occurs. This should help us determine how effective existing human subject regulations are in protecting those exposed to fieldwork from risk.

First, what is a subject in research? The question is more complex than it might seem and, as the National Commission for the Protection of Human Subjects of Biomedical and Behavioral Research discovered, it is difficult to define the term in a way that does not raise problems (Gray 1978:12).[1] Among the definitions of the term in the Oxford Universal Dictionary (1955), three are salient. The first involves

power and hierarchy: a <u>subject</u> is someone who is under do-
minion of a ruling power or bound to a superior by an obligation to pay allegiance. The second has to do with material
out of which things are made, with subjects of attributes
and of predicates; thus, in modern philosophy, a thinking
agent, or self, is a <u>subject</u>. The third definition involves
that which is or may be acted or operated upon, a person or
thing toward which action or influence are directed.

Of Subjects and Subjection

Two of these three meanings of subject are relevant in
traditional experimentation: someone who is subjected to
another more powerful person; and someone toward whom action
and influence are directed. Experimental subjects are characterized by a relative deficiency of power within the research situation: they are <u>subject</u> to the control of the
investigator. Experimenters usually define and direct the
situation in their own terms, with subjects having limited
opportunities to question procedures (Kelman 1972:991). The
superior power and control of the investigator is particularly clear in medical experimentation, where subjects may
be ill and need the doctors who wish to use them as experimental subjects. Subjects may also be prisoners, or belong
to other groups whose autonomy and power of choice are di-
minished by their situation. The status or power differential between experimenter and subject is related to the third
definition of subject, as that which is or may be acted or
operated upon. It is a one way flow: experimenters act;
subjects (or their disease or physiology) react.

Subjects are not entirely powerless. They can refuse
to take part in an experiment or they can leave. They can,
in short, refuse to be subjects. But once they have accepted
the role of experimental subject, they have relinquished control over the research setting and situation.

Symbolically, the depersonalized and hierarchical relationship between experimenter and subject is expressed in
the traditional terminology of psychological experiments,
where the subject is an S, and the experimenter an E. The
E manipulates the S, and the more parsimonious and elegant
the experiment, the less the irrelevant human attributes of
the S interfere with the measurement of the variables being
studied.

The two definitions of subject, involving the subjection of the relatively powerless subject to the experimenter
and the distinction between the person who acts and the person who is acted upon, are fundamental to medical and

behavioral experimentation. Neither is fundamental to the
practice of fieldwork, however, despite the fact that the
power differential between observer and observed has historically been common. Hughes says:

> Malinowski went out to the Trobriands and
> studied people whom he probably would not have
> liked to have to dinner. Radcliffe-Brown stud-
> ied the Andaman Islanders who ate pig which they
> cooked on sticks over a fire. It is called an-
> thropology, the study of anthropos, man. When
> finally we got around to studying the people here
> at home in our own cities we called that study
> "sociology," the study of our social companions.
> But in neither case did we as a rule study the
> people who are our closest companions. We are
> still studying people who are relatively deprived.
> We still keep, in practice, to the idea that there
> are those with the fate of being studied whether
> to be preserved, as were the aborigines, or to be
> enlightened and rehabilitated (1974:332).

Anthropology has been called "a child of Western imperialism," and we have the image of the ethnographer at the
outposts of empire, sitting on his verandah, sipping gin and
bitters, asking the District Officer to send over a few
"natives" to question. Whether this scene reflects myth or
history, such a relationship is entirely untenable in today's
"revolutionary and proto-revolutionary world" (Gough 1968:
405).

Intersubjectivity and the Flow of Interaction

I believe that the power differential between observer
and observed is not intrinsic to the fieldwork situation:
ethnographers can study peers (Cassell 1977, 1978); they can
study "up" (Nader 1974, 1976); they can study a large bureaucratic organization from top to bottom, focusing on the
power and opportunity structures that differentiate leaders
and the upwardly mobile from powerless individuals stuck in
dead-end jobs (Kanter 1977); or they can do what I suspect
most good fieldworkers have always done, which is to engage
in a cooperative enterprise with their informants in an atmosphere of respect and recognition of common humanity (Mead
1969).

In psychological experiments, subjects may attempt to
"read" investigators, reacting to subtle, unprogrammed
features of the research situation (Orne 1962; Orne and Evans
1965). This type of interaction is outside the experimental

paradigm. Because experimental research seeks to predict and measure responses, the human characteristics of subjects, which cause them to try to "read" or "please" experimenters, are irrelevant and distracting. What is being investigated are not individuals but <u>processes</u> (or variables), which can be delimited, measured and compared. No matter how humane the experimenters and how responsible their treatment of subjects, the basic interest is the process under study, with people conceptualized primarily as vehicles for, or carriers of, this process.

In fieldwork, on the other hand, the human characteristics which are considered irrelevant and distracting in the experimental situation are the objects of study. The distinction between action and acted-upon cannot be used to differentiate the person who studies from those who are studied. There is a two-way flow of interaction: action and influence must move in both directions if the observer is to learn anything about the observed. Both observer and observed are of necessity thinking or reflective agents, and the fact that each has a "self" is relevant to the research process. Both ethnographer and the people studied are busy trying to "read" and "manipulate" the other. Each has needs and ends; each interacts with the other to try to meet needs and achieve ends. And, in point of fact, those who are studied are frequently more sophisticated than the fieldworker in manipulating the other. (See R. H. Wax's hilarious account (1971: 181-220) of the experiences of her husband and herself when living on a reservation with a family of "professional" Indians who specialized in bamboozling unwary outsiders.)

Not only do members of so-called "simple" societies exhibit considerable expertise in manipulating fieldworkers, they also demonstrate ingenuity in blocking the curiosity of investigators from more complex and powerful societies. Consider the following interchange (Evans Pritchard 1971: 12-13), which occurred in Sudanic Africa, during the 1930s, when the British were politically the dominant force:

<u>I</u> (Evans-Pritchard): Who are you?
<u>Cuol</u>: A man.
<u>I</u>: What is your name?
<u>Cuol</u>: You want to know m<u>y</u> name?
<u>I</u>: Yes, you have come to visit me in my tent and I
        would like to know who you are.
<u>Cuol</u>: All right. I am Cuol. What is your name?
<u>I</u>: My name is Pritchard.
<u>Cuol</u>: What is your father's name?
<u>I</u>: My father's name is also Pritchard.
<u>Cuol</u>: No, that cannot be true. You cannot have the

```
          same name as your father.
I:   It is the name of my lineage.  What is the name of
     your lineage?
Cuol:  You want to know the name of my lineage?
I:   Yes.
Cuol:  What will you do with it if I tell you?  Will you
     take it to your country?
I:   I don't want to do anything with it.  I just want to
     know it since I am living at your camp.
Cuol:  Oh well, we are Lou.
I:   I did not ask the name of your tribe.  I know that.
     I am asking you to name of your lineage.
Cuol:  Why do you want to know the name of my lineage?
I:   I don't want to know it.
Cuol:  Then why do you ask me for it?  Give me some
     tobacco.
```

In experimental research, every possible attempt is made
to operationalize concepts, standardize measurements, isolate
the effects of the setting, and reduce as far as possible the
disturbing effects of observation upon that which is observed. Instruments are frequently used to measure and
record the changes in subjects (or their disease) which
occur as a result of manipulation; and, ideally, only those
changes which occur as a result of experimental manipulation
constitute the data of the experiment. The ethnographer, on
the other hand, carries on research amidst the "booming
buzzing confusion" of daily life. In fieldwork, unlike the
experimental situation, change is as likely to occur in the
observer as the observed; it is the ethnographer who alters
as a result of interaction with those who are studied and
these changes are part of the data. The fact that the
ethnographer is his or her own measuring instrument makes it
difficult to posit an absolute dichotomy between the mind of
the observer and that which is observed. Leach points out
that Malinowski, one of the first to carry out intensive
fieldwork, discovered that "there is a radical incompati-
bility between the demands of scientific objectivity and the
personal human involvement which participant observation
necessarily entails" (1974:2). Not only does the observing
interfere with the observation, but the interference itself
is a significant datum. Opposed to the objectivity, parsi-
mony and control which are the ideals of experimental research, in ethnography we have perhaps not subjectivity, but
surely intersubjectivity, where much of the basic data come
from an analysis of the interaction between the person who
studies and those who are studied, in a situation where both
"are at once observers to themselves and subjects to the
other" (Devereaux 1967:275).

Because (1) the hierarchy and power differential between
observer and observed is not intrinsic to fieldwork; (2) both
observer and observed are subject and object, since both are
thinking or reflective agents; and (3) that which is acted
upon is the observer and the observed, since action and influence flow in both directions; the term "subject" is inappropriate for those studied by participant observation. The
companion term "experimenter" is equally inappropriate,
since neither the observed nor the experimental parameters
can be experimentally manipulated or controlled. Those who
are observed and the context of observation both vary, and it
is impossible to isolate the y's from the x's so that the
researcher can write a proper function (Geertz 1973:22-23).

Regulating Fieldwork

Despite the fact that human subject regulations assume
an asymmetrical experimenter-subject role pair rather than
the reciprocal relationship between participant observer and
observed, this does not mean that regulations are entirely
unnecessary in fieldwork. Human subject regulations are
designed to protect those who are studied from risk. And, if
there is a group at risk in fieldwork, then in some ways they
are subjects, if only subjects of study. And people are at
risk in fieldwork. Both the person who studies and those
who are studied may be exposed to "physical, psychological,
sociological, or legal risks" (Code of Federal Regulations
1977), so each might be considered in need of some form of
protection.

Risk in fieldwork occurs at two different times, during
interaction, and when the data become public.

The Risks of Interaction

During the interaction between participant observer and
observed, various types of risk may be incurred. Deception
involves risk: those observed may be at psychic or social
risk if the observer deceives them about his or her purposes.
Some fieldworkers have performed covert research. In a pio-
neering paper Florence Kluckhohn (1940) defined "participant
observation" as if it were a form of deceptive role-playing
and illustrated the practice from her own research. Subsequent authors (Becker and Geer 1957; Gold 1958) regarded
covert research as one of the alternative (and legitimate)
modalities of participant observation. Happily, the literature does not contain many cases of deceptive research (the
most notable are Sullivan et al. 1958; Festinger, Riecken,

and Schacter 1958; Humphreys 1970), and the practice has been
sternly criticized (Erikson 1967; Barnes 1963). Nevertheless,
some covert research (e.g. Cavan 1974) has continued. M.
Brewster Smith points out that in cases involving deception,
there is a conflict between a potential harm, the invasion
of privacy, and an emerging value, that of the public's
"right to know." In such cases there is no clear solution
through abstract analysis or formula to the risk-benefit
calculus. In each case,

> complex human judgments are involved, ad hoc
> judgments guided by precedent and debate, in
> which movement toward consensus can be stimu-
> lated but hardly dictated by ethical analysis
> (1976:450).

Nor, it may be added, by governmental fiat. Certainly, more
flagrant cases of deception, such as that of an observer who
investigates illegal homosexual acts in public restrooms
without revealing his role as researcher, raise serious
ethical problems, which are compounded if later he follows
his subjects home and interviews them under false pretenses
(Humphreys 1970; see Warwick 1973 for a critique of
Humphreys' methods). Here not only privacies have been violated but the self-images of the actors have been threatened:
the researcher has taken pains to penetrate their "fronts" as
"solid citizens" in a way that could have exposed them publicly as people who take part in deviant, stigmatized and
illegal behavior. Deception threatens the ethnographer as
well as those who are studied; it is the ethnographer whose
ethical sensibilities are coarsened, on occasion, to the
extent where the validity of his or her work is jeopardized;
it may also threaten the work in progress, since people may
covertly recognize that they are being lied to and behave
accordingly (Mead 1969: 374-379; Erikson 1967; R.Wax 1952).

Interaction may put people at risk in other ways. There
is an emotional risk posed by an observer who has taken pains
to become part of a group's ongoing life and be defined as
a "friend," who then leaves abruptly, breaking off ties with
those who were studied (Harrell-Bond 1976). What are an
observer's obligations to the group when research is completed, and how long do these obligations last? Risk may be
involved when the observer introduces a higher standard of
living or a new technology to a group (Sharp 1952). How
much responsibility does the researcher bear for such a
situation? How technologically "pure" should the group be
kept? Should this "purity" extend to medical technology?

The Benefits of Interaction

Federal regulations for the protection of human subjects state that the risk to a population should not exceed the benefits of proposed research. Thus, in medical experimentation where the risks may be high, the possible benefits are also high. The risk which results from interaction during fieldwork is rarely as great as that from medical or other behavioral experimentation. But what are the benefits? There may be material benefits: the observer can supply scarce goods, medical help, money (Mead 1969:362). There are also intellectual benefits: the satisfaction of being able to perceive more about one's culture and the interrelations between various parts of it can be as important to informant as observer. "My best Sedang informant," says Devereaux, "once exclaimed, 'I never realized that there were so many things in our culture!'" (1967:139). And Kanter, when studying the modern corporation, had a small group of informants who told her about the history of the company, gave information about career issues, checked out stories gathered elsewhere and discussed concrete and philosophical issues relating to the new human problems of the corporation. She reports:

> Although occasionally they would seem embarrassed
> at not being "experts" in social science, I always
> found that they knew much more than they thought,
> and my discussions with them were very enjoyable.
> In some sense, they participated with me as "co-
> researchers" and our conversations always tended to be
> characterized by open exchange (1977:296).

The fact that the investigator places high value on the information is an intellectual and emotional benefit: we all like to be found interesting. There are emotional benefits to incorporating a new person with a fresh viewpoint into a group, if only temporarily. The ethnographic informant has on occasion been described as a deviant--this is supposed to explain why he or she "wastes time" talking to the observer, but this "deviance" may be related to the fact that the informant has dormant intellectual gifts which are stimulated by interaction with the observer. Thus Turner's unforgettable informant, Muchona, enjoyed their long philosophical discussions about the meanings of rites and symbols and mourned when the anthropologist left the field, lowering his status from "philosophy don" to "witchdoctor" (1970:150). (This, of course, accentuates the question of whether the benefit of deeply satisfying interaction is worth the risk of losing it, but this problem is not unique to fieldwork.)

Risks of Reporting Data

Interaction is just one source of risk in fieldwork. A more serious possibility occurs at a later date when the research data are made available to a larger public. There are two sources of risk at this time.

The Sponsor. One is the research sponsor. Although the power differential between observer and observed is not intrinsic to fieldwork, there is another power differential which almost always applies: the sponsor is more powerful than observer or observed, and both rarely have control over the sponsor's use of data (Kelman 1972). Counterinsurgency research sponsored by government agencies,"during the U.S. involvement in S.E. Asia" provides an outstanding example of research designed for social control. But there are less obvious examples, where research can be used in ways that harm those who were studied. Kelman points out that research on deviance, or on disadvantaged groups, can be used in ways to control these people, or to explain differences between them and the majority group in terms of "social pathology" (see Rainwater and Pittman 1967:302-303). The sponsor, or other powerful agencies, are then free to devise social work palliatives to correct this "pathology" and thus to avoid the attack on underlying economic causes (Kelman 1972:1009-1010; Ryan 1971:24).

Publication. A related risk is posed by publication. When research data become public the ethnographer can no longer control their use or misuse. Publication poses various levels of risk. These range from the characterization of a group in terms which many members of that group may find unacceptable (Moynihan 1965; Rainwater and Yancey 1967), to the violation of anonymity, subjecting an individual or group to unwelcome publicity (Gallaher 1964; Whyte 1973), to exposing people to legal, institutional or governmental sanctions because of behavior revealed by the fieldworker (i.e. studies of illegal massage parlor sex-for-money in a comparatively easily-identified college town; Rasmussen and Kuhn 1976). What are the responsibilities of ethnographers in such cases? Should material be "cleared" with the group under study, and if so, with which members or factions within the group? How does one weigh the public's "right to know" against an individual's or group's "right to privacy?"

Balancing Benefits Against Risks

Can we find benefits to balance against the sponsor and publication as sources of risk? The future possibility of having data misused by a sponsor is balanced by the immediate

benefit of having research funded. Here we have an uneven
risk-benefit calculus: the researcher gains while those who
are studied may possibly be put at risk. When one person or
group benefits from the risks of another, can risk and benefit be weighed against one another? In commenting on the
use of a risk-benefit calculus, May notes that the terms are
asymmetrical: "risk" implies the mere possibility or probability of harm, while "benefit" seems to describe virtually
certain payoffs. He suggests that it might be more accurate
to carry out risk-hope analysis or weigh harm against benefit (1978). The risk-benefit framework is particularly inappropriate for an activity such as fieldwork where interaction cannot be scheduled or planned in advance, and where
the most serious risks (or harm) occur at a later time when
data are reported. To weigh risks against benefits, a researcher must decide before a project is funded that the
personal (and immediate) benefit does not outweigh a possible future risk to the research population. This requires
a careful selection of sponsors, some clear thinking about
who is the "client" and what are the responsibilities of the
investigator (Rainwater and Pittman 1967)--and a crystal
ball!

     We can say that science benefits from the publication
of research data, and this is a legitimate benefit. The
researcher benefits as well, since his or her career is
advanced as a result. The research group may also benefit,
not only at the time of publication but at a later date as
well. For example, a number of current American Indian land
claims are based on earlier work by ethnographers studying
entirely different problems (Lurie 1977). There has been
much talk of ethnographers "taking away" or "stealing" information, but we must remember that on occasion the observer's work acts as the repository of material which may
not be valued by the group until a later date (Devereaux
1967:249). Such preservation is a benefit to science, to
society and to the observed group.

Conclusions

     I have pointed out that the relationship between ob-
server and observed in fieldwork is reciprocal and not necessarily hierarchical. In addition, there are two loci of
risk, one during interaction and another when the research
data become public. How do these differences between fieldwork and experimental research affect the results of human
subject protective regulations?

     Human subject regulations are designed to guard subjects
from risks which occur during the interaction between subject

and experimenter, rather than risks which occur at a later
date. Because of the hierarchical and asymmetrical nature
of the subject-experimenter relationship, protection involves
some attempt to equalize the power differential by giving the
subject the chance either to decline to enter this unequal
relationship or to leave it at any time. The asymmetry cannot be corrected, but the subject can be protected. The
process of informed consent provides information as to what
may happen and allows the subject to decide whether or not
to enter the research situation. Because of the limited,
controlled, and unidirectional nature of the relationship
between experimenter and subject in traditional experimentation, it is comparatively easy to foresee the risks a subject will be exposed to, and consequently, to describe them
in a consent form.

The concept of informed consent and the regulations
designed to keep an experimenter from misusing his or her
power over the subject are somewhat tangential to the reciprocal relation between the participant observer and the observed. In a truly reciprocal relationship, where action
and influence flow in both directions, it is impossible to
predict the course of interaction; consequently one cannot
obtain before-the-fact consent from those who interact as to
what will go on during that interaction. Even the subject
of study may change during fieldwork (M.L. Wax 1977). The
essential irrelevance of such protective regulations may
have been clouded by advocates of "scientific" sociology or
anthropology, whose terminology reflects their wish that
the research situation duplicate the biomedical model
(Vidich, et al. 1964: -- make a similar point).

There is a more serious problem than irrelevance, however. Human subject regulations are designed to control
against the most significant source of risk in traditional
experimentation, which occurs during or as a result of interaction between researcher and subject. We have seen that
there is a second, greater source of risk in participant
observation, however, which occurs when the data become
public. Here, human subject regulations do little to protect anyone.

Can regulations which conceptualize the research enterprise in a way which is inappropriate for a particular type
of research protect those who are studied by this technique?
How do inappropriate regulations affect researchers? Do they
ignore them? Falsify responses and permission, since it may
be impossible to obtain genuine ones?[2] Or do researchers
attempt to follow the spirit of the regulations even if the
letter does not apply? I can imagine a definite temptation

for an investigator to ignore regulations which do not
really apply and this could extend to a denial that there
are, in fact, any ethical problems at all associated with
the research. M. Brewster Smith points out that administrative regulation of research ethics inevitably focuses on the
extreme, unacceptable case, but that we might more properly
be concerned with the ethical level of what is generally
normative practice in our fields (1976:452). It is time to
start a dialogue among ethnographers, a dialogue which might
include ethicists as well as representatives of people frequently studied by fieldworkers, to discuss ethical problems
associated with fieldwork. We must heighten the sensibilities of ethnographers, and of students, to the difficulties
they may encounter. When fieldworkers are conscious of
ethical problems before these problems arise, then the ethical level of normative practice will improve and the extreme cases, which generate publicity, distaste and over-
regulation, will become less common.[3]

Notes

[1]Federal regulations for the protection of human subjects do not define what is meant by a "human subject." The
National Commission for the Protection of Human Subjects of
Biomedical and Behavioral Research finally solved the problem by defining it in terms of studies which they believe
should be reviewed by an Institutional Review Board. "The
provisional definition states that a human subject is a person about whom an investigator conducting scientific research
obtains (1) data through intervention or interaction with the
person or (2) identifiable private information" (Gray 1978:
13).

[2]I was told of a researcher who was required by a university review board to obtain consent signatures from an
entire tribe of American Indians before an ongoing study
could be resumed. Believing, after some time with the group,
that they would refuse to sign any sort of governmental form,
the ethnographer signed the forms with the names of the Indians and went back to live with the tribe.

[3]With the support of a grant from the Program in Ethics
and Values in Science and Technology, National Science Foundation, to Washington University, St. Louis, and the Center
for Policy Research, New York City, I shall be an Executive
Associate of a project devoted to "Ethical Problems of Fieldwork" (Murray L. Wax, Principal Investigator). The project
staff welcomes the interest and cooperation of our colleagues
and of professional associations.

References Cited

Abrahams, Roger
   1970   Deep Down in the Jungle...Negro Narrative Folklore
      from the Streets of Philadelphia. Chicago: Aldine.
Barnes, J.A.
   1963   Some Ethical Problems in Modern Fieldwork. British
      Journal of Sociology 14:118-134. Reprinted pp. 235-251
      in Qualitative Methodology, edited by William J.
      Filstead. Chicago: Markham, 1970.
Beals, Ralph
   1969   Politics of Social Research. Chicago: Aldine.
Becker, Howard S. & Blanche Geer
   1957   Participant Observation and Interviewing: A Compari-
      son. Human Organization 16:28-32.
Cassell, Joan
   1977   A Group Called Women: Sisterhood and Symbolism in
      the Feminist Movement. New York: David McKay.
   1978   The Relationship of Observer to Observed in Peer
      Group Research. Human Organization, 36:412-416.
Cavan, Sherri
   1974   Seeing Social Structure in a Rural Setting. Urban
      Life and Culture 3:329-346. Reprinted, pp. 269-281 in
      Sociological Methods: A Sourcebook, edited by Norman
      K. Denzin, 2nd edition. New York: McGraw-Hill, 1978.
Code of Federal Regulations
   1977   Protection of Human Subjects. 45 CFR 46, revised as
      of April 1, 1977. NIH, PHS, DHEW.
Deitchman, Seymour J.
   1976   The Best-Laid Schemes: A Tale of Social Responsi-
      bility and Bureaucracy. Cambridge: M.I.T. Press.
Devereaux, George
   1967   From Anxiety to Method in the Behavioral Sciences.
      New York: Humanities Press.
Erikson, Kai T.
   1967   A Comment on Disguised Observation in Sociology.
      Social Problems 12:366-373.
Evans-Pritchard, E.E.
   1971   The Nuer: A Description of the Modes of Livelihood
      and Political Institutions of a Nilotic People. New
      York and Oxford: Oxford University Press.
Festinger, Leon, Henry W. Riecken & Stanley Schachter
   1956   When Prophecy Fails. Minneapolis: University of
      Minnesota Press.
Gallaher, Art, Jr.
   1964   Plainville: the Twice-studied Town. Pp. 285-303 in
      Reflections on Community Studies. Arthur J. Vidich &
      Maurice R. Stein (eds.). New York: Harper Torchbooks.

Geertz, Clifford
  1973 Thick Description: Toward an Interpretive Theory of
     Culture. In The Interpretation of Cultures. New York:
     Basic Books.
Gold, Raymond L.
  1958 Roles in Sociological Field Observations. Social
     Forces 36:217-223. Reprinted pp. 30-38 in Issues in
     Participant Observation edited by George J. McCall &
     J.L. Simmons (Reading, Mass.: Addison-Wesley 1969).
Gough, Kathleen
  1968 New Proposals for Anthropologists. Current Anthro-
     pology, 9, 5:403-407.
Gray, Bradford H.
  1978 Human Subjects Review Committees and Social Research
     Paper presented at the annual meeting, American
     Association for the Advancement of Science.
Harrell-Bond, Barbara
  1976 Studying Elites: Some Special Problems. In Ethics
     and Anthropology: Dilemmas in Fieldwork. Michael A.
     Rynkiewich & James P. Spradley, eds. New York: John
     Wiley.
Horowitz, Irving Louis (ed.)
  1967 The Rise and Fall of Project Camelot. Cambridge:
     M.I.T. Press.
Hughes, Everett C.
  1974 Who Studies Whom? Plenary address of the 33rd
     annual meeting of the Society for Applied Anthroplogy.
     Human Organization, 33, 4:327-334.
Humphreys, Laud
  1970 Tearoom Trade: Impersonal Sex in Public Places.
     Chicago: Aldine.
Kanter, Rosabeth Moss
  1977 Men and Women of the Corporation. New York: Basic
     Books.
Kelman, Herbert C.
  1972 The Rights of the Subject in Social Research: An
     Analysis in Terms of Relative Power and Legitimacy.
     American Psychologist, 27:989-1016.
Kluckhohn, Florence
  1940 The Participant Observer Technique in Small Com-
     munities. American Journal of Sociology 46:331-343.
Leach, Edmund
  1974 Anthropology Upside Down. The New York Review,
     April 4.
Lewis, Oscar
  1968 La Vida: A Puerto Rican Family in the Culture of
     Poverty--San Juan and New York. New York: Random
     House Vintage Books.

Liebow, Elliot
    1967   Tally's Corner: A Study of Negro Streetcorner Men.
        Boston: Little, Brown.
Lurie, Nancy O.
    1977   Benefits--Mostly Unanticipated--Of Anthropological
        Research Among American Indians. Paper presented at
        the 76th annual meeting, American Anthropological
        Association, Houston, Texas.
May, William
    1978   The Right to Know and the Right to Create. M.I.T.
        Newsletter on Science, Technology and Human Values,
        forthcoming.
Mead, Margaret
    1969   Research With Human Beings: A Model Derived from
        Anthropological Field Practice. Daedalus 98:361-386.
Moynihan, Daniel P.
    1965   The Negro Family: The Case for National Action.
        Washington, D.C.: United States Department of Labor.
Nader, Laura
    1974   Up the Anthropologist--Perspectives Gained From
        Studying Up. Pp. 284-311 in Reinventing Anthropology.
        Del Hymes (ed.). New York: Vintage Books.
    1976   Professional Standards and What We Study. Pp. 167-
        182 in Ethics and Anthropology: Dilemmas in Fieldwork.
        Michael A. Rynkiewich and James P. Spradley (eds.).
        New York: John Wiley.
Orne, Martin T.
    1962   On the Social Psychology of the Psychological Experi-
        ment: With Particular Reference to Demand Characteris-
        tics and their Implications. American Psychologist,
        17:776-783.
Orne, Martin T.,& Frederick J. Evans
    1965   Social Control in the Psychological Experiment:
        Antisocial Behavior and Hypnosis. Journal of Personal-
        ity and Social Psychology, 1:189-200.
Rainwater, Lee,& David J. Pittman
    1967   Ethical Problems in Studying a Politically Sensitive
        and Deviant Community. Social Problems, Spring: 357-
        366.
Rainwater, Lee,& William L. Yancy
    1967   The Moynihan Report and the Politics of Controversy.
        Cambridge: M.I.T. Press.
Rasmussen, Paul K.& Lauren L. Kuhn
    1976   The New Masseuse. Urban Life, 5:271-292.
Ryan, William
    1971   Blaming the Victim. New York: Pantheon Books.
Sharp, Lauriston
    1952   Steel Axes for Stone Age Australians. In Human
        Problems in Technological Change. Edward H. Spicer, ed.
        New York: Russell Sage Foundation.

Sullivan, Mortimer A., Stuart A. Queen & Ralph C. Patrick, Jr.
  1958 Participant Observation as Employed in the Study of a Military Training Program. American Sociological Review, 23:660–667.
Turner, Victor
  1970 Muchona the Hornet, Interpreter of Religion. In The Forest of Symbols: Aspects of Ndembu Ritual. Ithaca and London: Cornell Paperbacks.
Vidich, Arthur J., Joseph Bensman & Maurice R. Stein
  1964 Preface. Pp. viii–xiv in Reflections on Community Studies. Arthur J. Vidich, Joseph Bensman, & Maurice R. Stein (eds.). New York: John Wiley.
Warwick, Donald P.
  1973 Tearoom Trade: Means and Ends in Social Research. The Hasting Center Studies, 1, 1:27–38.
Wax, Murray L.
  1977 On Fieldworkers and those Exposed to Fieldwork: Federal Regulations, Moral Issues, Rights of Inquiry. Human Organization 36, 3:321–328.
Wax, Rosalie H.
  1971 Doing Fieldwork: Warnings and Advice. Chicago: University of Chicago Press.
Whyte, William Foote
  1973 Freedom and Responsibility in Research: The "Springdale" Case. Pp. 39–41 in To See Ourselves: Anthropology and Modern Social Issues. Thomas Weaver (ed.). Glenview, Ill.: Scott, Foresman.
Wolf, Eric & Joseph Jorgenson
  1970 Anthropology on the Warpath in Thailand. New York Review of Books, 15, 9:26–35.
Wax, Rosalie H.
  1952 Reciprocity as a Field Technique. Human Organization 11(3):34–37.

Part III

Quantitative Methodology

Introduction to Part III

Murray L. Wax and Joan Cassell

Sociology has become the science of the interview.... Conversation of verbal and other gestures is an almost constant activity of human beings. The main business of sociology is to gain systematic knowledge of social rhetoric; to gain the knowledge we must become skilled in the rhetoric itself.... In the research interview, the assumption is generla that information is the more valid the more freely given. Such an assumption stresses the voluntary character of the interview as a relationship freely and willingly entered into by the respondent; it suggests a certain promissory or contractual element (Benney and Hughes 1970:190-191; 194).

Because their research procedures are more formalized, and their contacts with respondents ("subjects," "interviewees") more limited and more predictable, the ethical problems of quantitative methodologies are simpler to describe. As a result, the impact of federal regulations is more direct, so that it is easier to assess (as does Abt) the costs in time and monies, and the benefits (or lack of benefits) conferred on respondents. Compare, for example, the essays of Abt and of Olesen to perceive the differences between the ethical problems of federal regulations pertaining to quantitative and qualitative methodologies. Olesen is of necessity tentative and discursive, while Abt is able to be forceful and assured.

Because the interaction between investigator (here survey interviewer) and respondent is comparatively limited, ingenious technical devices can be used to protect privacy and confidentiality. Boruch and Cecil have considered and analyzed such devices: statistical indeterminacies, randomness, and computerized linkages of data, are intriguing examples of the elegance (or technique) of quantitatively based methodologies.

The gains in protection are clearly significant, providing that respondents and investigators are willing to adhere to the rules and procedures. Naturally, many of these protective systems cost more, and sacrifice some precision, and perhaps the presentation should be more specific about these so that they can be assessed against the overall cost of a project.

Singer's essay, focusing on the "informed" aspect of "informed consent," is even more encouraging. If the survey interviewer informs the respondent as to what may be expected during the course of an interview on "sensitive" topics, there seems to be little loss in willingness to participate, and an improvement in the quality of replies from those who do parti- cipate. Honesty (beforehand) seems to be the best policy for survey researchers. Singer also reports on the effects of various kinds of promises of confidentiality extended to respondents before the interview. The effects of differential promises seem to be comparatively small, and we might specu- late that respondents judge the nature of their participation, less by the initial verbiage, and more by their personal response to the interviewer. Indeed, if we stop to reflect on the nature of the interaction with the stranger at the door, the first judgment made is probably not confidenti- ality but whether the stranger portends personal danger (e.g. is the person an assailant?), or discomfort (a salesman?), or stimulating conversation. A generation ago, the Survey Research Center asked respondents to comment by mail about their reactions to being interviewed:

> Their replies were more often couched in terms of the personal relationship and personal qualities of the interviewer than in terms of the content of the study or the apparent purpose of the inquiry. Typical comments mentioned the fact that the interviewer was a very understanding person or that the interviewer had a keen insight into the respondent's situation (Cannell and Kahn 1953:356 as cited by Riesman and Benney 1956:11).

Or, from more recent survey research, the comment of a novice interviewer:

> People were on the whole quite willing to talk to me, but the distrust they expressed of others! Detroit homes seemed like fortresses (Converse and Schuman 1974:39).

Since respondents are preoccupied with assessing the character of the interviewer, it is only when they understand the situa- tion and feel safely in control of the interaction, that they can begin to worry about who (beyond the interviewer) will

have access to their responses to questions. Especially at
the start of the interaction--in the moments preceding the
interview proper--most respondents will not be concerned
about the confidentiality of questions which have not yet
been asked.

Where Singer, Boruch and Cecil focus on the interaction
between interviewer and respondent and how alterations may
(or may not) affect the survey process   , Abt focuses
on the survey process in large-scale, from the point of view
of the survey director concerned about time, monies, and
cost-efficiencies. From this perspective, significant aspects
of the various federal regulatory agencies and regulatory
systems appear reduplicative, inefficient and wasteful. Procedures designed to save federal money end up saving pennies
and wasting dollars; procedures designed to protect respondents instead expose them to federal investigators; procedures designed to minimize the imposition of federal paperwork
on citizens instead bring a social cost to the poorer sections
of the population. The indictment is severe, and unhappily
there is no court where the charges may be aired, rebutted,
and judged. In the present context, the most severe criticism
of all is that federal procedures may result in breaches of
the very confidentiality that the survey researcher has
promised to respondents. Frequently, it would appear that
the federal regulatory process, designed to protect respondents during research, may lead to crucial hazards from
government personnel, especially investigators of various
sorts.

References Cited

Benney , Mark, and Everett C. Hughes
  1970 Of Sociology and the Interview. Reprinted pp. 190-
    198 <u>in</u> Sociological Methods: A Sourcebook. Edited by
    Norman K. Denzin. Chicago: Aldine. Originally published
    American Journal of Sociology (1956) 62:137-142.
Cannell, C. F., and R. L. Kahn
  1953 The Collection of Data by Interviewing. <u>In</u> Research
    Methods in the Behavioral Sciences. Edited by Leon
    Festinger and Daniel Katz. New York: Dryden.
Converse, Jean M., and Howard Schuman
  1974 Conversations at Random: Survey Research as Inter-
    viewers See It. New York: John Wiley (out of print,
    available via Institute for Social Research, University
    of Michigan, Ann Arbor).
Riesman, David, and Mark Benney
  1956 The Sociology of the Interview. Midwest Sociologist
    18:3-15.

9

Federal Regulation
of Social Research
Survey Instrument

Clark C. Abt

Federal regulations intended for improving the quality
and efficiency of social research have too often strangled
it. They have sometimes improved it. Improvements have included better specified contract work statements, privacy
requirements for survey participants, and open competitions.
Multilayered clearances of survey instruments have been the
major strangulations. The potential benefits and costs to
social research sponsors, consumers, and producers of some of
the typical major federal regulations affecting social research, are sufficiently great to suggest reforms believed to
be in the interests of both the social research community and
the public.

A particularly important example of federal regulation
of social research is the Office of Management and Budget
(OMB) clearance review of evaluation and other research survey instruments. Every social researcher collecting survey
information from more than nine respondents for a government-
supported research and/or evaluation project is required to
have the survey instruments reviewed and accepted by OMB
before the survey can begin. OMB instrument review controls
much empirical policy research, because it can stop, delay,
or change the flow of survey data to government.

Power over the timeliness, form, productivity, costs and
degree of execution of much federally-sponsored social research is thus exercised by survey review regulations. This
effectively gives OMB considerable control of at least two
hundred million dollars' worth of evaluation and other policy
research every year. This is particularly significant when
one considers that this preponderance of federal social research thus controlled by OMB regulation is the only major
scientific source of information for the government and the
public on the effectiveness, efficiency, and equity of

federal social programs.

Great power for good and for harm may thus reside in this federal regulation of social research, suggesting a careful evaluation of this critical federal regulatory activity. Such an evaluation should include the costs and benefits of the OMB instrument review process for the constituencies most impacted.

There are at least eight distinct constituencies affected, or intended to be affected, by the OMB regulation of social survey instruments. First, there are the government consumers, whose programs are usually the topics of the surveys, such as social action and social services delivery agencies (e.g., HEW, DOL). Second, and overlapping the first group, are the government producers and consumers who initiate and fund the surveys. These include social research sponsors and research agencies. Third, the government producers and consumers such as regulatory agencies (e.g., OMB in this case), who control the direction and flow of the surveys. Fourth, the type of government consumers who are the research users who need the information produced by the surveys (e.g., executive, legislature -Congress-, judiciary). Fifth, independent researchers (contractors/producers) who do the surveys. These may be universities, non-profit institutes, or profit-making research or consulting companies. Sixth, the independent research users/consumers who also need the survey information (e.g., scholars, journalists, industry). Seventh, the general public (consumers) who pay for it all - surveys and their regulation - and are intended to get the benefits of both the surveys and the regulations. Eighth, the survey respondents, who are a subgroup of the general public as cooperating producers.

The eight affected constituencies may be categorized as consumers or producers of the government-regulated government social research, or both. Benefit-cost evaluation is complicated by the fact that, of those affected by the OMB survey instrument review, most partake to some degree of the roles of both consumers and producers of research. The ethics of social research would seem to require that all participants in the process share power over it, yet at this date the views and needs of several constituencies have not been solicited by the government's regulatory agency (in this case the OMB).

The survey respondents are directly involved in the production of the regulated survey research, by providing the responses to the questions put to them by the survey instruments. To a large extent, it was the legislative intent of

protecting respondents' rights to privacy and, more important, property, in the form of disposable time, that initiated the regulatory legislation many years ago, in 1942.
The purpose of the relevant law, the Federal Reports Act,*
is to minimize respondents' "burden" and costs. Section 3501
states: "Information needed by Federal agencies shall be
obtained with a minimum burden upon business enterprises,
especially small business enterprises, and at a minimum cost
to the government." Section 3509 of the Act states that the
director of the Bureau of the Budget (now OMB) must approve
the collection of information on identical items for ten or
more persons by any federal agency or federally sponsored
research contractor. Section 3502 defines information as
"facts obtained by the use of written report forms, application forms, schedules, questionnaires, or other similar
methods."

Political pressures behind this act may have been moti-
vated by the hope of deflecting the enforcement of other
federal regulations, such as those for equal employment
opportunity and environmental protection, and the paperwork
caused by non-research federal activities. These pressures
contributed to the Congress establishing the Commission on
Federal Paperwork (P.L. 93-556, 99 Stat. 1789) in 1974. The
Act states, "Congress hereby finds that federal information
reporting requirements have placed an unprecedented paperwork
burden upon private citizens, recipients of Federal Assistance, businesses, governmental contractors, and state and
local governments." The Commission reviewed the matter over
a two-year study period, and then reported to Congress on
what new remedial measures were required. On March 1, 1976,
President Ford wrote to the Director of OMB, saying,
"American citizens are understandably exasperated by the
complexity of reporting to the Federal Government." He then
added, "Specifically, I expect the number of reports which
collect information from the public to be reduced by 10 percent by next June 30 (1977). Further, I expect you to undertake a continuing effort to reduce the burden of government
reporting." President Carter has since asked the OMB to
further reduce paperwork burden, but also failed to define
it.

The constituencies that the regulatory action was probably intended to protect and the most common respondents to
social surveys are not all the same, although they may overlap slightly. This distinction is important for the evaluation of the cost and benefits to the affected consti-
uencies, because one group's benefits and costs, and their

*44 U.S.C. 3501-3512

political resources for modifying them, may not be the same
as that of another. The probable perceived benefits for the
originally intended constituency of small businessmen and
subsequently added institutional administrators may be a reduction in the costs of responding to federal questionnaires
used to help enforce other federal regulations, and possibly
the reduced or delayed or less probable enforcement of other
costly regulations, with an attendant reduction in this cost
of complying with those regulations.

For most respondents to social policy research surveys,
however, - typically poor people in need of diverse health,
education, employment, and housing services - the perceived
benefit of the OMB regulations may be nonexistent or negative.

Since the small businessmen and institutional administrators who were the intended beneficiaries of the OMB survey instrument review regulations constitute only a small
percentage of the commonly surveyed populations of social
policy research, it could well be that their total benefits
(if any) are more than cancelled out by the costs of the regulations to the much larger affected constituency of needy
respondents to whom the surveys can provide a net benefit by
offering information allowing social service programs to be
made more efficiently responsive to people's needs.

Research is badly needed on the typical unit costs and
benefits to both these survey respondent groups, and the
actual participation rates of both of them in the hundreds of
annual social surveys regulated by OMB. (Nor is it clear
that the same standards need to be applied both to program
monitoring and to social program research.)

The following example shows what a difference in net
benefits and benefit distribution small changes in the estimated unit costs and participation rates can make. Assume
that at least one half of the roughly 200 million dollars a
year's worth of federal evaluation surveys, or 100 million
dollars, is spent on the OMB regulated surveys for data collection on about 500,000 respondents, at an average total
unit cost of 100 dollars (including coding, cleaning and
processing, etc.). Assume further that 10 percent of these
half million respondents, or 50,000, are the hard pressed
small businessmen and institutional administrators that the
regulatory legislation was originally intended to protect
from excessive response burden. If individuals spent an
average of two hours a year responding to the surveys, and
their time is worth an average of $20 an hour ($15 salary,
plus 1/3 fringe benefit costs), the equivalent total cost of

this group of 50,000 individuals' response burden totals 2 million dollars. If the Federal regulations intended to reduce response burden and President Ford's appeal for a 10 percent paperwork reduction achieved its goal, we could assume that roughly 10 percent of these 2 million dollars response burden costs, or all of $200,000, would be saved by the OMB regulatory process for this particular group of respondents.

The costs of administering the regulations to achieve this saving are probably many times the savings gained. The regulations would thus have achieved an inefficient transfer payment out of the general revenues to higher income administrators and businessmen. This result, achieved at a substantial net national social cost, would hardly be embraced publicly as the intention of the legislation. Whether it was privately so intended or simply a perverse accident is a matter for speculation.

The possible costs to the preponderant proportion of the respondents - the other 450,000 in the illustrative example - also must be considered. It is very difficult to calculate the equivalent market worth of the time they spend in response to the surveys, since many of them are unemployed. Furthermore, many of them enjoy responding and regard it as a satisfying activity rather than a burden. Thus response "burden" could actually be "response benefit", or perhaps a mix of burdens and benefits whose net benefit or cost varies with time, place, population, and circumstances. Assume that the average wages of these respondents is $4 an hour, and that roughly one half are unemplyed. Then the average unit cost of respondents is $2 per hour, or a total of $1,800,000. Balancing this cost against the perceived and actual benefits to these individuals and their market worth, I would guess that their own view of the matter would conclude on a perceived net response benefit. This is a hypothesis, of course, and should be verified by empirical research on just how burdensome or beneficial surveys are for different kinds of respondents.*

---

* One could design a social experiment with random assignment of potential respondents to planned variations of response "burden" or benefit compensations to verify or reject the hypothesis that most respondents find survey interviews more of a benefit than a burden. The range of compensation should be from a positive $10 for those needing an incentive to compensate for a perceived burden, to a negative $10 or payment by respondents who consider it a benefit, to test what it is worth to them.

The majority of the survey respondents are the recipients of several billion dollars worth of Government social
services. Even a fraction of 1 percent of an improvement in
services delivery of this magnitude resulting from the
application of program knowledge gained by surveys would
more than compensate for the "worst case" of survey response
burden costing $1,800,000. Some survey experiences suggests
that the perceived benefit of responding on matters of concern can exceed the perceived equivalent time costs to the
individual. It should be apparent from this example that
the actual social costs of respondent burden to the overwhelming majority of the respondents simply cannot be large
in terms of the equivalent total market worth of the time
spent in responding. This logical conclusion needs to be
verified empirically.

Whatever the net benefit or cost of response benefit or
burden, it must be balanced against the indirect costs of
the regulation of social surveys to the majority of the survey respondents. This cost of regulation is likely to be
much greater than the costs of the survey response "burden"
being regulated. The regulations delay research an average
of at least two months, so improvements in the services
evaluated are also delayed at least two months. A delay of
two months multiplied across even a 1% improvement of 200
billion dollars' worth of services, or $2 billion times 2
months a year, generates social costs of 333 million dollars
to the recipient population, compared with the maximum cost
savings achieved through response burden reduction of 1.8
million dollars.

The net effect of the regulations is to create a transfer of benefits, or a reduction in relative costs, from the
poor to high income groups. If the actual data exist in
even roughly the same proportions as in the above illustrative example, one wonders, would the Federal legislators and
administrators support such a policy of Government regulation of social research with the perverse effect of trans-
ferring the burden from higher to lower income groups? At
least the stated social policy of the nation is to allocate
burdens in some proportion to the ability of the individual
to carry them, as in the progressive income tax. Government
regulation of survey research, however, appears to create
the perverse result of shifting the burden for improving our
social services to those least able to bear them.

There are at least four federal government constituencies affected by the federal regulation of social research
by the OMB survey instrument clearance process. Even a

crude qualitative review indicates that the government interest here is neither monolithic nor entirely identical
with the public interest, and that government itself, unhappily for both its supporters and critics, is neither the
hero nor the villain of the regulatory drama, or perhaps
both.

    May of the research agencies of the departments and
offices of planning and evaluation that sponsor survey research privately chafe at the OMB instrument review process.
However, they rarely oppose it openly because they fear that
their research budgets are vulnerable to OMB budget cutting
retribution. Major costs of survey clearance regulations
to government research sponsors are time delays of one to
twelve months, survey cost increases of 5 to 10 percent, and
reduced research productivity, relevance, quality, and validity.

    Research productivity is reduced by increased costs
and delays with a constant or reduced quantity and quality
of information obtained. Relevance of the research to current policy questions is reduced both by delays of survey
results further beyond the peak of policy decision-making
interest, and by diversions of research focus from controversial but essential research questions in (perhaps mistaken) anticipation of OMB reluctance to clear politically
"hot", "no-win" issues for survey research. Survey quality
is reduced by the shortcutting of the number and sample
sizes of pilot surveys for corrective feedback, as pilot
surveys are administered to inadequate samples of nine to
avoid the delays inherent in the full OMB clearance required for samples of 10 or more. Quality may also be reduced (as it can also be increased) by the half hour time
limit on telephone surveys and the one hour time limit on
personal interview surveys, sometimes forcing over-simpli-
fication or deletion of items significant for research
questions.

    Validity of survey research is reduced by the con-
straints imposed on efficient pilot testing, increasing the
risks of biased response; constraints on sample size increasing the risk of not obtaining statistically significant
findings on weak and interaction effects, and (usually cost)
constraints on multiple random samples reducing generalizability.

    The offsetting major benefits of the OMB survey instru-
ment clearance process include, paradoxically, an often increased quality of survey research, sometimes increased
productivity or efficiency in terms of non-duplicative

policy relevant findings, and sometimes reduced research
costs to both sponsoring agency and respondent publics.

Increased quality is often obtained by the mere threat
of OMB clearance and the requirement for justifying statements stimulating sponsoring agencies to demand better design
and execution of survey designs, instruments, and sampling
plans from their research contractors, and the research contractors responding with greater competence or losing bid
competitions to others that can meet the higher standards.
Quality of instruments is also sometimes improved by the OMB
imposed length or unit burden constraints forcing researchers
to better prioritize their information needs and relate
instrument items more precisely to specific research hypotheses, rather than asking too many vague questions in the
hope of covering all possible issues and thus risking negatively biasing exhausted respondents.

Increased productivity could be achieved by centralized
OMB clearance review if it really reduced duplication of
identical data gathering efforts across different agencies.
Duplication in time, however, which has sometimes been
erroneously disallowed by OMB, is usually very useful to survey research because it measures the temporal stability and
generalizability of the repeated items, and can be used to
establish social trends and forecasts. Increased productivity may also be achieved by the OMB enforcement or parsimonious instrument designs that concentrate on essential
information and thus produce more of it with less waste from
unessentials.

Costs may be reduced by the OMB "editing" out of unessentials, or the threat of this stimulating research sponsoring agencies or researchers to do it in anticipation of
the requirement.

Whether these regulatory benefits outweigh the costs to
the sponsoring agencies is doubtful. The OMB-imposed
response burden of lengthy and detailed written statements
supporting particular survey instruments submitted for
clearance on sponsoring agencies and researchers is substantial. The costs of this plus the costs of the delays
and design distortions engendered argue strongly that for
most government research sponsors, government regulation of
government· social research is at a net cost.

Government social action agencies, or social services
delivery agencies, such as social program operators, are
usually more interested in operating programs than research-
ing them, and do not always welcome evaluation research

in particular because it can threaten program expansion or survival. Most government program operators are heavily burdened with paperwork reporting requirements, and the additional time demand imposed by responding to surveys can seem costly. The <u>perceived</u> costs of time and threatened evaluative intervention of surveys thus may appear to be reduced by the OMB survey clearance process, precisely because such negatively perceived surveys are hindered.

The possible program-improving <u>benefits of formative evaluations using</u> surveys are likely to be underestimated by most program operators, so that from their point of view the regulation of social surveys, by constraining the amount of program evaluation, is often seen as a net benefit, or at least a reduction of the risks to the program advocates of objective program evaluation.

It should be said that many government program managers sincerely desire untramelled program evaluation because they want to increase their own cost-effectiveness, and because they can use external program evaluations to justify painful program cutbacks or changes. However, in the net, it seems probable that most program managers would find OMB restrictions on the quantity and intrusiveness of evaluation survey research productive from their point of view. In the sense that program managers are often the <u>subjects</u> of the regulated surveys, their threatened <u>organizational</u> response burden may be substantial enough to offer them significant net benefits from the slowdown on survey research caused by the instrument clearance process.

<u>Government regulatory agencies</u> (such as OMB in this critical case) find themselves in both an ambivalent and ambiguous position concerning survey clearance regulations. On the one hand they want to do their jobs well, and these include "saying NO" to plans for excessive or wasteful government spending, on survey research or any other activities. After all, the regulatory agency here is the Office of <u>Management</u> and <u>Budget</u>. On the other hand, OMB is itself charged with <u>the mandate of reducing waste in the execution of government programs</u>, including not only waste in survey research, but also the waste in <u>the regulation</u> of survey research.

The <u>benefits</u> to the regulatory agency of the regulatory mandate and process is of course the degree to which it helps to <u>actually regulate</u> the surveys in accordance with the legislative intent of the Federal Reports Act and the executive intent of the current administration. The costs to the

office are not only the administration and enforcement of the
regulatory survey clearance process, but also the extent to
which that activity creates perverse results, increasing
rather than decreasing response burden and costs.

There is also the benefit of one more kind of administrative "clout" by means of which the OMB can push for its
goals of efficiency in government, if that additional "per-
suasive" power for negotiating with the departments to
rationalize their budgets is not vitiated by the erosion
of legitimacy associated with a perceived non-credibility of
competence in achieving the regulatory goals. This last cost
to the OMB is at least a possibility, since it seems clear
that many "innocent victims" of the survey clearance process,
both in and outside government, are beginning to become
vocal, while the supposed beneficiaries of the intended and
alleged reduction in response burden, the businessmen and
institutional administrators, have yet to make any palpable
show of gratitude for the burden of social surveys that OMB
has supposed to have lightened for them. Thus the continued
regulation of social surveys by OMB in its present form probably promises increased policy embarrassment and administrative cost to OMB with few and unclear offsetting efficiency achievements.

The last but hardly the least of the four federal
government groups impacted by social survey regulation are
the research users or consumers, including the budget ana-
lysts in the OMB and research managers not directly sponsoring the research, the Congress, the General Accounting
Office and Congressional Budget Office, and the Judiciary.
For them, dispersed as they are, the regulated survey research is of interest chiefly for its policy relevance, its
contributions to politically useful knowledge about government programs and client populations.

For this diversified group of survey research findings
users, the issue is whether the administrative and other
costs of OMB regulation are more than paid for by improved
policy relevance, issue coverage, timeliness, and reliability in the sense of both validity and stability of findings.
Cost and efficiency of the research is of only marginal interest here, because the main concern is with the over 200
billion spent on the social programs, not with the less than
a quarter of a percent of this spent on social survey research.

Timeliness is certainly reduced by the regulatory process by an average of two months. Policy relevance is
reduced by delays, but may be increased by better concen-

tration of surveys on key issues, if that is indeed what the
regulatory process achieves (and there is doubt that it does,
in the absence of evidence to the contrary). Issue coverage
is probably reduced, although the possible sharpening of
focus could yield compensating gains. Reliability may be
increased or decreased--this depends particularly on the
individual survey design details. In the net, this important government audience of research findings users probably loses more than it gains from the OMB survey review
process, primarily because of the high policy relevance cost
of delays and the deflection of data gathering from some
important areas. A survey of these survey information users
is much needed to confirm or reject or qualify this estimate.

The independent researchers enjoy--perhaps this is the
wrong word--the most intensive costs and benefits of the OMB
survey clearance regulatory process. As the individuals
who must spend most of the efforts required by OMB to explain, justify, and if rejected, redesign the surveys and
survey instruments the researchers bear the heaviest direct
costs of this federal regulation of social research. Of
course as a researcher my view of this may be biased, but I
have a large sample of factual reports from several major
research organizations to substantiate this statement.

Naturally the researchers do their best to pass on some
of the costs imposed on them by survey clearance. The form
that this passing on of costs takes is the inflationary
one of research cost increases and productivity decreases.

A more subtle and eventually probably more damaging
form of externalizing these regulatory costs is the anti-
cipatory distortion of research designs from the scienti-
fically optimal to the administratively most feasible in the
context of the government regulations. In practice this
means elimination or inadequate sampling of pilot surveys,
reductions in the scope of the research questions addressed,
and reduction of the number of true experimental designs
achieving maximum validity by randomization to quasi- or
non-experimental designs limited to non-equivalent control
groups vulnerable to most of the more than 30 threats to
validity elucidated by Campbell and Stanley.

The actual amount of the survey research cost increases
passed on as increased costs of social survey research, are
variously reported as ranging from 3 to 20 percent. My own
estimate is that they total between 5 and 10 percent, but
this figure should be verified by actual audits and surveys
as soon as possible. If at least $200 million of social
policy research involving surveys is at issue, then the

added annual contracted research cost to the government
ranges from 6 to 40 million dollars, with my conservative
estimate being $10 to 20 million.

Added to these cost figures must be the administrative
costs of survey regulation within the government, both at
the regulatory agency (OMB) and in the departments responding to the regulatory requirements. The multiple layering
of this survey clearance process in large departments such
as HEW, Labor, Justice, and HUD incurs substantial administrative costs. Assuming even only one full time equivalent
staff at each of the clearance authority layers in each of
the affected departments, there must be on the order of at
least 100 high level federal employees required to adminis-
ter this regulation. Assuming that their average annual
cost is $35,000 salary plus 40 percent fringe benefit costs
or $50,000, the added annual government administration cost
of the survey review regulations is at least $5 million.

When this figure is added to the added cost of doing
the research, estimated at $10 to $20 million, we have a
minimum total added cost of regulation to the government of
$15 to $25 million, or about 10 percent of the social research budget involved. That is a substantial direct cash
cost of only one particular regulation, imposing heavy
responsibilities in the agencies administering the regulating to achieve corresponding savings and benefits justifying this expense.

What are the benefits of the regulation to the researchers, and of what magnitude are they? It must be said that
the OMB survey review and clearance process may have raised
the average quality and productivity of social surveys,
simply by requiring the thinking through of the needs for
and best form of the particular survey designs and individual questionnaire items. By causing to filter out some
of the more obviously incompetent survey attempts at the
sponsoring agency review level or even at the OMB level, the
quality distribution of social surveys by having its low
quality tail truncated has probably reached a higher mean.
(Unfortunately the continual shaking up of the survey
research designer population in an environment of unclear
and largely unstated OMB evaluative review criteria tends
also to result in a regression towards the quality/produc-
tivity mean, diminishing the high quality end that required
no regulation, but that is one of the perhaps inevitable
costs of indiscriminatingly uniform administrative controls
on anything).

The savings or benefits to researchers of the reduction
in incompetent surveys and the improved average survey quality is very difficult to quantify. Possibly the overall
state of the art is very slowly pushed forward. However,
balanced against this is the erosion of the first rate researcher population as they become frustrated and discourag-
ed by the indiscriminating regulatory process. In any case
it is difficult to find evidence for quantifiable benefits
generated for survey researchers, other than the additional
$20 million's worth of employment created for some 500 sur-
vey research professionals by the regulatory response activities. Surely the expansion of the social research industry job market was not an intended effect of the Federal
Reports Act or its administration by OMB in the survey
clearance process.

In the net, then, it seems clear that the researchers
have significant net costs imposed on them by the government
regulations, many of which they pass back to the government.
The following typical examples are illustrative.

"Increasingly, OMB's comments have focused
on survey design issues--the appropriateness of
the sampling plan, the adequacy of the plan for
analyzing the data, and even the wording of specific questions. While such comments and suggestions from OMB clearance officers are often
helpful, the process can be refined so that
contractors (who are usually responsible for
preparing the Supporting Statements) are more
aware of OMB's concerns."

***

"Interview length is almost totally dependent upon the information needs of the
particular project, and should not be (as it
sometimes has been) the main focus of concern."

***

"The limitations of pretesting questionnaires
with 9 or less respondents is a number that
has been picked out of the sky and is often
counterproductive to the development of solid
data-gathering instruments. While pretesting
with such small samples are helpful for identifying major difficulties with a questionnaire,
skilled professionals in survey research and

questionnaire design often find such limited
pretesting of little use. This limitation is
further aggravated by the fact that the majority of questionnaires often contain "skip"
patterns which direct the interviewer to omit
questions which are not relevant to that particular respondent; we have often conducted
pretests where the sample of 9 respondents has
been woefully inadequate for testing the specific questions contained within the skip
patterns."

"One important use of pretests is to ask
open-ended questions, obtain information on
the kinds of responses which are elicited from
them, and then use these responses as the basis
for developing a pre-listed set of response
categories in the final questionnaire. Answers
from only 9 respondents are of little help in
developing such closed-end questions."

***

"The limitation to 9 respondents is probably adequate for a questionnaire which will
be administered, in the full scale study, to
only a few hundred respondents. The 9 or less
limitation is also bearable when the proposed
questionnaire contains many questions which
have been used successfully in other projects.
However, if the questionnaire is to be administered, this limitation is foolish. OMB might
consider gearing this limitation to the size
of the full scale study--that is, the larger
the full scale study, the more pretest interviews which can be conducted without obtaining
Pre-clearance from OMB (which is just as time-
consuming as the regular clearance process,
and thus is avoided)."

***

"The interpretation of this 9 or less restric-
tion appears to differ drastically from one
Federal Agency (or OMB Clearance Officer?) to
the next. Some have interpreted this regulation
so that even if a single question is asked of
more than 9, then clearance is required beforehand. This is silly since there are many instances in which that single question is the

basis for determining which of several series
of questions should be asked. For example, "Do
you own or rent this house/apartment?" might
be the single filter question which determines
whether the respondent is asked about mort-
gage payments or about rent payments."

***

"During 1976 and 1977, we kept fairly comprehensive records of experience on OMB Clearance. This file showed that our average experience from time of submission to clearance was
approximately 55 days. The majority of delay
in OMB Clearance occurs between the time the
OMB statement is received by agency clients and
the time the agency submits the request for
clearance to OMB."

"OMB statements are seen as tasks for very
junior people within most projects. They rank
as some of our most poorly conceptualized requirements and written deliverables to the government. Occasionally, we will receive questions
on the sampling plans which appear to be reviewed by people with some degree of expertise.
Since these statements require significant invest-
ments of resources of both the contractor (up
to $10,000) and agency level, they rank as the
most systemized "waste of time" currently required by the government."

***

"The maximum delay we have experienced in
recent times was 13 days. The maximum cost of
a single OMB justifying statement was $10,000."

***

"We invested a great deal in preparing an
extensive clearance package. We did have pro
blems with regard to confidentiality clearance
with OMB. The Catch 22 was the following. We
planned to maintain separate computer files for
survey follow-up and for data. The former would
have names, addresses, and identification numbers and data. As soon as the data was cleaned,
we planned to destroy the name files. Thus, there

would be no problem with linking data to
individuals. However, the objection was
raised that we could not destroy that file
because the auditors would require the names
in case they wanted to do a postcard survey
to check on whether we had actually collected
data from these individuals. Obviously, there
are conflicting requirements stemming from con-
fidentiality/privacy versus auditing. Our
solution was to strip the identification numbers from the name tape."

***

"In December 1976, the instrument package
for the Study was submitted to HEW. This study
has two relatively independent purposes: (1) to
determine the long-term impact of the program
on participants in the Evaluation, and (2) to
determine the effectiveness of Centers which
were established at the conclusion of the Demonstration. At the request of HEW, all instruments were submitted in one OMB clearance
document. This requirement delayed the OMB
approval process considerably as well as the startup
of the Followup Study. The two-page "Background Questionnaire" was prepared in the
early stages of the project to facilitate the
selection of a comparison group of eligibles
who had not received program services, but
could not be submitted for OMB clearance until
all other instruments were developed. As of
December 1977, one year later, the instrument
package is still awaiting clearance by OMB.
This delay is attributable in part to an un-
usually long review by the HEW."

***

"In April of 1977, a copy of the instrument
package and the request for clearance for the
Followup Study was hand-carried to OMB in an
attempt to speed up the review process. Although some clearance requests are processed
simultaneously by HEW and OMB, this procedure
was not followed for this study. OMB made it
clear that the formal review process would not
get underway until the document had been
approved by HEW. Upon receipt of the hand-

carried instrument package, OMB requested information about sample attrition and sample
attrition effects. This information was supplied
in April. The HEW review was completed in
early December when the Followup Study was submitted to OMB for official review. As of
December 1977, no feedback has been obtained
from OMB concerning the clearance request,
and indications are that it may be some time
before OMB approval to proceed with the study
is granted.

These delays have created serious problems
for the Followup Study. First, it has caused
a year's delay in the full-scale implementation
of the study,. The data obtained in the spring
of 1977, for example, cannot be analyzed without
appropriate background information. Second,
outcome data will not reflect longterm impact
of the program on participants who were the
primary focus of the Demonstration. Third,
the one-year delay in data collection is expected to increase attrition from the original
sample and thereby potentially weaken study
findings. And fourth, the evaluation project
costs will be considerably higher since data
on all participants were not collected at the
same time. In order to complete the study,
it will be necessary to recruit and train a
new data collection staff and to spend additional resources in the re-tracking of evaluation
subgroups.

The OMB clearance package already contains
a justification statement explaining the need
for each item in the proposed instruments. As
a means of reducing respondent burden it seems
far more appropriate to review the need for
each of these items than to place an arbitrary
time limit on the entire package.

Finally, my major reservation about the
review process is the level of effort allocated
by OMB for reviews. For standard repetitive
surveys it is certainly feasible to review
both design and instrumentation quickly and
efficiently. However, for large complex studies
which may have taken a year or more to design,
the design factors are frequently very complex.

Long design reports are prepared to justify
these designs for HEW, yet OMB does not review
these reports. They review only a skeleton of
the design and in fact complain if the clearance package is too long. Under these circumstances relatively arbitrary reviewer comments
are not uncommon."

***

"The instrument review process is an
amalgam of HEW and OMB reviews. The former
is usually far more extensive and time consuming than the latter, and is generally more
responsible for study delays. In fact, my
overall experience with OMB has been quite
positive. Study reviews have generally been
prompt and to the point, clearly a consequence of the intelligence and responsiveness
of the particular reviewers I have encountered.
Nonetheless, I have substantial reservations
about the OMB review process. Reviewers are
well versed in standard sampling methodology
but they are not sampling specialists. This
means that for non-standard sampling designs
they are often uninformed. This leads to loss
of time in rounds of questions and answers on
sampling issues. Though in my experience
these issues have been correctly resolved, the
process does not guarantee such outcomes and
in any event the time lost has had substantial
cost implications.

***

I would recommend separation of the instrument review from review of the sampling design.
This has two advantages. First, some reviewers
would be able to specialize in design, others in
instrumentation. This should improve the quality
of design reviews. Second, the total review
process could be shortened by beginning the
design review earlier than the instrument review.
This is generally feasible as the design is frequently completed long before the instrumentation. In fact, in many cases design review
could begin immediately after contract award.

***

Another problem with OMB review is that
OMB seems to have placed an arbitrary time limit,
one hour, on respondent burden. This is independent of the number of interviews proposed
for each respondent or the importance of the
material covered in the interviews. Though
the intent of the limit on respondent burden
is laudable, the actual impact of the OMB guideline is counterproductive. It is now easier
to get OMB approval for several inefficient
small studies (with respondent burden under
one hour) rather than one large efficient study.
The OMB guideline seems more appropriate to
repetitive government reporting requirements
than one-time basic research studies.

***

Since the total respondent burden in
my study is longer than one hour, I have been
forced by OMB to seek a special exemption from
this guideline from the Office of the Secretary
at HEW even though HEW has already approved my
study instruments as they stand. Furthermore,
since OMB refused to review the instruments
before approval by HEW, this has created a
costly delay."

***

"Dear President Carter:

In a recent meeting with the Office of
Management and Budget, your new guidelines
on the reduction of paperwork were quoted with
almost liturgical repetition. I thought you
might be interested in knowing about the effect
of these guidelines as interpreted by OMB.

The particular survey we were discussing
required two hours from well under 100 respondents. Once the multitudes assembled--
there were fifteen people at the meeting--we
were able to proceed to a discussion of the
instrument. No changes of either substance
or form were discussed. Instead, the clearance
procedure focused on a portion of the contract
for which no survey respondents were involved.
OMB ruled, at about 1 p.m., that (1) a justification was required for this part of the study,

and (2) that no survey would be cleared until <u>all</u> parts of the study met OMB approval.

Since the survey was required by an act of Congress, and was, moreover, due about two months from the date of the meeting, we had no choice but to skip lunch and write a justi-fication on the spot. Inasmuch as the require-ment was exclusively a bureaucratic one, and not one of substance, this task was completed in about two hours. Feeling rather like bad school boys who had been kept after school, we drove to OMB's offices and submitted the addi-tional justification statement. The clearance officer looked our work over for about three minutes, asked one question--which indicated he had not read the first page--and granted his approval.

During this day no work of any value was accomplished by anybody. Fifteen grown-up men and women sat around a table for six hours playing political games. Four of us had traveled from a distant city to Washington. It is my estimate that the time involved in the clearance procedure (and associated paper-work) was at least three times that required for responding to the entire survey. As a researcher who is paid by the hour, I have no objection to this approach to paperwork on the part of OMB; as a taxpayer, I'm afraid that something may have been lost between your guidelines and their implementation of them.

Sincerely, a Researcher"

The above small random sample of comments by researchers who have actually experienced the OMB survey clearance pro-cess should give some concrete appreciation for the kinds of research operations costs imposed.

The <u>independent research users</u>, such as university scholars, journalists, industry researchers obtain only those benefits of the government regulation of survey re-search as accrue from greater quality, issue coverage, and timeliness. As we have seen from the above discussion, av-erage quality <u>may</u> be slightly increased but <u>top</u> quality may also be reduced by the regulatory process, so the net bene-fit on the quality dimension is uncertain. Issue coverage

is probably reduced by the OMB filtering process. Timeliness
is lost to the extent of at least the two months average clearance delay, and much more in a significant number of cases.

The overall quantity, quality, timeliness, and economy
of social survey research contributions to knowledge all
suffer from this survey clearance regulation. The few thou-
sands of individuals among the general public who may have
been saved a few hours of "response burden" are greatly out-
weighed by the millions of social services providers, recipients, and taxpayers who have had additional operational and
cost burdens imposed on them, in contradiction to the explicit
instruction of the Federal Reports Act to minimize survey
response <u>costs</u>.

In conclusion, it appears that this particular important
example of government regulation of social policy research is
counterproductive and costly to most of the affected constituencies, with few offsetting benefits. There is certainly
sufficient indication of the possibility of such a counterproductive result to justify a much more thorough cost accounting and impact evaluation than this necessarily brief
estimate based on only a small sample of experiences. It
would seem part of OMB's legitimate and important mission of
waste reduction to immediately initiate an independent benefit-
cost evaluation of its survey instrument clearance process.
OMB might then recommend revisions in the Federal Reporting
Act and its own administration of it that will reduce these
high, unnecessary, unintended, and largely accidental costs
of a misapplied government regulation. Such revisions, if
developed with the assistance of leading survey researchers,
might then enjoy the full professional support of the research community the regulations do not now obtain.

The most obvious specific revisions that would decrease
costs to all involved (including OMB) and increase research
quality would be:
  - the <u>consolidation of the too many redundant levels of
    review</u> to <u>one</u> at each department, whose effective
    operation could be audited by OMB with a time-saving
    sampling of inputs and outputs;

  - elimination of instrument completion time constraints
    and total respondent effort time limits;

  - the <u>expansion of the maximum pilot survey sample
    exempt from clearance</u> from 9 to 100;

  - the exclusion from review of all low-burden surveys
    (those that could demonstrate their <u>net</u> burden)
    (burden minus benefit) was less than 10 person years
    a year.

References Cited

Campbell, Donald, and Julian Stanley
  1960 Experimental and Quasi-Experimental Designs.
     Chicago: Rand McNally.

On Solutions to Some Privacy Problems Engendered by Federal Regulation and Social Custom

10

Robert F. Boruch and Joseph S. Cecil

Introduction

Our concern here lies with one class of problems: sustaining the privacy of individuals who must provide information to a social scientist, and assuring confidentiality of the information which they provide. Most often, the problems emerge as a conflict between privacy regulation, governmental or otherwise, and the scientist's need for high quality information. We restrict our attention further to social research, notably on the effectiveness of new social programs, rather than medical or technological investigations.

The paper sketches statistical, procedural, and empirical methods for resolving conflicts between regulation and research interests. The approaches have been developed over the past ten years by methodologists in North America and Europe, engaged in research on topics ranging from child abuse to voting behavior. We stress these approaches rather than legislative or judicial ones partly to reiterate the idea that new law and new regulation are not necessarily the best vehicle, certainly not the most accessible, for resolving privacy conflicts. We stress concrete solutions, rather than abstraction and complaint partly because scholarly work on the latter is already embarrassingly abundant. Our examination is brief because these solutions, as well as legal and managerial ones, their application, and their vulnerability, are discussed in relentless detail by Boruch

Background research for this paper was supported by National Science Foundation Grant No. APR-77-00349 and National Institute of Education Contract NIE-C-74-0115. A modified version of the paper, adapting other material from Boruch and Cecil (1978) was presented at the 1977 Annual Meeting of the American Bar Association.

and Cecil (1978); we've adapted some material from the
monograph.

A few readers may be unfamiliar with social experiments
which have been undertaken and their bearing on privacy. To
illustrate briefly, consider the Negative Income Tax Experiment which has run six years at a cost in excess of $13
million. It was designed to discover how alternative levels
of income subsidies affect employment, expenditures, and other
characteristics of subsidy recipients. Despite the confidentiality assurances made to research participants, a Senate
subcommittee and grand jury appropriated the research records
on identifiable respondents and used them for nonresearch
purposes. The Housing Allowance Experiments were designed
to run about 10 years and at a cost of about $280 million.
They were mounted to obtain better estimates of the impact of
alternative levels of housing subsidy on supply of good
housing and the demand for it. The experiment involved a
rather complicated disagreement between the researchers, who
had assured participants of the confidentiality of their
responses, and the U.S. General Accounting Office, which
sought to access research records on identifiable respondents
in order to assay the quality of sampling and record construction. Finally, the U.S. Census Bureau has mounted some
large scale trials to determine how different levels of
confidentiality assurance affect cooperation rate in surveys.
It's still not clear that the experiment itself was legal,
since Title 13 of the U.S. Code dictates exactly what level
of confidentiality applies to every Census record.

A Problem Elaborated

Consider research which is mounted to understand the
incidence of child abuse and to evaluate programs which are
designed to alleviate the problem. To establish incidence,
one might consider asking parents, their children, and perhaps others about corporal punishment in general and abuse
in particular. We'd need to identify parents in such a survey to permit long term follow-up study. It's obviously not
enough to know about abuse at one point in time; it is important to understand how consistent behavior of this sort is
over time. The difficulties in such a study include:

> • Under current HEW regulations, institutional
>   review boards may regard the survey as putting
>   parents who respond candidly at risk. I am
>   required by law, for example, to testify about
>   their responses if I'm subpoenaed. I can
>   appeal to no statute which will prevent a court's
>   compelling me to testify.

- Under the Privacy Act, if the risk of forced
  disclosure is high, I would have to tell the
  individual that subpoena could be issued and
  that I might be compelled to disclose information. This is unlikely to encourage candor
  in response, and in fact is likely to dis-
  courage cooperation. More importantly, if the
  risk is indeed high, I might subordinate my
  responsibility for generating scientific knowledge to my responsibility to protect my
  respondents, i.e., abort the project.

- Under the Family Educational Rights and Privacy
  Act (FERPA), I <u>might</u> have to elicit parental
  consent to survey children and that may be
  difficult to obtain. Especially if the people
  who consistently punish their children decline
  to participate, out of embarrassment or fear,
  the sample will be biased. If biased sufficiently in pilot surveys, one might abort the
  main study.

- The research may require that records maintained by crisis intervention centers,
  hospitals, and so on be linked to the survey
  data on the same individuals. Federal regulations governing federally supported archives,
  state law, and institutional rule or custom may
  prevent disclosure of archive records to the
  researcher. In the absence of any tactic to
  accomplish linkage without breaching privacy
  rules, this component of the research might
  be dropped.

Each of these problems is arguable on legal grounds. For instance, in a civil action suit, a court may forego appropri-
ation of the researcher's data as in <u>Richardson of Rockford
vs. Pacific Gas and Electric</u>. Rather than argue the likelihood of these problems, for they have indeed occurred, or the
legal niceties, we discuss methods for resolving parts of
each problem. The methods examined here help to assure
privacy of the respondent in a way that's consistent with
law or social custom, and without badly degrading quality or
scope of research.

A Statistical Solution to One Problem

In the simplest case, we might capitalize on one of the
new statistical approaches for resolving one problem. Adapting from a recent study by Zdep and Rhodes (1977), we might
present each parent in the sample with two questions:

- Within the past three days, have you intentionally injured or hurt one of your children by
  striking them?

- Have you contributed to a charity or church
  within the past three months?

The parent is told <u>not</u> to respond directly but rather to roll
a die. He or she is instructed to respond to the first question if a <u>one</u> turns up on the die and to the second question
if a number other than <u>one</u> turns up. The interviewer is not
permitted to see the die roll, nor is the interviewer told
which question is being answered. <u>Only</u> a "Yes" or "No"
response is provided; no other information aside from identification of the respondent is obtained. An analogous set of
questions can be set up to elicit information from children
or relatives of the parents in the sample.

Given a large sample, given the total number of <u>Yes</u>
responses, and given an estimate from an independent sample
of the number of charitable contributions, it takes only high
school algebra to compute the true proportion of individuals
in the group who've intentionally struck their children.
<u>The estimate is reasonable provided, of course, that respon-</u>
<u>dents adhere to the instructions</u>. Some of you may be amused
at the latter qualification. But you haven't heard the
evidence yet, dear reader, and we'll get to that in a moment.

The procedure's benefits with respect to government
regulation are that it reduces "burden on respondents": at
least for the economist's rationale decision-maker, it's less
embarrassing to answer the question simply because the interviewer doesn't know which question is answered. It reduces
risks of social or legal actions: there is no way to determine exactly <u>which</u> question was answered. If children are
respondents, their punishment cannot be linked to a particular parent in any deterministic sense. One has a <u>Yes</u> or <u>No</u>
response, but one cannot know the state of the individual
from the response.

About 30 variations of the technique have been invented
since Warner (1965) proposed the original method. Some are
undergoing field tests which generally compare the incidence
of a sensitive trait obtained under a "randomized response"
method, against recorded data on the same trait (e.g., police
records), or against response to direct interview. The tests
are being conducted in:

- the United States on abortions, racist attitudes
  and behavior, child abuse, alcohol abuse, drug
  abuse, and sexual behavior;

- Sweden: on sexual behavior, alcohol abuse, welfare;

- Taiwan: on fertility control;

- Germany: on police behavior;

- Canada: on drug abuse and fertility control.

All the field tests show the randomized methods work in the crude sense of providing no less accurate information than do direct questions; yet they protect confidentiality a great deal more. In about half the cases, the methods elicit more candid response than direct questions (Boruch and Cecil, 1978). The Zdep and Rhodes (1977) experiments, for example, yielded estimates of the incidence of corporal punishment which are about three times higher, under the randomized response approach, than estimated incidence under more orthodox methods of inquiry.

The methods have some shortcomings of course. Large samples, for example, are generally required, making research more expensive; further, the methods do not always work to increase candor (they may induce suspicion) and so other protection devices may be warranted, e.g., statutory protection. They require more technical sophistication to implement, and consequently increase the cost and complexity of research. Finally, applying the methods involves a presumption that privacy must be protected, and the presumption may be unwarranted.

That these methods are not always appropriate is clear. Case studies of particular families, for example, are essential for adding literal flesh to the statistical bone; the methods are useless in protecting case study material. Statutory protection is likely to be essential for assuring that the latter cannot be appropriated by the courts, executive agencies, or legislative bodies for non-research purposes. The developers of these techniques include Warner (1965) in Canada, Dalenius (1974) in Sweden, Horvitz, Greenberg, and Abernathy (1975), and Ajit Tamhane (1977) in the United States, and Moors in Holland (see Boruch & Cecil (1978) for references and a description of field tests).

Another Type of Problem and a Procedural Solution

Consider next a situation in which the researcher must link records from his or her own research with those in a restricted access data archive. Suppose, for example, that the research objective is to determine which of three different strategies is best at encouraging people to report particular forms of abuse or corporal punishment to a research archive or crisis intervention center. The strategies one might test include: appeals to moral conscience, threats of social embarrassment; and threats of legal action. In the interest of mounting a fair test, one might assign 300 people to each encouragement condition, then look at the later reports to the archive in order to determine which appeal led to highest reporting. The experiment would require that archive records be linked with the researcher's records on the same individuals.

Typically, the archive would not permit direct disclosure of records to the outside researcher. Rather than access them directly, the researcher might instead employ a device used by Schwartz and Orleans (1967), in related experiments on encouraging more honest reporting of income to the Internal Revenue Service (the archive). In particular, the researcher makes up little clusters of individuals within each condition, and computes means or averages of characteristics of individuals within each cluster. The averages, and the identification of each individual in the cluster are sent to archive; the archive finds its records for each individual in a cluster, computes average reported incidence of abuse or corporal punishment by cluster, then links that information to the file sent to them by the researcher. Identification of individuals is stripped off the tape by the archive custodian and the data returned to the researcher for analysis. The product is a data set which links archive information and research information without breaching privacy rules governing each source.

One benefit of the technique is that it can be used with any archive which restricts access to data. It has been used, for example, with bank records, employment records, and school files to accommodate restrictions on each, yet still meet research needs. In the Schwartz and Orleans experiment on IRS records, for example, the investigators found that appeals to moral conscience worked best for low income groups, threats of legal sanction worked best for middle income groups, and threats of social embarrassment worked best for high income groups. The parallel experiment in reporting child abuse has not yet been undertaken.

The possible variations on each strategy are large. They are demonstrably useful in some but not all institutional settings and can meet the restrictions on access to individual records imposed by law or by interpreters of the law. Inventors of alternative approaches of this sort include Joseph Steinberg, Richard Schwartz, Donald Campbell and others (see Campbell, et al. (1977)). Variations and their vulnerability are reported by Boruch (1974) and applications in a variety of settings are reported by Boruch and Cecil (1978).

That such methods may be insufficient is also clear. Many regulations are formidable even for the good bureaucrat, and the archivist who simply does not understand the method or who interprets access rules naively may prevent their use. The methods are cumbersome and so may increase the costs of research. Further, the methods may be unnecessary: we know of no significant instance in which a legitimate researcher, when given access to proprietary records, has exploited the record at a cost to the individual on whom the record is kept. This latter problem can only be ameliorated by creating special provisions, in institutional rules governing record disclosure, which permit access to records for research purposes. Finally, it may be possible for the archivist or the researcher to deduce new information about specific individuals within cluster from strictly statistical data. So-called deductive disclosure is possible only under certain conditions which cannot always be verified. The procedures are also vulnerable to corruption by the fraudulent researcher.

Partial Solutions and Rigidly Interpreted Regulation

It's clear that even where formal restrictions are generally legitimate, their interpretation in the special case may be unnecessarily conservative. The same spirit of finding solutions to problems, reflected in our earlier remarks, can be employed in this instance. For example, in 1976 we elicited the names of researchers who received testimonial privilege under the Drug Abuse Act from the Drug Enforcement Administration. DEA refused to disclose the identities of the researchers on grounds that disclosure would violate their privacy. We then made an appeal and simultaneously asked for detailed information on the topic for which the researcher got the privilege and his or her home institution. The latter are customarily a matter of public information. By the time we got the identifiers (a year later) from DEA based on our appeal, we had already deduced the identification of 75% of the researchers, based on the information DEA supplied earlier on home institution research topic (Boruch and Cecil, 1978). The example illustrates three points. First, deductive disclosure is indeed possible and if an agency is uninformed about the problem, as DEA appears to have been, then privacy controls will be weak. Second, deductive disclosure can be a useful device to the legitimate researcher who must rely on multiple methods, rather than a single method, to achieve an end. Third, bureaucratic privacy control may be unwarranted: the conservative interpretation of privacy law, as in this instance, is persistent. We believe conservative, even stupid interpretation must be recognized for what it is, and where it's unwarranted, action must be taken to eliminate it or get around it.

Still Another Problem and Another Type of Solution

In 1976, the U.S. Congress considered changing the law governing confidentiality of Census Bureau records. A proposal was made to permit greater access to records on identifiable individuals, but the relevant committee took no action on it in view of testimony, asking that action be delayed until some pertinent research could be done, by the Director of the Census Bureau. The Bureau staff were concerned that a change in law on confidentiality of Census records would affect cooperation rate. In particular, staff believed it is plausible to expect refusal rate to increase if records were made public after 25 years, rather than 72 years as they are now. In the interest of obtaining a fair estimate of the effect of legislative change, Census mounted a randomized field test. In that experiment, five types of confidentiality assurance were used by interviewers prior to eliciting information from a sample of respondents:

1. Confidentiality of records assured forever;
2. Confidentiality of records assured for 75 years;
3. Confidentiality of records assured for 25 years;
4. No statement of confidentiality offered to the respondent;
5. Explicit statement that records would be available to other federal agencies.

Members of the national probability sample were randomly assigned to one of the five interview conditions. They were interviewed by regular census staff about conventional census topics, such as income, housing, and marital status. The interviewee was informed that response was voluntary and was read a statement about the pertinent confidentiality assurance.

The percent of sample members who consented to respond under each of the five conditions were:

Condition: 1   2   3   4   5

Response: .982 .981 .977 .973 .972

The conclusions we draw are:

(a) there is indeed a change in cooperation rate as a function of confidentiality assurance level.

(b) the change is small on a percentage basis, but
     moderate in terms of the number of people in
     the entire population who would refuse to co-
     operate.

(c) we cannot generalize the result immediately to
     a future survey in which, say, privacy is more
     salient to respondents, interviewers are less
     competent, or topics of inquiry are more
     intrusive.

After the interview, people were asked to recall exactly
what type of confidentiality promise was made. The general
recall rates are generally high, 80% or so, but many people,
40% or so, simply did not recall all important details, e.g.,
the duration of the confidentiality assurance. If we estimate the proportion who both recall all specific details of
the assurance and who cooperate by responding, we dramatize
the evidence of the link between cooperativeness and confidentiality assurance.

Condition: 1   2   3   4   5

Response & Recall: .76   .64   .67   .15   .30

This seems to imply that to the extent people really assimiil-
ate the statement of confidentiality, the more likely it is
that they'll cooperate with a positive assurance and fail to
cooperate with a negative or absent promise. We use the
cowardly phrase "seems to imply" since the overall response
rates are astonishingly high--the Swedes don't achieve that
level in their regular population censuses. And the high
response rate, governed primarily by appearance, auspices,
and training of the interviewer, and probably by respondents'
trust in the process, swamps the influence of information.

Singer's work, described in Chapter 11 of this volume
and in Singer (1978a, 1978b) is different from, but related
to, the Census experiments. A weak effect of confidentiality
assurances is also evident in her experiments. Recognizing
how well the respondent is informed doesn't appear to affect
the results much.

Concluding Remarks

Privacy problems are diversified and they demand diverse
solutions. Here, we've sketched some approaches to clarifying various problems and achieving at least a partial
solution:

• Statistical strategies, useful in large scale
  surveys;

182 Boruch and Cecil

- Procedural strategies, useful in linking records from different archives, in experimental or survey research;

- Empirical approaches, including field tests to anticipate the impact of privacy law or new regulation on the quality of research data.

There are at least four implications to all this. First, we need not rely exclusively on law or public trust in the social scientist to resolve conflicts between privacy regulations and the scientist's need for information. We can develop alternative approaches to resolving them. Second, these approaches, however useful, are not always appropriate or sufficient. It is imperative that law itself be employed to minimize or eliminate conflict in these instances. This may include, for example, the development of statutory privilege for social researchers engaged in research not currently covered by legal protection. It should also include provisions, in law and institutional rule, to permit disclosure of archived records for research purposes, when the risk to the individual on whom records are kept is clearly negligible and where procedural devices for access are clearly inappropriate. The third message is simpler: it is to remind the law maker and interpreter of law that researchers are indeed toiling at invention of their own solutions to problems engendered by research and by federal regulation of research.

Finally, we ought to recognize that a sizeable state of the art has developed in this area, despite the orthodox social science community's tedious lack of interest prior to the 1970's. It's emerged with increasing sophistication in the 1970 Conferences on Conflicts between Law and Social Research, sponsored by West Germany (Nejelski, 1976), in more recent Swedish Conferences on Personal Integrity and Data Protection Research (Dalenius and Klevmarken, 1976), and still more recently in the efforts of the Social Science Research Council in the United States (Riecken, et al. 1974). The construction of multiple solutions to other ethical and legal problems in social research is also rigorous (Boruch, Cecil, Ross, 1978). This suggests emergence of a new subdiscipline in research methods and research law, a subsequent growth in treatment of the topic in university education, and ultimately a coherent theory and set of practices for eliminating unnecessary conflicts and resolving the necessary ones.

References

Boruch, Robert F.
  1972 Strategies for eliciting and merging confidential
     social research data. Policy Sciences, 3: 275-297.

Boruch, Robert F. and Cecil, Joseph S.
  1978 Assuring Privacy and Confidentiality in Social
     Research. Philadelphia: University of Pennsylvania.

Boruch, Robert F., Cecil, Joseph S., and Ross, Jerry (Eds.)
  1978 Proceedings of a Conference on Solutions to
     Ethical and Legal Problems in Social Research, Evanston,
     Illinois: Psychology Department, Northwestern Univer-
     sity.

Campbell, Donald T., Boruch, Robert F., Schwartz, Richard D.,
and Steinberg, Joseph
  1977 Confidentiality preserving modes of access to files
     and to interfile exchange for useful statistical
     analysis. Evaluation Quarterly, 1: 269-299.

Dalenius, Tore
  1974 The invasion of privacy problem and statistics
     production: An overview. Satryck ur Statistitisk
     Tidskrift, 3: 213-225.

Dalenius, Tore and Klevmarken, Anders
  1976 Privacy Protection and the Need for Data in the
     Social Sciences. Stockholm: Swedish Council for
     Social Science Research.

Horvitz, Daniel G., Greenberg, Bernard G., and Abernathy,
James R.
  1975 Recent developments in randomized response designs.
     Pp. 271-286 in A Survey of Statistical Design and
     Linear Models. J. N. Srivastava (Ed.) Amsterdam:
     North-Holland.

Nejelski, Paul (Ed.)
  1976 Research in Conflict with Law and Ethics.
     Cambridge: Ballinger.

Riecken, Henry W. and others.
  1974 Social Experimentation. New York: Academic.

Schwartz, Richard D. and Orleans, S.
  1967 On legal sanctions. University of Chicago Law
     Review, 34: 274-300.

Singer, Eleanor
   1978(a) Informed consent: Consequences for response rate
   and response quality in social surveys. American
   Sociological Review, 43: 144-162.

Singer, Eleanor
   1978(b) Informed consent procedures: Some reasons for
   minimal effects on response. Presented at the Northwestern University Conference on Solutions to Ethical
   and Legal Problems in Social Research, Washington, D.C.,
   February 27-29.

Social Science Research Council, Committee on Evaluation
Research
   1978 Report of the Committee. New York: SSRC.

Tamhane, Ajit C.
   1977 A randomized response technique for investigating
   several sensitive attributes. Proceedings of the
   American Statistical Association: Social Statistics
   Section. Washington, D.C.: ASA, Pp. 273-278.

Warner, Stanley L.
   1965 Randomized response: A survey technique for eliminating evasive answer bias. Journal of the American
   Statistical Association, 60: 63-69.

Zdep, S. M. and Rhodes, I. N.
   1977 Making the randomized response technique work.
   Public Opinion Quarterly, 41: 531-537.

Informed Consent Procedures in Surveys

Some Reasons for Minimal Effects on Response

Eleanor Singer

11

Introduction

It is generally accepted that the best, if not the only, way to obtain accurate information about the consequences of some hypothesized cause is by means of a randomized experiment. For certain categories of causes--e.g., social programs with social consequences--it is sometimes claimed that experiments in situ, otherwise known as field trials, are preferable to experiments carried out in the laboratory. In the first place, it is impossible to simulate the complexity of the real world in the laboratory; and second, the artificiality of the laboratory setting may create its own spurious effects (e.g., Miller 1972).

In 1976, I carried out such a field experiment to determine the effects of informed consent procedures on response rate and response quality in social surveys (Singer 1978a, 1978b). The experiment was on a large scale, using as its subjects a probability sample of the adult noninstitutionalized population of the continental United States. The factors were complex, manipulated by means of a classic factorial experimental design, unobtrusively administered as part of a routine survey.

Nevertheless, with one exception, the experimental variables produced findings that were for the most part unimpressive, indicating little effect on response of the procedures used to secure informed consent.

This situation is not uncommon. The question is, why does it occur? One possibility, of course, is that the hypothesized causal variables really make no difference, and that the minimal effects observed are correctly estimated. Another possibility, however, is that conditions in the field attenuate "true" effects, so that the experimental outcomes

misrepresent reality. This suspicion is especially likely to
arise if findings initially demonstrated in the laboratory
fail to be supported in the field, and Boruch and Gomez
(1977) have recently proposed what they call "a small theory"
to account for such attenuation. Their theory permits one to
estimate the decline in power of a field trial as a function
of (1) an imperfect fit between "response" as conceptualized
and as measured, and (2) an imperfect fit between "treatment"
as intended and as experienced. They list some reasons for
what they refer to as the degradation of the treatment variable, and advise evaluators, among other things, to measure
programs as implemented and received as well as intended.[1]

Fortunately, such information is available for the
informed consent study mentioned above. Two sorts of sup-
plementary measures were built into the research design.
First, respondents' perceptions of what the interviewer had
said were obtained. And second, several mechanisms, or intervening variables, were conceptualized by which the experimental variables could affect response, and measures of
these were incorporated into the design as well.

One purpose of the present paper is to use these supple-
mentary measures to elucidate treatment effects. That is, if
we look only at respondents for whom the experimental treatments work as intended, do we get the effects we predict? A
related purpose is to examine the implications of this procedure for informed consent in particular and the use of
field trials in general.

I begin by briefly describing the design of the informed consent study and the major findings. Then, I report
on an "internal analysis" of two of the three experimental
variables, in order to see whether such an analysis leads to
conclusions different from those based on the experimental
treatments themselves. Finally, I turn to the implications
of both sets of analysis.

The Informed Consent Study: Design and Major Findings

The study I am about to describe, funded by a grant
from the National Science Foundation and carried out under
the auspices of the National Opinion Research Center, was
designed to investigate the effects of three factors that,
together, may be said to constitute "informed consent" procedures in social surveys.

The first of these factors was the amount of information
initially given to respondents about the content of the

interview. Half the respondents were given a brief, vague
description of the survey as a study of leisure time and the
way people are feeling. The other half were given a fuller
description of the interview, which contained a large number of questions generally considered sensitive: e.g., questions about drinking, marijuana use, sex, and income.

The second factor that was experimentally varied was the
assurance of confidentiality given to respondents. One third
of the respondents were told nothing about the confidentiality of their replies; one third were given an absolute
assurance of confidentiality; and one third were given a
qualified assurance of confidentiality.

The final factor varied in the study was whether or not
a signature was required to document consent, and, if so,
whether the request for a signature came before or after the
interview.

Aside from these three factors, which can also be
thought of as representing different levels of risk, or
cost, to respondents, certain elements of the introduction
to the interview were kept constant. All respondents were
told that the study was being done by the National Opinion
Research Center; that the interview would take about half an
hour, and that they would then be asked to fill out a short,
self-administered form; that participation was voluntary and
that they could refuse questions within the interview. Every
introduction also included a plea for honesty of response if
the person decided to participate.

The three factors described above were combined in a
2 x 3 x 3 factorial design, superimposed on a national probability sample of 2084, drawn within 50 primary sampling
units of NORC's master sample.

The interview schedule was substantially the same as
that used a year earlier by Sudman and Bradburn in a study
of the effects of question threat and question wording on
response (Blair et al. 1977; Bradburn et al. 1978; Sudman
et al. 1977). Following some questions about conventional
leisure activities were sections dealing with emotional well-
being and mental health, drinking, marijuana use, and sexual
behavior. A number of demographic items, among them income,
were also included.

Also measured in the study were respondents' reactions
to the interview, ascertained by means of a self-administered
questionnaire filled out immediately following the interview
and handed to the interviewer in a sealed envelope (Singer

1978c), and interviewers' expectations about and reactions to
the study, assessed just prior to and after the completion of
field work (Singer and Kohnke-Aguirre 1978). After all interviewing had been completed, each respondent was sent a
letter thanking him or her for participating, explaining that
the study had had a methodological as well as a substantive
purpose, and briefly describing that purpose.[2]

With one exception, only experienced NORC interviewers
--almost a third of whom had worked on the Sudman-Bradburn
study a year earlier--were used on the survey. They were
trained in the special experimental procedures for the study
through a combination of written materials, group telephone
briefings by area supervisors, and specially developed training exercises that had to be completed before interviewing
could begin. Interviews were edited in the New York office,
and 20 percent of each interviewer's cases were validated by
means of telephone interviews.

Interviewers were told about the methodological purposes
of the study but not about any specific hypotheses, and were
urged to keep an open mind about the effects of the experimental variables. Those who felt seriously uncomfortable
with either the substantive or the methodological aspects of
the study were asked not to take on this particular assignment; about five withdrew for this reason.

The primary purpose of the study was to investigate the
effect of each of the three experimental variables on three
different types of outcome: over-all response rate to the
survey, response rates to individual questions, and response
quality. Major findings, which are reported in detail in
Singer (1978a), can be summarized as follows:

1. The over-all response rate to the survey was 67 percent; of the three variables investigated, only the request
for a signature had a significant effect on the probability
of responding. The response rate was seventy-one percent
for those not asked for a signature, compared with 64 and
65 percent for those asked to sign before and those asked to
sign afterwards. Even so, it should be noted that refusals
were limited to the signature itself. Only a handful of respondents actually refused to be interviewed; the rest agreed
to the interview but refused to sign the consent form, or
signed after the interview rather than before.

2. Only the assurance of confidentiality had a significant effect on item nonresponse. Despite the sensitive
nature of the interview, nonresponse to individual questions
was very low. On those questions to which the nonresponse

rate totaled more than 3 percent--all of them questions about behavior rather than attitudes--respondents given an assurance of absolute confidentiality had lower nonreponse rates than those in the other two experimental groups, in some cases by a statistically significant margin.

3. None of the three independent variables had either consistent or large effects on the quality of response. However, there are suggestions in the data that asking for a signature before the interview has a sensitization effect, so that better data are obtained if the respondent is asked to sign a consent form afterwards rather than before.

Except for the request for a signature, the experimental variables appear to have had little effect. As noted earlier, such an outcome is not uncommon in field experiments.[3] The question is, why does it occur? Are there really strong effects of the experimental variables which we are somehow failing to measure, or are the weak effects which we measure, real?

One way to get at this problem is to conceptualize the processes by which the experimental treatments are supposed to bring about results, and to measure (a) the relationship between the experimental treatments and the hypothesized processes, and (b) the relationship between the processes and the predicted results.[4]

In the informed consent study, two such sets of processes were conceptualized and measured. One set linked variations in prior information about the content of the study to response patterns; the other did the same for variations in the assurance of confidentiality given to respondents. The analysis is based on responses to the self-administered questionnaire, completed immediately following the main interview.[5]

The Effect of Variations in Information about Content

We had predicted that giving respondents more information about the details of the interview should heighten the salience of the topics mentioned in the introduction, and that increased salience should result in responses of better quality among those who decided to participate. The data supported our prediction concerning the behavior of the intervening variable. People who were given more information ahead of time were more likely to anticipate questions about the various topics mentioned in the introduction (Table 1), and those who anticipated[6] such questions--i.e., those for

Table 1: Expectations about Content by Amount of Information Received Ahead of Time

Topic	Long Introduction % Expecting Questions	Short Introduction % Expecting Questions	Significance[b]
Sports activities	81% (610)[a]	73% (596)	< .01
Gambling with friends	28	24	n.s.
Drinking beer, wine, or liquor	66	47	< .01
Getting drunk	41	29	< .01
Using marijuana	46	32	< .01
Sexual intercourse	51	24	< .01
Masturbation	16	10	< .01
Mental health	58	49	< .01
Education	79	76	n.s.
Income	71	70	n.s.
Religion	70	70	n.s.

[a]Percentages are based on all those who filled out the self-administered questionnaire, scoring one point for each "expected" and zero for all other answers (including no, don't know, and no answer). If the last two categories are excluded, so that percentages are based only on those who said either that they expected the question or else that they did not, the percentage expecting increases for both groups and each question, but the pattern of expectations does not change.

[b]Based on chi-square.

Table 2: Percent Nonresponse,[a] by Whether or Not Respondent Expected Questions About Topic[b]

Question	Percent Nonresponse			Significance[c]
	Expected	Did Not Expect	Don't Know or No Answer	
1. Ever smoked marijuana 3 times a week	8%(154)	7%(135)	6%(17)	n.s.
2. No. of pipes, joints smoked	5 (154)	6 (135)	12 (17)	n.s.
3. Intercourse during past month	5 (453)	10 (627)	12 (126)	p < .01
4. Frequency of intercourse	5 (339)	13 (382)	17 (58)	p < .01
5. Intercourse in last day	2 (339)	6 (382)	7 (58)	p < .05
6. Masturbated in past month	6 (160)	9 (892)	14 (154)	p = .05
7. Frequency of masturbation	7 (15)	9 (68)	0 (8)	n.s.
8. Masturbated in last day	7 (15)	6 (68)	0 (8)	n.s.
9. Amount of earned income	7 (851)	14 (246)	15 (109)	p < .01

[a]"Nonresponse" includes don't know, refused, and not asked.

[b]All topics asked about on the self-administered form to which the nonresponse rate on the main interview totaled more than 3 percent are included in this table.

[c]Significance levels are based on chi-square.

Table 3

Responses to Selected Questions[a], by Respondent's
Expectation of Question Topic

Question	Eta/ Partial Beta	Responses (Mean Scores)[b]			Significance[c]
		Expected	Did Not Expect	Don't Know or No Answer	
1. Probability of walking in past month	.06/.05	.58(928)	.49(178)	.53(100)	n.s.
2. Probability of watching sports event in past month	.06/.04	.20(928)	.14(178)	.17(100)	n.s.
3. Probability of bowling in past year	.07/.02	.32(928)	.27(178)	.20(100)	n.s.
4. Gambling Scale score	.11/.07	1.14(313)	.85(746)	.80(142)	p(F) < .01
5. Probability of drinking liquor	.21/.14	.91(677)	.76(408)	.73(121)	p(F) < .01
6. No. of 3 closest friends drunk in past year	.15/.04	1.16(413)	.87(629)	.59(141)	p(F) < .01
7. Probability of smoking marijuana	.15/.06	.33(468)	.22(606)	.13(132)	p(F) < .01
8. No. of 3 closest friends who smoke	.15/.06	.86(461)	.55(598)	.44(129)	p(F) < .01

9. Probability of intercourse in past month	.19/.09	.75(453)	.61(627)	.46(126)	$p(F) < .01$
10. Probability of masturbating in past month	.04/.05	.10(160)	.08(892)	.06(154)	n.s.
11. Positive Affect	.05/.07	13.68(647)	13.98(429)	13.88(130)	$p(F) < .05$
12. Negative Affect	.02/.04	9.96(647)	9.90(429)	10.16(130)	n.s.
13. Langner Scale	.07/.07	3.28(645)	3.01(429)	3.71(128)	n.s.
14. Years of school	.18/.06	12.34(933)	12.26(158)	10.72(114)	$p(F) < .05$
15. Income[d]	.11/.02	8.07(791)	7.69(211)	6.38(93)	n.s.

[a]Table 3 includes virtually all questions asked of the total sample about the morethreatening of the 11 topics included on the self-administered form but, for economy, only a sampling of items on sports, drinking, and mental health.

[b]Based on unadjusted deviations. Deviations adjusted for the other independent variables (social desirability, upset, importance of truthtelling, and certainty of confidentiality) and for the covariates of sex, education, and age are usually, but not always, smaller than those shown here, the reduction being due about equally to the independents and the covariates.

[c]Significance levels are based on an F-test among the means, adjusted for the effect of the other independent variables.

[d]The analysis here is based on numbered response categories rather than dollar amounts. "8" corresponds to an earned income of $7,500—8,900; "5", to an earned income of $4,000—4,999.

Table 4

Percent Somewhat or Very Embarrased, by Different
Question Topics and Amount of Prior Information
about Content

Question Topic	Percent Very or Somewhat Upset	
	Long Introduction	Short Introduction
Sports activities	1.2%	2.1%
Gambling with friends	4.5	6.2
Drinking beer, wine, or liquor	6.6	8.1
Getting drunk	13.5	19.2
Using marijuana	14.3	18.7
Sexual intercourse	42.2	50.1
Masturbation	47.8	53.1
Mental health	8.0	10.3
Education	2.1	3.6
Income	13.3	14.4
Religion	2.6	3.1

whom the questions were more salient--had a lower rate of item nonresponse (Table 2). They also tended to give responses of better quality[7] to sensitive questions (Table 3).[8] Expectations significantly affected responses to 8 of the 15 questions shown in Table 3, and on all but one of the 15, those who expected the question were more likely to acknowledge the behavior, even though most of the behaviors can be construed as sensitive.[9]

But all of these relationships were modest. Only half of the respondents in the "informed" condition, for example, expected questions about sexual intercourse, even though they had been told explicitly to expect them, and as many as a quarter of the respondents in the "uninformed" condition expected such questions as well. In consequence, differences in response between information conditions (i.e., the experimental treatment as intended) are less clear-cut than differences between expectation conditions (i.e., the experimental treatment as perceived).

We had also predicted that giving respondents more information about the content of the interview ahead of time would result in less upset or embarrassment at sensitive questions, and that this, too, would enhance the quality of response.

Again, predictions concerning the relationship of advance information to self-reported upset or embarrassment were supported (Table 4),[10] as were those concerning the relationship of upset to item nonresponse (Table 5). But, as with salience, differences in reported upset between information conditions were not large, and since very few respondents claimed to have been upset, the effect on response tendencies between experimental conditions is very small. Furthermore, the relationship of upset to response quality is complex. On the most sensitive questions in the interview schedule, both those respondents who were very upset, and those who were not at all upset, tended to acknowledge less of the behavior asked about than respondents experiencing an intermediate degree of threat (data not shown; cf. Bradburn et al. 1978; Singer 1978b: ch. 7).

For these and perhaps other reasons, we found no significant or consistent differences in item nonresponse rates or response quality by information condition. In large part, this appears to be true because of the modest relationships between the experimental treatment and the hypothesized intervening variables of salience and upset. In the concluding section, we return to the question of whether or not such modest relationships are to be regarded as "attenuated."

Table 5: Percent Nonresponse[a], by Self-Reported Upset with Question Topic[b]

| Question | Not Upset | Percent Nonresponse | | | Significance[c] |
		Somewhat Upset	Very Upset	Don't Know, No Answer	
Ever smoked marijuana 3 times per week	9%(213)	4%(70)	8%(13)	0%(10)	n.s.
No. of pipes, joints smoked	7 (213)	4 (70)	0 (13)	0 (10)	n.s.
Intercourse during past month	3 (612)	7 (403)	25 (119)	31 (72)	p < .01
Frequency of intercourse	5 (404)	11 (290)	30 (61)	25 (24)	p < .01
Intercourse in last day	2 (404)	6 (290)	15 (61)	4 (24)	p < .01
Masturbated in past month	5 (553)	6 (371)	22 (191)	28 (91)	p < .01
Frequency of masturbation	3 (34)	8 (40)	13 (15)	50 (2)	p < .10
Masturbated in last day	0 (34)	8 (40)	7 (15)	50 (2)	p < .05
Amount of earned income	6 (972)	15 (109)	43 (47)	21 (78)	p < .01

[a]"Nonresponse" includes don't know, refused, and not asked.
[b]All topics asked about on the self-administered form to which the nonresponse rate on the main interview totaled more than 3 percent are included in this table.
[c]Significance levels are based on chi-square.

Table 6

Percentage of Respondents Reporting
Upset, by Expectation of Question Topic

Question Topic	Percent	Somewhat or Very Upset	Significance[a]
	Expected	Did Not Expect	
Sports activities	1.0% (904)	2.3% (172)	n.s.
Gambling with friends	2.6 (306)	6.7 (726)	p < .05
Drinking beer, wine, or liquor	5.7 (662)	9.7 (391)	p < .05
Getting drunk	12.9 (411)	18.6 (628)	p < .05
Using marijuana	12.4 (453)	19.2 (588)	p < .01
Sexual intercourse	31.9 (439)	57.0 (607)	p < .01
Masturbation	24.3 (152)	56.8 (862)	p < .01
Mental health	6.3 (631)	13.4 (411)	p < .01
Education	2.1 (913)	5.3 (150)	p < .01
Income	10.7 (822)	23.0 (235)	p < .01

[a]Significance levels based on chi-square.

Table 7

Perception of Confidentiality, by Confidentiality Condition

Perception of Confidentiality	No Mention	Qualified	Absolute
No mention	20%	3%	6%
Confidential except as required by law	17	63	29
Results public, answers confidential	26	21	49
Don't remember	33	10	12
Other	4	3	4
Total	100% (403)	100% (397)	100% (404)

The Effect of Varying Assurances
of Confidentiality

Reviewing prior research on the effects of anonymity and confidentiality, Boruch and Cecil (1976) concluded that, for sensitive information, "strong" assurances of confidentiality (by which they mean technical, in addition to verbal, guarantees) improve response rate as well as quality. However, their review of the literature, as well as that by Singer (1978a), suggests that verbal assurances, and assurances attached to innocuous information, produce little difference in response. For example, variations in a verbal assurance of confidentiality had trivial effects on over-all response rates in a recent field experiment by Goldfield et al. (1977), and none in the present study. Item nonresponse rates, however, were consistently and sometimes significantly lower in the present study when respondents received an absolute verbal assurance of confidentiality, and such an assurance may have improved the quality of response to the most sensitive items on the questionnaire.

It was hypothesized that the effects associated with variations in the assurance of confidentiality might be weak for one or more of three reasons: respondents might not hear or understand what the interviewer had said about confidentiality; even if they heard, they might not believe; and even if they believed, they might not care. The hypotheses were tested by examining the effect of the experimental variations in confidentiality on these intervening variables, and the effect of the intervening variables on response.

In fact, we found that misunderstanding was widespread, but that correct understanding resulted in effects no stronger than misunderstanding did. As can be seen from Table 7, less than half of those given an absolute assurance of confidentiality correctly perceived the assurance they had been given,[11] and only 20 percent of those in the "no mention" condition correctly reported this fact after the interview.[12] However, the respondent's perception of the amount of confidentiality the interviewer had promised appears to have little effect on response (Table 8). Only with respect to income do these perceptions make a significant difference, and in only two of fifteen comparisons is the perception that one's answer will remain confidential associated with the highest estimates of the behavior or characteristic.

On the assumption that it might be the accurate perception of confidentiality which makes the difference, we examined the responses of those who both perceived that their answers would be held in confidence and were in fact given

Table 8

Cognitions Concerning Confidentiality, and
Responses to Selected Questions[a]

	Eta/ Partial Beta	Responses (Mean Scores)[b]					Significance[d]
		Answers Confidential (386)[c]	Answers Public (14)[c]	Confidential Except by Law (434)[c]	Interviewer Didn't Say (118)[c]	Doesn't Recall (223)[c]	
1. Probability of walking in past month	.03/.01	.56	.58	.54	.57	.58	n.s.
2. Probability of watching sports event in past month	.01/.02	.20	.17	.20	.19	.21	n.s.
3. Probability of bowling in past year	.05/.05	.28	.34	.32	.30	.34	n.s.
4. Gambling Scale score	.04/.05	.89	.50	.95	.93	.98	n.s.
5. Probability of drinking liquor	.06/.07	.85	.67	.86	.87	.83	n.s.
6. No. of 3 closest friends drunk in past year	.08/.06	.89	.67	.91	1.12	1.12	n.s.
7. Probability of smoking marijuana	.08/.04	.25	.25	.23	.30	.32	n.s.
8. No. of 3 closest friends who smoke	.08/.04	.62	.92	.62	.84	.80	n.s.

9. Probability of intercourse in past month	.06/.06	.67	.84	.65	.71	.62	n.s.
10. Probability of masturbating in past month	.05/.05	.10	.00	.08	.07	.07	n.s.
11. Positive Affect	.05/.05	13.82	14.75	13.88	13.47	13.74	n.s.
12. Negative Affect	.05/.03	10.01	10.09	9.73	9.85	10.06	n.s.
13. Langner Scale	.07/.08	3.29	2.42	2.93	3.16	3.48	n.s.
14. Years of school	.05/.06	12.27	11.50	12.50	12.47	12.12	n.s.
15. Income	.10/.10	8.17	6.09	8.10	8.03	7.20	$p(F) < .05$

[a] Questions are identical to those in Table 3.

[b] Based on unadjusted deviations. Deviations adjusted for the other independent variables (confidentiality condition, certainty of confidentiality, and worry about confidentiality) and for the covariates of age, sex, and education are usually, but not always, smaller than those shown here, changes being due in part to the other independent variables and in part to the covariates.

[c] N's shown are for all 1175 respondents who answered the self-administered form and the question about perceptions of confidentiality, and may vary somewhat from question to question because of nonresponse.

[d] Significance levels are based on an F-test among the means, adjusted for the effect of the other independent variables.

Table 9

Certainty of Confidentiality, by
Confidentiality Condition

Degree of Certainty	No Mention of Confidentiality	Qualified Confidentiality	Absolute Confidentiality	Total
1 (Not at all)	26%	21%	18%	22%
2	9	12	8	10
3	24	27	22	24
4	13	17	15	15
5 (Very)	24	22	35	27
D.K., N.A.	4	2	3	3
Total	100% (403)	101% (397)	101% (406)	101%(1206)

$X^2 = 31.11$ with 10 df; $p < .01$

an assurance of absolute confidentiality, and contrasted them
with those who accurately perceived that their responses
would be accorded lesser protection. However, this comparison provides no more evidence for the effect of cognitions
about confidentiality than the analysis immediately preceding.

We also found that some people believed the assurance of
confidentiality they had been given, whereas others did not.
Asked to indicate, on a five-point scale, how certain they
were that answers would remain confidential, some 27 percent
of the sample professed a great deal of certainty; at the
other extreme, 22 percent said they were "not sure at all"
(Table 9). Those who were assured of absolute confidentiality professed the highest level of certainty, but, although the difference among confidentiality conditions was
significant, in absolute terms it was not very large.[13] Less
than half a point on the five-point scale, or 11 percentage
points in Table 9, separates those who had been given an absolute assurance of confidentiality from those to whom the
matter had not been mentioned at all, suggesting that respondents either did not hear, or else did not believe, very
much of what the interviewer had told them about the confidentiality of their replies.

Turning now to the effects of certainty, we note that,
with one exception, item nonresponse rates of those who were
certain about the confidentiality of their answers are lower
than those of respondents who were not certain (Table 10).
Four of the comparisons reach statistical significance,
though the relationship is linear only for those items asked
of the total sample. This finding is consistent with the
conclusion drawn on the basis of the experimental treatments
themselves--namely, that an assurance of confidentiality has
a modest but consistent effect on response rates to sensitive
questions--but offers no stronger support for it. Differences between those who claimed to have been certain, and
those who said they were not, averaged 4.2 percentage points
on the nine questions with the highest nonresponse rates;
differences on the same nine questions between those given an
absolute assurance of confidentiality and the average of the
other two experimental groups averaged 4.3 percentage points.

The relationship between certainty and response quality
is more complex. On theoretical grounds, one might expect
those who are very certain of the confidentiality of their
replies to be more likely to acknowledge engaging in sensitive or threatening behavior than other respondents, and
those who are not at all certain of confidentiality to be
less likely to do so. Differences in response, by certainty

Table 10: Item[a] Nonresponse by Certainty of Confidentiality

| Question | Percent Nonresponse | | | | Significance[c] |
	Not Certain (1,2)	(3)	Certain (4,5)		
1. Ever smoked marijuana 3 times a week	9% (104)	7% (77)	7% (121)		n.s.
2. No. of pipes, joints smoked	4 (104)	8 (77)	6 (121)		n.s.
3. Intercourse during past month	11 (380)	7 (292)	6 (503)		p < .05
4. Frequency of intercourse	10 (229)	15 (200)	6 (338)		n.s.
5. Intercourse in last day	4 (229)	9 (200)	2 (338)		p < .01
6. Masturbated in past month	13 (380)	9 (292)	7 (503)		p < .05
7. Frequency of masturbation	11 (18)	4 (26)	9 (47)		n.s.
8. Masturbation in last day	11 (18)	0 (26)	6 (47)		n.s.
9. Amount of earned income	15 (380)	9 (292)	5 (503)		p < .01

[a]All topics asked about on the self-administered form to which the nonresponse rate on the main interview totaled more than 3 percent are included in this table.

[b]"Nonresponse" includes refused, don't know, and not asked.

[c]Significance levels are based on chi-square.

of confidentiality, are shown in Table 11. Differences are significant on six of the fifteen items: the probability of having gone bowling in the past year; of ever having smoked marijuana; the number of three close friends who smoke; the probability of having had intercourse during the past month; the number of years of schooling; and the amount of earned income. On all of these, however, both those who are very certain about confidentiality, and those who are not at all certain, give lower estimates than intermediate groups. This curvilinear pattern, which is not confined either to the most sensitive items or to those asked about behavior rather than attitudes, characterizes the responses to two-thirds of the items in Table 11, and suggests that, while skepticism about confidentiality may lead to underreporting, certainty is not necessarily associated with the reporting of high levels of sensitive behavior. Thus, the failure of variations in the assurance of confidentiality to affect the quality of response cannot be attributed to disbelief, any more than it can be attributed to misunderstanding.

Finally, we found that some people cared whether or not their answers remained confidential, whereas others did not. Asked to indicate, on a five-point scale, how much they would care whether anyone knew the answers they gave, 36 percent of the sample claimed they "would not care at all," but 21 percent said they "would care very much." The assurance of confidentiality given to respondents had no effect on the importance they attached to it.[14] But since the effects of importance resemble those reported for certainty, they provide no evidence for the hypothesis that if confidentiality had mattered more, the experimental treatments would have produced a stronger effect.

To summarize this section: It was hypothesized that the observed effects of confidentiality on item nonresponse rates and response quality might be weak for one or more of three reasons: people might not hear; they might not believe; or they might not care. Although it is true that relatively few people heard correctly, believed implicitly, or cared very much, the effects of confidentiality would have been no stronger had the numbers been larger. This is true for several reasons. First, there is no relation between correct perception and response. Second, the relationships between certainty and importance, on the one hand, and response quality, on the other, are not linear. Finally, the effects of certainty and importance on item nonresponse rates are no greater than those of the confidentiality conditions themselves--i.e., the treatments as perceived have effects no greater than the treatments as intended.

Table 11

Certainty of Confidentiality and Responses to Selected Questions[a]

Question	Responses (Mean Scores)[b]					Eta/Partial Beta	Significance[d]
	Not at all Certain (1) (N=262)[c]	(2) (N=118)[c]	(3) (N=292)[c]	(4) (N=178)[c]	Very Certain (5) (N=325)[c]		
1. Probability of walking in past month	.56	.56	.52	.63	.56	.07/.06	n.s.
2. Probability of watching sports event in past month	.21	.27	.16	.21	.20	.08/.07	n.s.
3. Probability of bowling in past year	.25	.39	.32	.34	.31	.09/.06	$p(F) < .05$
4. Gambling Scale score	.92	1.08	.93	1.00	.84	.06/.02	n.s.
5. Probability of drinking liquor	.82	.87	.86	.86	.85	.05/.04	n.s.
6. No. of 3 closest friends drunk in past year	.98	1.13	.98	.97	.86	.06/.06	n.s.
7. Probability of smoking marijuana last year	.24	.35	.27	.31	.21	.11/.01	$p(F) < .01$
8. No. of 3 closest friends who smoke	.66	1.00	.67	.78	.53	.12/.04	$p(F) < .01$

9. Probability of intercourse in past month	.59	.67	.69	.78	.62	.13/.09	$p(F) < .01$
10. Probability of masturbating in past month	.04	.07	.09	.10	.09	.08/.08	n.s.
11. Positive Affect Scale	14.01	13.64	13.45	13.84	13.98	.08/.09	n.s.
12. Negative Affect Scale	9.91	10.06	9.95	9.70	9.90	.03/.04	n.s.
13. Langner Scale	3.35	2.95	3.14	2.79	3.34	.07/.06	n.s.
14. No. of years of school	12.02	12.66	12.52	12.83	12.06	.09/.06	$p(F) < .05$
15. Amount of earned income	7.53	8.18	8.16	8.58	7.56	.10/.05	$p(F) < .05$

[a]Questions are identical to those in Table 3.

[b]Based on unadjusted deviations. Deviations adjusted for the other independent variables (confidentiality condition, perception of confidentiality, and worry about confidentiality) and for the covariates of age, sex, and education are usually smaller than those shown here, the reduction being due almost entirely to the effect of the covariates.

[c]N's shown are for all 1175 respondents who answered the self-administered form and the question about certainty of confidentiality, and may vary somewhat from question to question because of nonresponse.

[d]Significance levels are based on an F-test among the means, adjusted for the effect of the other independent variables.

Conclusions and Implications

In this concluding section, I would like to stress certain limitations on the findings derived from the informed consent study, and consider some more general issues in drawing inferences from field trials.

First, of course, there are the conventional caveats. All of the findings reported here concerning the effects of informed consent procedures derive from one kind of survey only. It is entirely possible that certain types of questions, asked of certain specialized categories of respondents, might interact with the independent variables to produce results other than those reported here. For example, if welfare clients were asked about their income, refusals under several of the experimental conditions might be higher than those in the present study; the same is true if we asked employees of a large corporation about their drinking habits.

Furthermore, although the study provides information about the effects of informing (or failing to inform) respondents about the content of the interview ahead of time, it says nothing about the effects of other kinds of deception. For example, respondents were not told about the survey's methodological purpose until after the completion of field work, and, ironically, the study could not have been carried out successfully without this deception. More research to specify the conditions under which responses are affected by disclosure, and those under which they are not, is clearly needed. Note, however, that any research designed to get at this question is bound to use deception in one or more experimental conditions.

Granted these limitations, what conclusions can be drawn from the findings? At least two sorts of questions can be addressed to the data that have been presented. First, since the introduction to the interview was designed to provide respondents with sufficient information on which to base a decision about participating, how adequately were they in fact informed? That is, how adequately were the ethical imperatives of informed consent met by the procedures employed? Second, which set of findings--those based on the experimental treatments, or those based on the internal analyses reported here--should be used in drawing inferences about the consequences of these procedures for survey research?

So far as alerting respondents to potential risks in the interview is concerned, the evidence presented is not very reassuring. Although people who were told to expect certain kinds of questions did in fact expect such questions more often than other respondents by absolute standards they were not especially well informed. Only two-thirds of those who had received the detailed introduction said they had expected questions about drinking alcoholic beverages, and only 50 percent expected to be asked about sexual intercourse, despite the explicit mention of these topics in the introduction to the interview.

Nor were respondents especially well informed about the degree of confidentiality their answers would be accorded. Overall, only 44 percent of the sample correctly heard or recalled what the interviewer had said about confidentiality. Thus, when we talk about the "effect of informed consent procedures" in this study, it ought to be clearly understood that many--perhaps most--of the respondents were not accurately informed with respect to at least some elements of the interview, and in that sense certainly cannot be said to have given their informed consent. This is true despite the fact that between 80 and 90 percent of those who completed the self-administered form claimed they had not found the introduction unclear or confusing in any way.[15] The only element of the introduction remembered correctly by the overwhelming majority--93 percent of those who completed the self-administered form--was the interviewer's statement concerning the voluntary nature of the interview.

These findings indicate a need for research to discover how best to inform respondents about the risks and benefits associated with their participation in research. Such a study is currently under way for informed consent in the medical field (Mellinger et al. 1976); it would clearly be useful for social research as well. The findings also raise questions about the extent of the researcher's responsibility for assuring that the information presented is in fact correctly understood. They also suggest that exclusive reliance on "informed consent" may be relatively ineffective in protecting the subjects of research against harm.

Aside from their ethical implications, however, what should one conclude about the effects of the procedures used in the present study? Is the attenuation of treatment effects which is observed in the field, in this study, and in others, to be "corrected for," like attenuated correlation coefficients, or is this attenuation an integral part of the phenomenon we are trying to appraise, so that it is the corrected estimate which is misleading?

The answer depends on one's purpose. If one is trying to demonstrate certain conceptual or theoretical linkages-- for example, if one is trying to establish the precise relationship between salience and accuracy of recall--then obviously one wants to refine these concepts as much as possible, stripping away all extraneous influences. Or, if one is trying to pinpoint the reasons for program failure, one would pay particular attention to the linkages among the concepts and mechanisms postulated by the theory underlying the program, and to the relationship between the program and those concepts. That is the message of the Boruch-Gomez paper (1977).

But that is not the situation we are dealing with here, or in many other field trials. So far as informed consent is concerned, it seems clear that there will always be a less than perfect fit between what is said and what is understood or believed, just as different procedures for informing subjects are bound to have different utility for subgroups varying in age, education, race, and perhaps other character-istics. The finding that the procedures used in the present study have little discernible net effect on response there-fore deserves to be treated as real, not as a mishap of measurement. Whether one regards it optimistically, conclud-ing that because effects are small, practical considerations do not conflict with ethical imperatives, or pessimistically, as indicating that even the procedures used in this survey fail to assure truly informed consent, is a separate question.

The same argument probably applies to most social pro-grams. In the real world, teachers lose motivation, children interrupt their television viewing to play with a friend, go to the bathroom, have a snack. Respondents trust interview-ers even in the face of a weak guarantee of confidentiality. For these and other reasons, the effects of social programs are attentuated in the field. This doesn't mean that the theories linking concept to concept, or proposition to propo-sition, are correct. It does mean that theories about effects in the real world will have to be much more complex, including many more variables, than theories about what happens in the laboratory. It also means that many simplified theories, translated into programs in the real world, will fail to produce effects. Often that is a misfortune; but sometimes, perhaps, it is, on the whole, a good thing.

Notes

[1]Such advice is by no means new in the evaluation literature. See, for example, Hyman, Wright and Hopkins (1962:
72-86), and Hyman and Wright (1967).

[2]This method was decided on in preference to personal
debriefing in order to keep interviewers from receiving
feedback that might affect their future performance.

[3]It has been pointed out, for example, with respect to
the "fairly substantial experimental evidence" linking television violence and subsequent aggression by children,
contrasted with the "much less certain evidence from field
studies." Cited from Television and Growing Up: The Impact
of Televised Violence, Report to the Surgeon General,
U.S.P.H.S., from the Surgeon General's Advisory Committee on
Television and Social Behavior, Washington, G.P.O., 1972,
by Bogart (1972:497).

[4]Such an analysis resembles what is sometimes referred
to as an internal analysis in social psychological experiments, in which the experimenter eliminates those subjects
for whom the treatment failed to have the intended effect.
For this purpose, social psychologists normally obtain
measures of treatment effectiveness, by which they mean not
whether it led to certain hypothesized consequences, but
simply whether it aroused the psychological condition hypothesized as the independent variable in the experiment
(Rommetveit and Israel 1954; Schachter 1954). Unless an
experimental manipulation succeeds in arousing anxiety, for
example, there is no use in expecting it to evoke affiliative
behavior (Schachter 1959).

[5]Of the 1321 respondents to the main interview, 1206, or
91 percent, completed the self-administered questionnaire.
Five percent refused, and the remainder claimed they could
not read or write well enough to perform the task. Those
respondents who had refused to sign the consent form (74 of
the 1321) were also more likely to refuse to fill out the
self-administered questionnaire (26 percent, versus about 3
percent for those who either signed or were not asked to sign;
chi-square = 83.75 with 6 df; $p < .01$). Respondents given an
absolute assurance of confidentiality, and those given a
qualified assurance, were equally likely to complete the self-
administered form (93% and 92%, respectively), whereas respondents to whom confidentiality was not mentioned at all were
less likely to do so (88%; chi-square = 9.82 with 4 df; $p < .05$).
Prior information about content had no measurable effect on
willingness to complete the self-administered questionnaire.

[6]Since "expectations" were ascertained after the interview itself, they are contaminated by its content. This con-
tamination should serve to reduce differences between respondents who heard the more detailed and the vaguer introduc-
tions, so that any differences we observe are a conservative
measure of effect.

[7]Previous research has indicated that for sensitive or
threatening questions, more reporting is better reporting.
For a citation of studies, see Blair et al. (1977).

[8]Accuracy with respect to expectations does not enhance
the quality of response. That is, those who accurately expect certain questions do not give better replies than those
who expect such questions in the absence of prior warning by
the interviewer. Putting it a different way, expectations
have a significant independent effect on response, but the
interaction between experimental condition and expectations
is not significant.

[9]The column headed "eta/partial beta" in Table 3 indicates that a substantial portion of the correlation between
expectations and reported behavior derives from the relationship of expectations to the three covariates of age, sex, and
education (i.e., is spurious) and to their intercorrelation
with four other independent variables controlled simultaneous-
ly--social desirability, upset at a particular question, concern with honesty, and concern with confidentiality. In general, about half the reduction in eta is accounted for by the
other independent variables, and half by the covariates.
The net effect of expectations is, thus, often considerably smaller than that shown in Table 3, but the effect is
nevertheless to elicit better data from respondents who expected a question than from those who did not. This is true
even though most of the questions concern sensitive behavior,
where one might suppose that respondents who are forewarned
would alter their replies in a socially desirable direction.

[10]This effect appears to be mediated by the role of expectations. As we have just seen, respondents who were given
the more detailed introduction were more likely to expect
questions about such sensitive topics as drinking and sex.
At the same time, those who said they expected questions about
a topic invariably reported having been less upset by the
questions (Table 6). For all topics except sports, differences in reported upset between those who did and those who
did not expect the questions are statistically significant,
and in some cases substantial: 11% vs. 23% upset by questions
about income, for example; 24% vs. 57% by questions on mastur-
bation; and 32% vs. 57% by questions on intercourse.

[11] The question was, "What did the interviewer say about who would find out the answers you gave in the interview?", with the following response alternatives provided: "The results would be made public but my answers would be confidential; the interview would be a matter of public record and anyone who wanted could find out the answers I gave; the research organization would try to keep my answers confidential except as required by law; the interviewer didn't say anything about this; I don't remember."

[12] Goldfield and his colleagues (1977) concluded, on the basis of questions asked after the interview, that most respondents had accurately understood what the interviewer had said to them about confidentiality. However, the probabilities of perfect understanding, conditional on response, vary from .76 for the condition in which the respondent was promised confidentiality forever, to .14 for the condition in which no mention was made of confidentiality at all.

[13] Of the five demographic variables we examined, only two--sex and race--proved to be significantly related to the respondent's certainty that confidentiality would be maintained. Men were more skeptical than women, and black respondents more skeptical than those of other races, most of whom were, of course, white.

[14] It is entirely possible, of course, that different survey topics would arouse greater levels of concern, and that under certain conditions the assurance of confidentiality might affect the concern expressed.

[15] Some 31% of respondents with less than four years of high school found the introduction unclear or confusing in some respect, compared with 19% of highschool graduates or those with some college and 16% of college graduates; and 19% of those with less than four years of highschool failed to answer the question. Similarly, as many as 35% of the oldest (66+) group had some trouble with the introduction, compared with 14% of the youngest (18-25). These findings have clear implications for attempts to ensure truly "informed" consent on the part of respondents, and raise practical as well as ethical questions about the extent of the researcher's responsibility to bring this about.

It would have been desirable to explore the reasons for the lack of understanding, perhaps by means of unstructured interviews with a sub-sample of respondents; but we did not do this.

Acknowledgments

The work reported here owes much to many people. I would like especially to thank James R. Murray and Martin R. Frankel for helping to design the experiment; Steven M. Cohen for advice in planning the analysis; Luane Kohnke-Aguirre for carrying it out; and Herbert H. Hyman for reading and commenting on an earlier draft of this manuscript. I would also like to express my appreciation for the grant from the National Science Foundation (No. Soc 75-22889) which made it possible to translate a proposal for research into a completed experiment. The study was carried out as a Visiting Senior Study Director at the National Opinion Research Center in New York.

An earlier version of this paper was presented at a National Science Foundation sponsored conference on Solutions to Ethical and Legal Problems in Social Research, held in Washington, D.C. February 23-25, 1978.

References Cited

Blair, E., et al.
  1977 How to Ask Questions about Drinking and Sex. Journal
     of Marketing Research 14:316-321.
Bogart, Leo
  1972 Warning: The Surgeon General Has Determined That TV
     Violence Is Moderately Dangerous to Your Child's Mental
     Health. Public Opinion Quarterly 36:491-521.
Boruch, Robert F., and Joseph S. Cecil
  1977 On the Need to Assure Confidentiality. Ch. 3 of
     Methods for Assuring Confidentiality of Social Research
     Data. Boston: Cambridge University Press.
Boruch, Robert F., and Hernando Gomez
  1977 Sensitivity, Bias, and Theory in Impact Evaluations.
     Professional Psychology, November, pp. 411-434.
Bradburn, N.M., et al.
  1978 Question Threat and Response Bias. Public Opinion
     Quarterly 42:221-234.
Goldfield, Edwin D., et al.
  1977 Privacy and Confidentiality as Factors in Survey
     Response. Paper presented at 1977 meeting of the Ameri-
     can Statistical Association.
Hyman, Herbert H., Charles R. Wright, and Terence K. Hopkins
  1962 Applications of Methods of Evaluation. Berkeley:
     University of California Press.
Hyman, Herbert H., and Charles R. Wright
  1967 Evaluating Social Action Programs. In Paul F. Lazars-
     feld, William H. Sewell, and Harold Wilensky, eds. The
     Uses of Sociology. New York: Basic Books 741-782.
Mellinger, Glen, et al.
  1976 Public Judgments about Ethical Issues in Research.
     Proposal submitted to the National Institute of Mental
     Health.
Miller, Arthur G., ed.
  1972 The Social Psychology of Psychological Research.
     New York: Free Press.
Rommetveit, Ragnar, and Joachim Israel
  1954 Notes on the Standardization of Experimental Manipula-
     tions and Measurements in Cross-National Research.
     Journal of Social Issues, No. 4, pp. 61-68.
Schachter, Stanley S.
  1954 Interpretative and Methodological Problems of Repli-
     cated Research. Journal of Social Issues, No. 4, 52-60.
  1959 The Psychology of Affiliation. Stanford: Stanford
     University Press.

Singer, Eleanor
  1978a Informed Consent: Consequences for Response Rate and
    Response Quality in Social Surveys. American Sociologi-
    cal Review 43:144-162.
  1978b Informed Consent: Consequences for Response Rate and
    Response Quality in Social Surveys. New York: National
    Opinion Research Center, xerox.
  1978c The Effect of Informed Consent Procedures on Respon-
    dents' Reactions to Surveys. Journal of Consumer Re-
    search, forthcoming.
Singer, Eleanor, and Luane Kohnke-Aguirre
  1978 Interviewer Expectation Effects: A Replication and
    Extension. Paper presented at the annual meeting of
    AAPOR, Roanoke, Va., June 3.
Sudman, Seymour, et al.
  1977 Modest Expectations: The Effects of Interviewers'
    Prior Expectations on Responses. Sociological Methods
    and Research 6:177-182.

Part IV

Epilogue

12

Case Study

An Undergraduate's Experience
with Human Subjects Review Committees

Lynne Kipnis

> While much has been written about the dangers of
> research for the participants, both in medical
> and social science research, there is almost no
> attention paid to the effects of different 'con-
> trol systems' on the creation of science. Parti-
> cipants will not be harmed if no research is
> conducted, but then there will be no empirically
> based scientific knowledge. If the creation of
> scientific knowledge is brought to a standstill
> by procedures designed to protect the subjects,
> is the problem solved? (Reynolds 1972:706)

As I approached my junior year in "Elite College," I
began to plan to do a senior honors thesis in the Department
of Psychology. Instead of completing the thesis, I spent
approximately one-and-a-half semesters trying to get my proposal through a variety of bureaucratic review committees,
including two "Human Subjects" Committees. In this endeavor,
I was repeatedly misguided about forms I should submit, when,
and to whom. When at last I got the final "go ahead," I did
not have sufficient time even to begin the actual testing of
my subjects, let alone conduct the project.

My proposed research project, "The Psycho-Social Impact
of Juvenile Diabetes Mellitus on Diabetic Children Between
the Ages of Five and Twelve," was to evaluate the attitudes
of juvenile diabetics towards their disease and its treatment,
as well as to evaluate their own view of the effect of diabetes on the usual events in their lives. Specific emphasis
was to be placed on these children's self-concepts, body-
images and behaviors. I was interested in testing the following hypothesis:

1. Children with diabetes would show a greater degree
of emotional and social disturbance in terms of their

self-concept than would children in the epileptic or
control group.
2.   Children with diabetes would show a greater
degree of emotional and social disturbance in terms
of their perception of body-image than would children in the epileptic or control group.
3.   Children with diabetes would show a greater
degree of maladaptive behavior than would children
in the epileptic or control group.

Although in all of the above it was hypothesized that
the diabetic child would show an increased degree of disturbance, it was my assumption that this degree of disturbance
would be closer in proximity to the epileptic population
(like diabetes, a chronic illness) as opposed to the control
population.   It was my hope that while the chronic illness
groups might present similar "clusters" of difficulties, that
certain problems would be specific to each of the two groups.

The rationale behind doing such a study rested on the
fairly wide consensus among professionals that there was a
relationship between juvenile diabetes mellitus and difficulties in child development.   It seemed reasonable to me that
the implications of this relationship were important in that
if one could establish definite problem areas that resulted
from having diabetes, one could then attempt to take preventa-
tive measures to help insure these children of relatively
normal psycho-social development.

Early in the Fall of 1976, I spoke to the Chairman of
the Department of Pediatrics at Metro Children's Hospital
about my proposed research.   He already knew of my interest
in the field of child development because I had been working
part-time as a research assistant in that department for four
years.   He assured me that the proposal was indeed a sound
one and that it was fine with him if I began the project.   I
explained that I planned to hold off beginning because I
hoped the project would be accepted as the topic of my senior
honors thesis.

In November 1976, I pre-registered in Psychology 489;
"Study for Honors."   It was listed in the course catalogue
as follows (see Form F):

Acceptance into the Honors program is based on a
superior performance as evidenced by the record of
the student in his undergraduate course work and the
written agreement (petition for permission to enroll)
of a member of the faculty of the department or other
approved supervisor to supervise an Honors project.

> The student must complete 6 units of Honors work
> (3 units of Psych. 489 and 3 units of Psych. 490),
> submit an acceptable project report and be recommend-
> ed by the department. Recommendation for cum laude,
> magna cum laude, or summa cum laude will be based on
> the evaluation of the project report and the student's
> overall performance as an undergraduate. Petition
> for permission to enroll is available in Room ___ .

Nobody ever questioned whether or not I "qualified" to register in this course, nor did I ask, since I already had a set idea concerning the project I wished to carry out. Instead of seeking permission, I simply asked my undergraduate advisor how I should go about petitioning for the course; I was told that all I needed to do was to pick up the proper forms (see Form A) in the Departmental Office and "find an advisor." I also asked him if he could specifically tell me what was expected of students in Psych 489 as opposed to Psych 490. Again, his response was brief and to the point, "You write a proposal, do your study, and then write it up." He added, "In theory you must also take oral exams, but in all the years I've sponsored students doing their senior thesis only one kid got stuck taking orals, because by the end of the year we're (faculty) all busy and nobody has the time." I feel it is important for me to mention that my undergraduate advisor's specialty was Child Psychology--the only child psychologist in the Department. Although my project was clinical in nature and involved children, he refused to sponsor me because 1) he didn't have enough time, and 2) he planned to take a semester sabbatical. He advised me to "make the rounds" of clinical professors and verbally propose my project to them until I could find a thesis sponsor and "get his or her signature"! So, I made appointments with five clinical professors; each told me they were too busy to sponsor my "original" research proposal, but they would sponsor me if I worked under them doing research they were interested in, or if I worked under one of their graduate students.

Frustrated, I made an appointment with the Chairman of the Psychology Department and explained that although all the professors I contacted felt my proposal to be of interest, none had the time to sponsor me, unless I did his or her research. He nodded a lot and said that he would check into it --I never did hear from him again.

During the next week a graduate student in the department told me that there was a new faculty member that I "might try." At this point I decided to commit the proposal to paper even though I was told that there was no reason to do so until someone accepted sponsorship.

222 *Lynne Kipnis*

After listening to my case, the new faculty member said that, since I obviously had the project well thought out, he would advise me as long as I recognized that (1) he had never "sponsored" a student before and therefore didn't know what a senior honors thesis entailed (I still didn't either), (2) child psychology was not his forte, (3) he knew little about measures of self-concept, body-image, and behavior disorders, and (4) he knew nothing about the psychology of chronic illnesses. His promise was to direct me, when necessary, to sources who could provide me with the information--assistance I might need. The fact that someone was willing to sponsor me at all was a tremendous relief.

During the Spring semester of 1977 I met with my thesis advisor every two weeks just to let him know what I was doing. I did a complete literature review (reviewed the literature on Juvenile Diabetes, Cystic Fibrosis, Epilepsy, Asthma and Kidney Disease), spoke with a variety of professionals (i.e. pediatricians, endocrinologists, child psychiatrists, child psychologists, pediatric neurologists, social workers, and dieticians) and wrote the final draft of my proposal. This was completed by the end of the semester (May). My thesis Advisor then suggested that instead of taking Psychology 490 "Study for Honors" the following semester (Fall 1977), I take a semester of Psychology 500, "Independent Study"--the idea being that I would need to get my proposal approved by the department and/or the Human Studies Committee (my advisor wasn't sure what the protocol was) and I could also use this time to select and test all of my subjects. This would allow me to analyze my data and write my thesis when I took Psych. 490 in the Spring of 1978. This sounded like a good idea to me and I enrolled for three credits of Independent Study (see Form B). Little did I know what problems I was about to face.

The first set of forms I had to fill out were the "Human Subjects Evaluation Form; Departmental Review of Nonfunded Activities." These forms were to be turned in in triplicate; since I always made a copy for myself and for my thesis advisor as well, I needed five copies of these forms (a total of 15 pages). I also had to draw up a consent form for my subjects to sign, and to answer specific questions regarding confidentiality of my data, as well as to write an "abridged proposal," since my thesis advisor stated that nobody in the department would need or want the type of detailed proposal I had submitted to him. I was told that this "screening" was conducted by members of the Psychology Department so that "inadequate" proposals could immediately be weeded out and "adequate" proposals could immediately be started. I submitted the forms to the departmental chairman on May 15, 1977 (Form C).

Approximately two weeks later I received a phone call from the departmental secretary telling me that there had been a "split" concerning the acceptance of my proposal and therefore it was rejected. She added that I was welcome to pick up copies of each reviewer's critique. The next day I learned that the two professors who reviewed my proposal were both Animal Behavioralists; the one who "accepted" made no comment on the form, the one who "rejected" wrote,

> The subjects, all victims of a chronic illness, will be interviewed about their attitudes toward the disease, a stressful topic, in a hospital, a stressful environment. I feel that this invites more than minimum risk (see Form C).

In coping with the critique and rejection, I found it terribly upsetting that animal behavioralists were reviewing a clinical psychology proposal and failing to examine its design. The fact was I did not plan to "interview" my subjects--they were to be administered standardized psychological tests and inventories that had nothing to do with whether a person had a chronic illness or not. Secondly, it was specified in my proposal that "the room reserved for the testing of subjects is not near any clinical section of the hospital."

I wanted to know how the two men who reviewed my proposal were chosen and why two clinical psychologists familiar with the measures I proposed to use had not been selected as reviewers. It turned out that the Departmental Secretary arbitrarily assigned reviewers to projects (whether submitted by undergraduates or by graduate students or faculty). In consequence, people who have no expertise in an area may be asked to pass judgment on exactly what they know little or nothing about.

My thesis advisor thought that, once he explained to the reviewer who had rejected my proposal what were the measures that I planned to use, he would "change his mind." Unfortunately, the reviewer had left the country for three weeks!

Next, my advisor contacted the Psychology Department's representative to the Human Studies Committee of the Arts and Sciences' faculty. She told him that she thought my proposal would pass with little or no difficulty. All I needed to do was make 13 copies of the form and the proposal (Form C) for the 13-member committee, and she would try to get it on the agenda "as soon as possible." This was done (a total of 130

xeroxed pages at 6¢/page). For about three weeks I was in
limbo, the Committee meeting was coming up and I had yet to
hear whether or not my proposal was on the agenda. At 3:00
p.m. on the afternoon of October 22, 1977, my thesis advisor
called me at home and told me that it was important that we
meet right away. When I arrived at his office, I was handed
a letter he had just received from the Vice-Chancellor for
Research (see Letter, Form D). He had called my thesis advisor earlier in the day to tell him that my proposal should
never have been sent to the Human Studies Committee of the
Arts and Sciences' faculty. Because it involved the Medical
School, it had to be sent to their Human Studies Committee.
If I wanted my proposal to be on the agenda of the next Medical School Human Subjects Committee meeting, a new set of
forms and another version of the proposal had to be at the
Medical School by 9:00 a.m. the next morning. Since it was
impossible for me to complete the Medical School forms in
less than 24 hours, the commencement of my project was again
postponed.

On October 25, I submitted the necessary forms, explanations, proposals, etc., to the Medical School Human Subjects
Committee (see Form E). (I needed the Chairman of the Psychology Department's signature on one of the Medical School
forms. When I found him and asked him to please sign on the
dotted line, he responded, "Are you sure this shouldn't go
through the Arts & Sciences Committee?")

On November 11, the School of Medicine's Human Studies
Committee approved my proposal without any questions. Nine
months had passed between my original discussion with the
Chairman of the Department of Pediatrics (who had unoffici-
ally approved the project) and its "official approval."

I again spoke with the Chairman of the Department of
Pediatrics at Metro Children's Hospital to give him copies of
all the approved forms and to let him know that I planned to
begin work in mid-December (Form E). The reason I postponed
beginning was that my final exams were coming up. My plan
was fine with him; however, he informed me that since we had
last spoken, Metro Hospital had established its own internal
committee in order to review research proposals such as mine,
and, although he thought it would be approved quickly and
without question, it was "policy" and I had to submit my proposal in triplicate to the hospital. I gave them the same
packet of information I gave Elite University's Medical
School Human Studies Committee and on December 5, I received
a letter (see letter Form G) giving the Hospital's approval.

   In mid-January, 1978, I began the job of going through
several hundred medical files--to which I now had "legal"
access--in order to select my subjects. Within three weeks
I realized that my thesis would be impossible to complete
during the semester. The time it would take for me to 1)
select subjects, 2) have the M.D. following the case notify
the family that I would be calling to ask them to participate
in a study, 3) call the families and ask them to participate,
and set up appointments, 4) "run the subject" (2 hour maximum per subject), 5) analyze data and finally 6) write the
thesis would require dropping all other courses as well as
my part-time job at Metro Children's Hospital. Therefore,
after presenting my case to an undergraduate Dean, Psych. 489
was dropped from my record in March.

   Aside from the frustration and anger I felt (and still
feel) about the entire process of trying to get approval for
what I still maintain to be a good research proposal, I am
now three credits short of the total number I need to graduate. In my case, it seems clear that the number of reviewing
committees set up to protect human subjects and to promote
research accomplished just the opposite--my research project
was not done and the fact that my findings may have helped
human subjects got lost somewhere among the pages of forms.

<u>Reference Cited</u>

Reynolds, Paul Davidson
   1972 On the Protection of Human Subjects and Social
       Science. International Social Science Journal 24:
       693-719

U N I V E R S I T Y

DEPARTMENT OF PSYCHOLOGY

RECOMMENDATION FOR ACCEPTANCE INTO HONORS PROGRAM
AND PERMISSION TO ENROLL IN PSYCHOLOGY 498

> Submit IN DUPLICATE to Miss

Mr.
Ms. _____, whose signature appears below,
has petitioned me to supervise his work in Psychology 498 (Study
for Honors) for 3 units of credit in the _____ of _____.
                                                      semester   academic year
He has satisfactorily completed Psychology 100 and 101. I have apprised
him that his acceptance into the Honors program is contingent on his
candidacy being acceptable to the Department and his successful completion of 3 units of Psychology 498 and 3 units of Psychology 499.
I accept his position.

         _____   _____
         signature, faculty member   date

         _____   _____
         signature, candidate   date

         _____   _____
         signature, Chairman of Department   date

> RECEIVED BY MISS
>
>   _____
>   date

                                    semester level for
                                    which this petition
                                    is submitted, e.g.,
                                    1st-semester senior,
                                    2nd-semester junior,
                                          etc.

FORM A

U N I V E R S I T Y

DEPARTMENT OF PSYCHOLOGY

PETITION FOR SUPERVISION OF INDEPENDENT STUDY

Submit IN DUPLICATE to Ms.

Mr.
Ms. _____, whose signature appears
below, has petitioned me to supervise his work in Psychology 500 (Independent Study) in the _____ of
                                       semester
_____ for _____ of credit. He
academic year   number of units
understands that Psychology 500 is an upper level course and
must have the prerequisite of satisfactory completion of
Psychology 100 and 101. I accept his petition.

_____   _____
signature, faculty member   date

_____   _____
signature, student   date

APPROVED: _____
                   Chairman of Department

RECEIVED BY MS.

_____
date

FORM B

HUMAN SUBJECTS EVALUATION FORM

Departmental Review of Nonfunded Activities

Name of Activity Director(s) Lynne Kipnis   Date: May, 15, 1977

Period Covered by this Sheet: 5/15/77 - 5/15/78   Supervisor: Dr.

Committee (List all faculty members connected with this project):

Title of Project: The Psycho-Social Impact Of Juvenile Diabetes Mellitus On Diabetic Children Between The Ages Of
Five and Twelve.

INFORMATION FORM FOR SOCIAL AND BEHAVIORAL ACTIVITIES USING HUMAN SUBJECTS

(To be completed by reviewer)

1. Has the activity director provided you with sufficient information to
    determine if subjects are at risk? Yes ✓   No ____
    (If no, return to activity director with your comments)

2. As defined in the Departmental Guidelines, does the activity involve
    subjects at risk? Yes ✓   No ____
    (If yes, review will continue with outside evaluation. Use University-
    wide FORM B available in Psychology Department Office)

FORM C-1

Comments (Use additional sheet if necessary):

The subjects, all victims of a
chronic illness, will be interviewed about
their attitudes toward the disease, a stressful
topic, in a hospital, a stressful environment.
I feel that this invite more than minimum risk.

Review should be made semi-annually ____
annually ✓

_____
(Signature of Reviewer)

Washington University

Information Sheet Concerning Social and Behavioral
Activities Using Human Subjects

Name of Activity
Director: ___Lynne Kipnis___

Department
or School ___Psychology___

Date: ___May 15, 1977___

Period Covered by
This Information Sheet: 5/15/77 - 5/15/78

Title of Project: Psycho-Social Impact of Juvenile Diabetes Mellitus on Diabetic

Children Between the Ages of Five and Twelve.

Grant, Contract, or Fellowship
Funding Agency: DHEW ☐ Other: __unfunded__ Number, if available: _____
Disciplines and/or Professional Expertise Most Appropriate for Review of This Project:_____
Psychology, Medicine (Pediatrics)

ATTACH A DESCRIPTION OF THE OPERATIONAL ASPECTS OF THE PROJECT.

Answer the following questions. (Use other side or additional sheets if necessary).

1. Methods of protecting confidentiality:

   [X] a. Describe methods.

   [ ] b. If none required, specify reason.

2. Methods of approaching subjects and securing their cooperation:

   [ ] a. Behavior to be studied is public.

   [ ] b. No data to be collected from human subjects in this period.

   [X] c. Informed consent to be obtained. Specify: written or oral; before or after the fact; reasons if not written and before the fact. Attach copies of consent forms and summaries of oral explanations.

3. Extent of risk:

   [ ] a. None.

   [X] b. Only in connection with the preservation of anonymity.

   [ ] c. Other; specify the risk, the procedures for handling the risk, and the justification of the risk.

4. Funding Agency Requirements re Human Subjects

   [ ] Are met by conforming with Washington University Guidelines

   [ ] Differ from Washington University Guidelines; attach copy of requirements.

Signed: _Lynne Kipnis_
(Activity Director)

ACTIVITY
   DIRECTOR: { Prepare 6 copies
             { Submit 5 copies to the Department Chairman/Dean
DEPARTMENT   { Forward 1 copy to the Standing Committee (Box 1054) and
   CHAIRMAN/ { 1 copy to each member of the review panel.
   DEAN: { Retain 1 copy.

PANEL
   REVIEWER: Retain for your file.

Form C-2

Consent Form

I hereby authorize Lynne Kipnis to subject me and my child
_____ to the following procedures in
connection with her research project; " The Psycho-Social
Impact of Juvenile Diabetes Mellitus on Children Between the
Ages of Five and Twelve". The procedures encompass my filling
out The Missouri Children's Behavior Checklist and the Two Factor
Index of Social Position and my child being administered the
following battery of tests: Peabody Picture Vocabulary Test, The
Piers-Harris Children's Self Concept Scale, Self-Esteem Scale,
and The Children's Manifest Anxiety Scale.

I understand that the results of the procedure in which me and
my child participates will be confidential and will be reported
only in group form.

I understand that the investigator is willing to answer any questions
I may have concerning the procedures herein discribed; all inquiries
I have at this time have been answered.

I understand that I am free to withdraw my consent and to discontinue
my, as well as my child's, participation in the project at any time.
I also understand that I may ask a question or state a concern to the
faculty advisor, Dr. Karl Wilson, Department of Psychology (889-6511)
or to the Chairman of the Standing Committee for Review and upon
my request the investigator will tell me how to reach the above two
mentioned people.

I have read and understand the above and I thereby consent for my
child _____ as well as myself to be subjected
to the above procedures.

_____   _____
     Date   Signature of Parent

I have explained the above to the parent(s) of the participant on
the date written above.

                                           _____
                                                Investigator

Form C-3

OFFICE OF THE ASSOCIATE VICE CHANCELLOR
FOR RESEARCH

Box   Ext.

Assoc. Vice Chancellor for Research

DATE: October 21, 1977

TO:

FROM:

RE: Lynne Kipnis' Research Proposal

Enclosed are the forms for a Med School review. When
you have them completed, send them to
Box   in Dr.   's office at the Med School.

Also enclosed is a copy of the Med School guidelines.
Contrary to what I told you on the telephone, I would
appreciate it if you would return them to me as they
appear to be the only copy we have at the present time.

Thanks very much for your cooperation. If you need
any further help just give me a call.

CES

Enc.

Form D

FORM E-1	UNIVERSITY SCHOOL OF MEDICINE	APPENDIX C
	STATEMENT TO HUMAN STUDIES COMMITTEE	Revised 7/7/75

From __Lynne Kipnis__   Date __October 25, 1977__

Department __Psychology__   Telephone Extension____

Return Approval to __Dr.__   Address or Box __Psych. Dept.__

Title of Project: "The Psycho-Social Impact of Juvenile Diabetes   New __X__
                  Mellitus on Diabetic Children Between the Ages of   Renewal_____
Grant Identification No.: Six and Twelve"   Continuation_____
                  (Name of agency and project number, if any)

1. Does this project involve human subjects?   NO_____   YES __X__

2. If no, what animal(s) used_____

3. Submit two (2) copies of Appendix C. If human subjects are involved, include
   two (2) copies of either Appendix D or Appendix D_1.

4. A copy of the plan of investigation as it appears in the grant application must
   be attached to each copy of Appendix C. Budgetary data is not required.

5. If radioactive material is used, include two (2) copies of the letter of approval
   from the Radiation Hazards Committee, Dr.   Chairman.

6. In addition to Washington University Human Studies Committee approval, research
   from either   Hospital, V.A. Hospital or City Hospital must also be approved
   by the Human Studies Committee of their respective institution.

7. If research involves patient interviews submit two (2) copies of the interview(s).
   Also, submit four (4) copies of the protocol and four (4) copies of interview(s)
   to the Ad Hoc Committee on Research Interviews, Dr.   , Chairman.

8. If research involves using a new drug, the Committee must be assured of clearance
   by the Food and Drug Administration. Also, submit two (2) copies of pertinent
   literature on the use of the drug in animals and humans, including all anticipated
   side effects and toxic properties.

9. Principal investigators of all research projects that will necessitate the use of
   human subjects please read and complete the reverse side of this Appendix C.

10. Submit to Washington University Human Studies Committee one month prior to desired
    date of approval.

11. Send to: , M.D., Medical School, Box

_____   _____
Signature of Department Chairman   Signature of Principal Investigator

ACTION OF COMMITTEE

NO HUMAN SUBJECTS	HUMAN SUBJECTS				
Approved	Disapproved	Reviewed Not At Risk	Reviewed At Risk, Approved	Duration of Approval	

No.:_____

_____
Signature of Committee Chairman

1. In accordance with the policy of the School of Medicine, assurance is given that rights and welfare of human subjects in this investigation and methods to be employed for securing informed consent of subjects will be carried out in conformance with guidelines adopted by the School of Medicine.

2. The following are six regulations regarding risks and benefits which were implemented as policy of DHEW on July 1, 1974 for grant applications. These are to be answered on a separate page and two (2) copies submitted to the Human Studies Committee.

   a. Describe the requirements for a subject population and explain the rationale for using in this population special groups such as prisoners, children, the mentally disabled or groups whose ability to give voluntary informed consent may be in question. Also, indicate if the experimental subject is to be remunerated for participation and the amount of remuneration. In the case of mentally incompetent individuals, if consent is to be obtained by proxy, indicate the relationship of the proxy to the experimental subject.

   b. Describe and assess any potential risks--physical, psychological, social, legal or other--and assess the likelihood and seriousness of such risks. If methods of research create potential risks, describe other methods, if any, that were considered and why they will not be used.

   c. Describe consent procedures to be followed, including how and where informed consent will be obtained.

   d. Describe procedures (including confidentiality safeguards) for protecting against or minimizing potential risks and an assessment of their likely effectiveness.

   e. Assess the potential benefits to be gained by the individual subject, as well as benefits which may accrue to society in general as a result of the planned work.

   f. Analyze the risk-benefit ratio.

Form E-2

THE WASHINGTON UNIVERSITY SCHOOL OF MEDICINE

Project:

" The Psycho-social Impact of Juvenile Diabetes Mellitus
on Diabetic Children Between the Ages of Six and Twelve"

CONSENT FOR PARTICIPATION IN RESEARCH ACTIVITIES

This form is to be used only in connection with research approved by the
Human Studies Committee.

Participant:_____   Date:_____

1.   I hereby authorize Dr._Lynne Kipnis_____, and/or such assistants as may
be selected by him for use now or at a later time, to perform upon me the
following procedures in connection with a research project:

The procedures encompass my filling out the Missouri Children's Behavior
Checklist and the Two Factor Index of Social Position and my child being
administered the following battery of tests: Peabody Picture Vocabulary Test,
The Piers-Harris Children's Self Concept Scale, Coopersmith's Self Esteem
Scale and the Children's Manifest Anxiety Scale.

(State nature of procedures, including any drugs to be
administered. Identify those which are experimental.)

2.   I am informed of possible benefits to myself or others associated with the
procedure described above. These are:

Identification of developmental disorders associated with chronic illness

and the institution of appropriate treatment.

(State the possible benefits)

3.   I am informed of certain hazards and discomforts which might be associated
with the procedures described above. These are:

There are no identifiable hazards. If anxiety is produced by the testing

situation, testing will be promptly stopped.

(Describe possible hazards and discomforts)

4.   I am informed that the following alternative procedures are available that
would be advantageous to me:

There are no alternative procedures.

(Describe alternative procedures and advantages)

Form E-3

(continued)

5. I understand that the investigator is willing to answer any inquiries I may have concerning the procedures herein described. All the inquiries I have at this time have been answered.

6. I understand that I am free to withdraw my consent and to discontinue participation in the project or activity at any time. I also understand that I may ask a question or state a concern to the School's Chairman of the Human Studies Committee, and that the investigator will, on request, tell me how to reach the Committee Chairman.

7. I have read and understand the above, and I hereby consent to the performance of the above procedures upon me.

_____
Participant

_____
Parent or legal guardian on participant's behalf if participant is less than 21 years of age or not legally competent.

_____
Auditor Witness

I have explained the above to the participant (or parent or guardian) on the date stated on this Consent for Participation.

_____
Investigator

Form E-4

U N I V E R S I T Y

DEPARTMENT OF PSYCHOLOGY

PETITION FOR PERMISSION TO ENROLL IN PSYCHOLOGY 490

> Submit <u>IN DUPLICATE</u> to Miss

Mr.
Ms. _____, whose signature appears
below, has petitioned me to supervise his (her) work in
Psychology 490 (Study for Honors) for 3 units of credit in
the _____ of _____. He has satisfactorily
       semester   academic year
completed Psychology 498. I accept his petition.

           _____   _____
           signature, faculty member   date

           _____   _____
           signature, candidate   date

           _____   _____
           signature, Chairman of   date
                Department

> RECEIVED BY MISS
>
> _____
> date

semester level for
which this petition
is submitted, e.g.,
2nd-semester senior,
1st-semester junior,
etc.

FORM F

CHILDREN'S HOSPITAL

DATE: 12/5/77

To: Miss Lynne Kipnis

From: M.D.

This will confirm that the Human Studies Committee of   Children's
Hospital has approved your proposed study: THE IMPACT OF JUVENILE
DIABETES MELLITUS ON CHILDREN'S PSYCHOSOCIAL DEVELOPMENT.

Form G

13

Final Words

Murray L. Wax and Joan Cassell

Within organized society a classical problem is that of controlling groups with special powers, notably priests, shamans and sorcerers, physicians, scientists, and scholars. How can the powers of such persons be controlled so as to be used to help and not to harm other members of the community?

In the modern industrial (or "post-industrial") world with its complicated interdependence, intricate division of labor, and growth of specialized and arcane sciences, the powers in the hands of scientists seem ever more awesome. Phrases such as recombinant DNA, nuclear fission and fusion, have become not only symbols of progress and hope, but of public anxiety, which has been translated into restrictive legislation. Devices such as computers, originally perceived as liberating humankind from drudgery, now become feared because of their potentialities for breaching confidentiality and privacy. Social research, too, acquires new potentialities for harm because of the increase in the kinds of intimate knowledge that its methods may gather and because of its potentialities for disseminating knowledge about those who are the subjects, respondents, informants or hosts of its research investigators.

Within the United States, there are a number of alternate political traditions or models to which there may be recourse in an effort to monitor the conduct of scientists and ensure that their activities are beneficial rather than harmful to the community at large. In the 17th and 18th century settlements of North America, some enthusiasts attempted to found communities of the righteous, governed by religious or ethical principles. While Puritan New England is archetypical, there were a large number of other commonwealths ruled either by divine law or by utopian codes and ranging from the Shaker and Amana communities to Brook Farm and New Harmony. The same tradition has been influential in political life, where

there have been successive waves of effort to establish high
levels of public conduct and to transform the United States
into a moral commonwealth.

Professional or disciplinary self-regulation has been
established with the same spirit: the association--or order--
bound by a common discipline, instituted with sacred oaths,
has been a classical modality for restraining the conduct of
those seen as possessing both special powers and special
responsibilities, be they monks or nuns, healers or lawyers.
Some of these orders denied to their members the privilege of
owning personal property or of establishing a heterosexual
family; organizationally, they were to be set apart from conventional society and freed from certain of its temptations.
In the modern U.S., the association, with its ethical code,
has become characteristic of many professions, and in some
cases has acquired legal recognition (as,notably, physicians
and lawyers). Yet, reformers and skeptics have judged that,
rather than protecting the public, the process of disciplinary
self-regulation has been utilized so as to shelter members of
the order who were under critical attack.

Those who framed the federal Constitution were dubious
of efforts to institute a religious or moral commonwealth
through the force of government. The federalists thought of
governmental power as both necessary and yet dangerous, and
so the Constitution was devised with an intricate division of
responsible political functions and a system of checks and
balances, designed to restrain any arm of government, or any
person, from acquiring excessive powers, no matter how moral
was the goal.

In his review of the process of creation of the Human
Subjects Protective System, Gray reminds us that the spirit
of the venture was toward the tradition of the moral commonwealth. The ethical principles which should govern the treatment of human subjects were to be spelled out and enforced.
Unhappily, the task was large and complex, given the incred-
ible variety of methodologies and researches. In the haste
to formulate desirable ethical principles, there was a tendency to overlook the caution urged by philosophers since the
time of Socrates: in the absence of knowledge, it is difficult
to act--or legislate--morally; if one must commence action in
a state of ignorance, one's duty is to remedy that condition
as rapidly as possible. Yet, there has been no systematic
search to discover--for each area of research and for each
variety of methodology--cases (or examples) where those who
had been studied had been subjected to significant abuse or
morally wronged. Had there been such researches, the regulatory system could have been established in a more economical

fashion: rather than seeking generally to improve the moral
tone of scientific activity, the system could more sensibly
have been designed to lessen the likelihood of specific abuses.
(Note the considerable literature on morality and law from
the celebrated 1917 essay of Roscoe Pound to the volumes by
Devlin and Feinberg excerpted in Kipnis [1977].)

Federally established regulatory commissions can be
viewed as compromise efforts in the struggle to institute a
higher level of conduct in a specific area of social activity,
such as commerce or drugs. Each commission has been instituted amid waves of popular discontent with the establishment,
and then, once in operation, has generated waves of criticism
from those affected. The latter complain of "red-tape,"
excessive costs for modest benefits, denial of due process,
and of the elimination of the possibilities of choice by
autonomous action. Meanwhile, the original complainants
criticize the regulatory process for being weak, indecisive,
and unwilling or unable to cope with the most serious ills.
In recent years, we have witnessed these public debates in
connection with a variety of commissions and a range of topics:
protecting workers from asbestos and benzene, consumers from
red dye and saccharin, not to mention related issues of air-
line fares, television broadcasts, and stock market trans-
actions. The same processes are manifested in the Human
Subjects Protective System, which is but another variant in
the genus of federally established commissions designed to
improve the level of conduct in a specific area.

The present volume has been intended to raise questions
about the ethical import of federal regulatory systems, not
to propose a particular alternative and certainly not to dis-
miss the issue of the ethical conduct of social research.
Nevertheless, it would be appropriate to conclude by noting
some of the risks and harms to social research of the present
system of federal regulations, while suggesting that this
might be the proper time for a systematic review leading to a
"risk/benefit" evaluation of the Human Subjects and related
regulatory systems: have they altered the conduct of scientists, and, if so, in what ways and with what consequences for
the --moral and scientific--quality of their researches?
Meanwhile, from the essays of the present volume we may note
the following:

Researchers of little experience and low institutional status may find (as did Kipnis) their time
wasted and their energies exhausted by a series of
bureaucratic reviews, in which no person or agency is
willing to assume the responsibility for helping the
petitioner to do the research.

A variety of state and federal agencies (OMB, district attorneys, investigatory committees, program directors of federal funding agencies, et al.) have the legal sanction to force investigators to violate pledges of confidentiality and privacy made to their respondents. Investigators have no legal grounds for withstanding most of these demands and can only attempt to forestall such attempts by either trickery or techniques--such as outlined by Boruch and Cecil-- which increase the costs and diminish the efficiencies of the research. If they have not taken such pre-cautions--or, if their research design does not permit them to be taken--researchers may be put in a position where they must choose between going to jail or breaching a promise of confidentiality. In qualitative research there is a well documented case where the fieldworkers were forced to choose between violating their promises to their respondents and hosts or losing their research contract with a federal agency (Colfer 1976; Everhart 1975; Miller 1974).

Much research has become so specialized that it is difficult for someone outside the field to comprehend the process completely. Especially in qualitative social research, even the investigator may not know the proximate risks and hopes, harms and benefits, while the long-range effects are anyone's guess. Under these circumstances, it becomes diffi-cult--or an exercise in creative imagination, or a temptation to intellectual dishonesty--to frame research summaries with risk/benefit calculations as required for adequate review by an IRB.

That variety of social research which is denominated as "interpretive sociology" or "qualitative methodology (including fieldwork)" thus eludes most of the categorization employed by the federal regulatory systems. No claim is here made that its practitioners are more moral or responsible than other researchers, or that the research process is governed by purer motives. What is significant is that in some varieties of fieldwork the process of interaction be-tween fieldworker and host people is longer-lasting, more intense, and generically more "human," so that an uninformed attempt by an outside agency to regulate the interaction beforehand can turn into a nuisance, either foolish or time-consuming.

In addition, the regulatory system proceeds on the assumption that those who are studied by social research, (whether as subjects, informants, respondents, or hosts) have been unable to protect their own interests. That assumption

is based on little empirical evidence, but derives from the
typical instance of biomedical research where indeed subjects
have usually been unable to protect their interests because
they are ill. In most social research, those who are studied
are not ill, but are adults in reasonable possession of their
faculties. Nevertheless, neither the government, nor any body
of scientists, nor any spokespersons for special groups have
done research to determine how people feel about the kinds of
social science studies in which they have participated or
been involved. We do not know whether we may be trying to
protect people from risks and opportunities from which they
do not wish to be protected.

   True, there are occasions when the legislature of the
courts may decide that it is essential to protect people,
regardless of their personal wishes (a significant instance
being the pressures by state and federal governments to
insist on the use of seatbelts by motorists). But, in a well-
run and responsibe democracy, such occasions should be
approached with discretion.

   As we indicated initially, the purpose of this volume
was to inform and to raise issues for discussion. All the
authors are conscious of the ethical implications of social
research, and none would wish to declare that these be ignored.
But, at the same time, many of us are critical of the present
governmental systems for coping with ethical problems, and we
should wish to see further informed discussion, refined
analysis, and empirical investigations of the risks, harms,
hopes, and benefits of social research to those who are
studied.

References Cited

Colfer, Carol J. Pierce
    1976 Rights, Responsibilities and Reports: An Ethical
        Dilemma in Contract Research. Pp. 32-46 in Rynkiewich
        and Spradley (1976).
Devlin, Patrick
    1965 Morals and the Criminal Law. Reprinted, pp. 54-65 in
        Kipnis (ed.) (1977).
Everhart, Robert B.
    1975 Problems of Doing Fieldwork in Educational Evaluation.
        Human Organization 34(2):205-215.
Feinberg, Joel
    1973 From Social Philosophy. Reprinted, pp. 71-86 in
        Kipnis (ed.) (1977).
Kipnis, Kenneth, editor
    1977 Philosophical Issues in Law: Cases and Materials.
        Englewood Cliffs: Prentice-Hall.
Miller, Judith
    1974 Scuttling Education Research. Change (November)
        46-47; 62.
Pound, Roscoe
    1917 The Limits of Effective Legal Action. International
        Journal of Ethics. 27:150-167.
Rynkiewich, Michael, and James P. Spradley, editors
    1976 Ethics and Anthropology: Dilemmas in Fieldwork
        New York: John Wiley.

Index

Latané, B., 14, 22
Law Enforcement Assis-
  tance Administration
  (LEAA), U.S., 34
Leighton, Alexander H.,
  120, 127
Leighton, Dorothea C., 120
Lerman, Lindsey Miller, 39
Lewis, Anthony, 98, 101
Lowry, Ritchie P., 75-76,
  80
Lurie, Allison, 112, 117
Lurie, Nancy O., 138, 143
Lyons, Gene M., 69, 80

Malinowski, Bronislaw, 86,
  131
Mansfield Amendment, 67
Matos Mar, Jose, 73
Mauksch, Hans, 58
May, William, 138, 143
McCulloch, Donna Hansen, 59
McNamara, Secretary Robert
  S., 63
Mead, Margaret, 97, 131,
  135, 136, 143
Mellinger, Glen, 209, 215
Mering, Otto von, 76, 80
Meyer v. Nebraska, 30, 40,
  42
Milgram, Stanley, 14, 17,
  18, 20, 22
Miller, Arthur G., 185, 215
Miller, Arthur R., 25, 41
Miller, Judith, 242, 244
Millstein, Eugene J., 59
Miner, Horace, 98
Moore, Sally Falk, 113, 117
Moos, Felix, 75
Moynihan, Daniel P., 137,
  143
Murray, James R., 215
Musto, David F., 112, 118

Nader, Laura, 131, 143
National Association for the
  Advancement of Colored
  People (NAACP), 28, 42;
  NAACP v. Alabama, 28, 42
National Commission for the

Protection of Human Sub-
  jects of Biomedical and
  Behavioral Research
  (NCPRHSBBR), U.S., 5, 7,
  44, 46-48, 51-58, 85, 104,
  106-107, 112, 115, 129
National Institute of Educa-
  tion (NIE), U.S., 173
National Institute of
  Health (NIH), U.S., 45, 58
National Opinion Research
  Center (NORC), 186, 187,
  214
National Science Foundation
  (NSF), U.S., 173, 186, 214
Nejelski, Paul, 35, 39, 41,
  59, 182-183
Nisbet, Robert A., 76, 80
Northwestern University, 58
Nutini, Hugo, 65, 68

Office of Economic Oppor-
  tunity (OEO), U.S., 125
Office of Management and
  Budget (OMB), U.S., 151-
  158, 162-171
Office of Strategic Services
  (OSS), U.S., 74
Olesen, Virginia, 5, 58, 83,
  84, 105, 111, 117, 147
Olmstead v. United States,
  26-27, 42
Oppenheimer, Jules Robert,
  76, 80
Orlans, Harold, 75, 79, 80
Orleans, S., 178, 183
Orne, Martin, 131, 143

Parent-Teachers Association
  (PTA), 123-124
Paris Adult Theatre 1 *et al.*
  v. Slaton, 30, 42
Park, Robert Ezra, 93-94, 97
Personality and Social
  Psychology Bulletin, 11
Pierce v. Society of Sisters,
  30, 40, 42
Pincus, Walter, 66
Pittman, David J., 137-138,
  143

Uhlaner, J.E., 80
Uliassi, Pio, 66
University of California-
  Berkeley, 107
U.S.S.R., Soviet Foreign
  Ministry, 6

Vallance, Theodore, 63, 69
Veatch, Robert M., 58
Vidich, Arthur J., 139, 144

Warner, Stanley L., 176, 177,
  184
War Relocation Authority
  (WRA), U.S., 74
Warren, Samuel D., 25, 41
Warwick, Donald P., 135, 144
Washington, Booker T., 93
Washington Star, 66
Wax, Murray L., 4-6, 33, 83,
  86, 102, 103, 115, 118,
  139, 140, 144

Wax, Rosalie Hankey, 86, 98,
  102, 111, 118, 132, 135,
  144
Weaver, Warren, Jr., 98, 102
Weber, Max, 83
Weinberger, Secretary Cas-
  per, 47
Westin, Alan F., 24-25, 28,
  32
Whittaker, Elvi, 111, 118
Whyte, William Foote, 73, 80,
  98, 102, 137, 144
Whyte, William H., Jr., 94
Withers, Carl (James West),
  89, 102
Wright, Charles R., 211, 215

Yancey, William M., 137, 143
Yarmolinsky, Adam, 63, 80

Zdep, S.M., 175, 184
Zurcher v. Stanford Daily, 98